The Dead Sea Scrolls

The Dead Sea Scrolls

A Textbook and Study Guide

Menahem Mansoor

Second Edition

Baker Book House
Grand Rapids, Michigan 49506

The author acknowledges with gratitude the generous support of the Wisconsin Society for Jewish Learning for the Hebrew Literature Projects of the Department of Hebrew Studies

BM
487
.M27
1983

Copyright 1964, 1983, *by Menahem Mansoor*
All rights reserved. No part of this book may be reproduced or translated in any form, by print, photoprint, microfilm, or any other means, without written permission from the copyright owner

Paperback edition issued 1983 by
Baker Book House with permission
of copyright owner

ISBN: 0-8010-6152-0

Printed in the United States of America

This work is dedicated to Professors
H. B. MC CARTY AND C. A. WEDEMEYER
but for whose encouragement and inspiration it would not have been undertaken

TABLE OF CONTENTS

Introduction. IX
    I. The First Discovery 1
   II. The Qumran Library 5
  III. Excavations at Khirbet Qumran. 11
  IV. The Dating of the Scrolls 23
   V. Discoveries at Wadi Murabbaat. 28
  VI. Discoveries at Khirbet Mird and Later Discoveries. . . . 38
 VII. The Copper Scrolls 43
VIII. The Genesis Apocryphon. 52
  IX. The War Scroll. 57
   X. The Isaiah Scrolls 69
  XI. The Scrolls and Biblical Studies. 82
 XII. The Commentaries. 88
       General Review of Chapters 1-12. 98
XIII. The Thanksgiving Hymns 99
XIV. Doctrines of the Qumran Sect 105
XV. Jewish Sects: Part I—Assideans, Pharisees, Sadducees and Zealots 109
XVI. Jewish Sects: Part II—Essenes and Therapeutae. 125
XVII. The Manual of Discipline 137
XVIII. The Essenes and the Identification of the Sect. 143
XIX. Qumran Writings and Christianity. 153
XX. Discoveries Pertaining to Bar Kochba's Revolt 164
XXI. Discoveries Pertaining to Bar Kochba's Revolt (Continued) 171
XXII. Discoveries Pertaining to Bar Kochba's Revolt (Concluded) 185
XXIII. The Temple Scroll 194
XXIV. Masada 204
XXV. The Case of Shapira's Missing Dead Sea (Deuteronomy) Scroll of 1883 215
General Review 225
Topics for Further Study 226

Glossary of Terms and Proper Names 227
List of Main Scrolls Discovered in the Dead Sea Regions . . 234
Recommended Bibliography on the Scrolls 236
Chronological Table of Major Events 237
Index of Subjects 239

INTRODUCTION

This work represents the first in a series which surveys biblical archaeology, beginning with the momentous discoveries in the caves of the Judean Desert in the vicinity of the Dead Sea. It includes the discoveries of the Bar Kochba scrolls in the southwestern regions of the Dead Sea coastal region.

The story of the discoveries of the scrolls is as extraordinary as it is fascinating. It has been hailed as "the greatest manuscript discovery of all time."

In the early summer of 1947 an Arab shepherd, searching for his straying goat near the Dead Sea, stumbled upon a cave containing seven ancient scrolls. They proved to be part of the library of a Jewish community—probably the Essenes—living before and during the time of Christ. Later discoveries, in at least eleven different caves in that area, have produced the remains of about four hundred scrolls represented by over forty thousand fragments. There are biblical fragments dating back to the pre-Christian era which are one thousand years older than any other clearly dated biblical manuscript hitherto in our possession. These are of tremendous importance to biblical studies for these biblical scrolls have confirmed the authenticity of the Hebrew Bible.

The nonbiblical scrolls also throw a flood of light on a relatively obscure period—that immediately preceding the advent of Christianity—and thus give us a better understanding of the background of Christianity. They have once and for all confirmed the Palestinian-Jewish background of the New Testament.

These outlines have been very carefully prepared and numerous sources have been consulted in their preparation. They do not necessarily reflect the opinion of the author, but are more or less a distillation of all the most important work done in the field. You must study them thoroughly. The outlines on the Jewish sects (Chapters 15 and 16) and discoveries relating to Bar Kochba (Chapters 20-22) are given in detail, since not enough information is given in your textbooks on these subjects.

The present textbook includes two review tests. These are generally similar in content and standard to those given to resident students at The University of Wisconsin, enrolled in the course Hebrew Literature in Translation.

I would like to express my warmest thanks to Mrs. Naima Wallenrod Prevot, M.A., project assistant in the Department of Hebrew and Semitic Studies, whose constant help in research and patient correction of the manuscript were invaluable. But for Mrs. Prevot's painstaking care and assistance, it would not have been possible for me to have completed this work without considerable delay.

I also wish to express my indebtedness to my project assistants who edited and proofread the manuscript, Miss Carolyn Hillier, Mrs. Helene Isaacs, and Mr. L. Duane Willard. Mr. Willard compiled the glossary under my guidance.

My sincere gratitude is also due to Mrs. Agnes Rapp, secretary of the Department, whose help and patient correcting and typing of the manuscript were invaluable.

The enthusiasm and generous support of the Wisconsin Society for Jewish Learning and the Correspondence Instruction Program authorities of the University of Wisconsin have given me great encouragement.

I am also deeply thankful to my wife for her indispensable help, especially in the German works of reference.

A final word before you begin your adventure: this work is written on a strictly nonsectarian basis. The purpose is to introduce you to a legitimate and wonderful body of literature, as you have been introduced to other national literatures, and to show its place in world literature and its contribution to western civilization. We sincerely hope that the book will fulfill these aims.

MENAHEM MANSOOR

February, 1963
Madison, Wisconsin

I

THE FIRST DISCOVERY

This unit is concerned with general background material on the discovery of the Dead Sea Scrolls. Specific topics discussed include circumstances of the first discovery, location of the discovery, purchase of the original finds, and an introductory description of the scrolls found in the first cave. This information provides a sufficient background for future detailed study of the scrolls. Read at least two books from the following list. Make copious notes. You will notice that there are conflicting accounts about the discovery, but this should present no difficulties for your study of the scrolls. Pay more attention to the brief descriptions of the seven scrolls of Cave One. Memorize the names of the scrolls, since constant reference is made to them in future units.

RECOMMENDED READING

Allegro, J. M., *The Dead Sea Scrolls*, pages 15-34
Burrows, Millar, *The Dead Sea Scrolls*, pages 3-28
—, *More Light on the Dead Sea Scrolls*, pages 3-19
Cross, F. M., Jr., *The Ancient Library of Qumran*, pages 1-8
Milik, J. T., *Ten Years of Discovery in the Wilderness of Judaea*, pages 11-19
Van der Ploeg, J., *The Excavations at Qumran*, pages 1-28
Yadin, Yigael, *The Message of the Scrolls*, pages 15-52

A. The initial finds

1. Muhammad el Dīb ("Muhammad, the Wolf"), an Arab shepherd of the Ta'amireh tribe, stumbled upon a cave in the wilderness of Judea one spring day in 1947 while searching for a stray goat. The cave is in the vicinity of a site now called Qumran, located in the northwestern region of the Dead Sea in Palestine. Today the cave is known in the scholarly world as "Cave One."
2. The Arab Bedouin and a fellow shepherd, crawling through a narrow hole in the cave, discovered several earthenware jars, some with their lids still on, standing in rows.

3. Only one of the sealed jars yielded decaying rolls or bundles of leather. The rolls were later found to comprise seven large scrolls, wrapped in linen, and several fragments. These scrolls, written in Hebrew and Aramaic, are the first of the now-famous Dead Sea Scrolls. (For a list of the scrolls, see section B, below.)

B. *Ownership of the scrolls*

1. Archbishop Samuel of the Syrian Orthodox Monastery of St. Mark purchased the following scrolls in Jerusalem through a Bethlehem dealer:
   a. A complete scroll of Isaiah, 24 feet long, written in Hebrew and *almost* identical with the Book of Isaiah in the Hebrew Bible. This scroll is sometimes known as *St. Mark's Monastery Isaiah Scroll*.
   b. The *Manual of Discipline*, a scroll containing rules and regulations by which members of the sect of the Dead Sea Scrolls were governed.
   c. *Commentary* (Heb. *pesher*) *on the Book of Habakkuk*, the text of the first two chapters of Habakkuk with a running interpretation. It contains some interesting historical allusions.
   d. The *Genesis Apocryphon*, first known as the *Lamech Scroll*, containing apocryphal accounts in Aramaic about some patriarchs in Genesis such as Noah and Abraham and other biblical personalities such as Sarah and Lamech, but with more details.
2. The Syrian archbishop brought the above scrolls to the United States. They were eventually sold in 1955 in New York for $250,000,[1]) to General Yigael Yadin, son of Prof. E. L. Sukenik, and professor of archaeology at the Hebrew University of Jerusalem. The scrolls were then flown to the Hebrew University.
3. The remaining three scrolls from Cave One, sold to E. L. Sukenik, professor of Palestinian archaeology at the Hebrew University of Jerusalem, are as follows:
   a. An incomplete scroll of Isaiah, also known as the *Hebrew University Isaiah Scroll*.

---

[1]) The United States tax court has upheld the contention of the Internal Revenue authorities that the $250,000 received from the sale of the scrolls is subject to the capital gains tax. The matter came to light when the archbishop sought tax-exemption status for the Archbishop Samuel Trust to which the ownership of the scrolls was transferred. The trust listed as its tasks the financing of education for Syrian monks and the maintenance of St. Mark's Monastery in Jerusalem.

THE FIRST DISCOVERY 3

b. The *War Scroll*, whose full title is the *War of the Sons of Light Against the Sons of Darkness*. It gives directions for the conduct of an actual or eschatological war between members of the sect and their enemies.
c. The *Thanksgiving Hymns*, containing about thirty hymns resembling the Old Testament Psalms.
4. These seven scrolls are now at the Hebrew University of Jerusalem. For information on the publication of the scrolls from Cave One, see Unit 2, "The Qumran Library."

C. *Names given to the scrolls*

1. The scrolls are generally known as the "Dead Sea Scrolls" because they were found in the vicinity of the Dead Sea.
2. The scrolls are also referred to in scholarly works as the "Qumran Scrolls," or "Qumran Writings," since they were found near the ruins of an ancient site now called Qumran.
3. Other names for the scrolls are as follows:
   a. "Scrolls from the Wilderness of Judea."
   b. "The Jerusalem Scrolls."
   c. "'Ain Feshka Scrolls." 'Ain Feshka is a stream in that region about seven and a half miles south of Jericho, a mile from the western shore of the Dead Sea and about 1,000 feet above sea level.
   d. The "Dead Sea Scriptures."
   e. "The Sectarian Writings." The term sometimes refers to the non-biblical scrolls.

D. *Similar discoveries in the Dead Sea region recorded in antiquity*

1. Bishop Epiphanius of Salamis, fourth century A.D., refers to Old Testament manuscripts in Hebrew and Greek found concealed in earthenware jars near Jericho in A.D. 217. Both Origen (second to third century) and Eusebius (third to fourth century) refer to this find. According to Origen, a Greek version of the Psalms was among the manuscripts.
2. Nestorian Church Patriarch Timothy I (780-823) in a Syriac letter addressed to Sergius, Metropolitan of Ela, tells of books found near Jericho in a house on the rocks. Timothy goes on to say that "more than two hundred psalms of David" had been found among the books.

E. *Other items found in Cave One*

1. The cave contained many fragments of parchment and scraps of papyrus.
2. Linen measuring 16 to 20 inches on each side, some of it decoratively interwoven with narrow blue stripes and having hemmed borders, was used to wrap the scrolls.
3. Cylindrical earthenware jars, the lids of which are in the shape of shallow bowls appear to have been made for protecting the scrolls.
4. Parts of two Hellenistic-type lamps with elongated muzzles were found.
5. The cave contained sherds of numerous jars.
6. A handful of potsherds and nozzles of two lamps of the Roman period were found when Cave One was rediscovered by archaeologists in 1949. Most of this material is in the Palestine Museum of Jerusalem.

F. *General evaluation of the discovery*

1. "The greatest manuscript discovery of modern times"—William F. Albright.
2. "A phenomenal discovery; the most important discovery ever made in Old Testament manuscripts"—G. Ernest Wright.

TOPICS FOR STUDY AND DISCUSSION

A. Describe the Dead Sea and the region in which the scrolls were found.
B. List and give a brief description of the scrolls found in Cave One.
C. Give an account of the circumstances and the contents of the discovery of Cave One.
D. Describe the sequence of events leading to the purchase of Archbishop Samuel's scrolls by Yigael Yadin.
E. Write a brief note on each of the following:
   1. Qumran
   2. 'Ain Feshka
   3. A scroll
   4. Hellenism
   5. Apocrypha
   6. The Dead Sea
F. Give accounts of two similar discoveries of manuscripts made in antiquity.

II

THE QUMRAN LIBRARY

About three hundred caves in the region of Qumran have been excavated and eleven of these yielded thousands of fragments believed to contain different manuscripts. The many different types of discovered manuscripts consisted chiefly of biblical writings, apocryphal manuscripts, Old Testament Pseudepigrapha, sectarian literature, and commentaries on biblical books. Only about ten scrolls have been preserved complete, and some texts are represented by only one fragment.

Several of the books found at Qumran were in more than one version, such as the Book of Isaiah. Some of the versions represent the Massoretic, that is, traditional Hebrew text, some reflect the tradition of the Septuagint, and others include such traditions as that found in the Samaritan Pentateuch. A few of the biblical books are relatively close in date to their original composition, such as the Book of Daniel (generally believed to have been written about 165 B.C.), and some of the books were found in versions hitherto unknown to biblical scholars. As a result, you will see in the other units, the Qumran library provides valuable material for contemporary biblical scholarship in the areas of history, paleography, and linguistics. The sectarian literature and the other non-biblical manuscripts that were found are also extremely important. These, too, are examined further in other units to show how these provide us with new and significant information about the period between approximately 150 B.C. and A.D. 70.

RECOMMENDED READING

Allegro, J. M., *The Dead Sea Scrolls*, pages 35-49
Burrows, M., *The Dead Sea Scrolls*, pages 54-69
Burrows, M., *More Light on the Dead Sea Scrolls*, pages 5-8 and 20-36
Cross, F. M., Jr., *The Ancient Library of Qumran*, pages 1-36
Milik, J. T., *Ten Years Discovery in the Wilderness of Judea*, pages 21-43
Van der Ploeg, J., *The Excavations at Qumran*, pages 150-188
Yadin, Y., *The Message of the Scrolls*, pages 57-59

A. *Quantities found*

So far, the Qumran caves have produced parts of almost four hundred different manuscripts, but only some ten scrolls have been preserved complete, and some texts are represented by only one fragment.

B. *Types of material*

1. Cave Four seems to contain the main library of the "monastery." It appears to have been a hermit's cell.
   a. The lack of jars in this cave suggests that material was left there in a hurry.
   b. The extremely fragmentary state of the manuscripts, the fact that some of the tears in the manuscripts are indubitably old, and the survival of long strips believed to have been torn off the rolls seem to indicate a violation of the caves in antiquity.
2. Caves One and Three appear to have been hiding places.
3. All the other caves in which manuscripts were found were probably inhabited by individual hermits. Manuscripts and domestic utensils in the keeping of each hermit were found as he had left them.

C. *Types of manuscripts*

1. Biblical manuscripts
   a. A quarter of the manuscripts consists of copies of books of the Bible.
   b. Every book of the Hebrew Bible, except the Book of Esther, is represented in the Qumran finds. The Book of Esther fails to appear, while parts of books such as Deuteronomy, Isaiah, or the Minor Prophets and the Psalms are represented by more than ten copies.
   c. Some of the copies of the biblical books are relatively close in date to the original composition.
      (1) The manuscript of Daniel from Cave Four is believed to be only half a century removed from the generally accepted date of composition of the original (ca. 165 B.C.).
      (2) Only a century separates the manuscript of Ecclesiastes from the author's copy. (Generally believed to have been written, at the latest, between 250 and 300 B.C.)

d. Pentateuch. The Massoretic text is followed in most of the fragments. The exceptions (which are more closely related to the Hebrew text underlying the Septuagint) are a copy of Exodus, a copy of Numbers and a small roll containing the Song of Moses (Exodus 15). In another manuscript of Exodus we come into contact with the recensions found in the Samaritan Pentateuch.
e. Fragments of the Former Prophets have been found in four of the caves.

   (1) They seem to be derived from the same Hebrew Tradition as seen in the Septuagint; this is especially clear in a manuscript of Samuel I.

   (2) Another Samuel manuscript dates towards the end of the third century B.C. and it seems to be superior in places to both the Septuagint and the Massoretic text.

f. Of the Latter Prophets, Isaiah is the most frequently found, but all the others are well represented.

   (1) One complete and one incomplete yet large scroll of Isaiah were found in Cave One; one reflects a Massoretic tradition and the other (the complete) a more popular edition.

   (2) The Septuagint type of text is found in one case—Jeremiah. This text is one-eighth shorter than the Massoretic text.

   (3) Most of the manuscripts of the Latter Prophets belong to the Massoretic tradition.

g. The Writings—Hagiographa

   (1) The Book of Job was found in normal square Hebrew characters, in paleo-Hebrew script, and in an Aramaic translation. All three are fragmentary. The Aramaic translation of Job is of particular interest because it appears to be the translation condemned by the Rabbi Gamaliel I (Paul's alleged teacher, compare Acts 22 : 3) and is believed to be among the earliest translations committed to writing.

   (2) There are a dozen fragmentary scrolls of the Psalms.

   (3) The Book of Daniel must have been read a great deal: two manuscripts of it were found in Cave One, four in Cave Four, and one in Cave Six. Most of them follow the Massoretic text, apart from a few variants related to the Hebrew archetype of the Septuagint.

2. The Apocrypha

   a. It is well known that the canon of the Alexandrian Jews included certain additional books, which are also found in the liturgy and Bibles of the early Church but not in the Hebrew Bible. b. At Qumran three examples of these books have been found---Tobit, Ecclesiasticus (or Ben Sira), and the Epistle of Jeremy.

3. Old Testament Pseudepigrapha
   a. A sizable section of the Qumran manuscripts represents this category.
   b. Only one of the major Pseudepigrapha—The Book of Jubilees—is found in the same textual form underlying the early translations which were, until recently, our only sources of these works. Caves One, Two, and Four have produced fragments of about ten manuscripts of this work.
   c. The Book of Enoch is also represented by about ten fragmentary manuscripts from Cave Four.
   d. No trace of the testament of the Twelve Patriarchs has been found at Qumran of the Hebrew or Aramaic archetype which some scholars have assumed to be the basis for our present Greek text, but fragments have been found which enable us to identify some of the sources used.
   e. The *Genesis Apocryphon*, the last to be unrolled, was found in Cave One. (See Unit 11 on this scroll).
   f. Other apocryphal writings are these:
      (1) A pseudo-Jeremiah work, which has only loose connections with the rest of the known literature attributed to the prophet or his secretary, Baruch.
      (2) The Psalms of Joshua.
      (3) A Vision of Amram, the father of Moses and Aaron.
      (4) Beginnings of a small Aramaic scroll entitled *The Prayer of Nabonidus*, which seems to be the source used, in either written or oral form, by the author of the Book of Daniel when he wrote of Nebuchadnezzar's illness.

4. Sectarian literature
   a. The *Manual of Discipline* in virtually complete form was found in both Caves One and Ten, and fragmentary manuscripts were found in Cave Four.
   b. The *Damascus Document* had been known for fifty years, ever since two manuscripts representing two distinct recensions of it were discovered in the *Cairo Geniza* and published by S. Schechter. Copies were found in Caves Four, Five, and Six.

(1) The work consists of two parts: the first comments on God's plan for salvation and the second gives detailed rules for the lives of members of the New Covenant in their camps in the land of Damascus.

(2) The Qumran manuscripts, the oldest of which should be dated between 75 and 50 B.C., give us these two parts in one continuous text.

c. The *War of the Sons of Light Against the Sons of Darkness* was first found in Cave One. Fragments from the War Scroll of three different manuscripts from Cave Four seem to follow the same text but two other manuscripts from the same cave, one of them fairly well represented, attest to the existence of a different recension.

d. The *Thanksgiving Hymns*, a long roll from Cave One, is badly damaged. Most of these hymns begin with the phrase, "I thank Thee, O Lord."

5. Commentaries on biblical books
   a. Biblical commentaries of the sect have a uniform pattern. The biblical text is transcribed and then commented upon, verse by verse, the comment being introduced by a formula such as "The explanation (pesher) of this is . . ."
   b. Three types of biblical commentaries exist. (They are not kept rigidly separated although one type predominates in each commentary.)
      (1) The commentaries on Habakkuk, Micah, and the Psalms. The text is explained in relation to the sect's own history.
      (2) The Nahum commentary. The explanation again concerns the sect but in its relation to some ethnic groups in Palestine and its part in contemporary events.
      (3) The commentaries on Isaiah. The prophet's words are interpreted eschatologically.
   c. Other documents containing quotations and short passages from Exodus, II Samuel, Isaiah, Psalms, Amos, and Daniel.
      (1) The text is often quoted with the formula, "As is written in the book Isaiah, Daniel," etc.
      (2) All manuscripts containing *pesher* (commentary) material come from later periods of the Qumran community.
      (3) No one work seems to have existed in more than one copy.

6. Other writings found at Qumran

a. Many fragments from Cave Four contain hymnal material or have a liturgical or sapiental character.
b. Also found was a series of manuscripts called *Mishmarot* or "Courses", which describe in detail the rotation of the priestly families' service in the Temple geared to the solar calendar and synchronized with the lunar calendar.
c. An Aramaic work was found which can be titled *A Description of the Heavenly Jerusalem*. It contains an exceedingly detailed vision of the Holy City and Temple—obviously inspired by the last chapters of the Book of Ezekiel.
d. Two fragmentary columns from Cave Four give the signs of the Zodiac distributed over the days of the month, and following that, predictions that can be drawn from thunder.

Topics for Study and Discussion

A. Name the five main types of manuscripts discovered in the Qumran area and describe one specific text representing each type.

B. Discuss the three main biblical traditions represented in the Qumran texts and discuss an example of each.

C. Discuss the following:
1. Three of the important finds among the biblical manuscripts and the reason for their importance.
2. One of the Old Testament Pseudepigrapha found and its importance.
3. Three of the manuscripts that come under the heading of "Sectarian Literature" and their importance.
4. One of the biblical commentaries and its importance.
5. List three of the other writings found at Qumran which do not fall into any of the above categories.

D. Discuss what, in your opinion, are two of the most interesting and important manuscripts found at Qumran.

III

EXCAVATIONS AT KHIRBET QUMRAN

The ruins called Khirbet Qumran were found about 1,000 yards southeast of Cave One. These ruins show four distinct phases of occupation:

1. Occupation in the Iron Age II (eighth to seventh centuries B.C.)
2. Occupation by a religious community from the second century B.C. to A.D. 68
3. Occupation by a Roman garrison between A.D. 68 and 86
4. Occupation by Jewish insurgents in the second war against Rome, A.D. 132-135

The ruins have proved interesting and valuable to scholars for many reasons, but primarily it has been established that the religious community which occupied the ruins from the second century B.C. to A.D. 68 is the community which wrote and copied the Dead Sea Scrolls found in the neighbouring caves.

The history of the ruins known as Khirbet Qumran and the archaeological evidence which has enabled scholars to reconstruct the history of the ruins are discussed in this unit. In addition you will see what the buildings must have been like at the time of the sect, that is, how they have been reconstructed and what phases the buildings went through in their long history.

RECOMMENDED READING

You are required to read at least TWO of the following:

Allegro, J. M., *The Dead Sea Scrolls*, pages 35-40 and 73-93
Cross, F. M., Jr., *The Ancient Library of Qumran*, pages 1-36
Milik, J. T., *Ten Years of Discovery in the Wilderness of Judaea*, pages 44-49
Van der Ploeg, J., *The Excavations at Qumran*, pages 27-28
Vermes, G., *Discoveries in the Judean Desert*, pages 10-23

A. Discovery of Khirbet Qumran

1. During the excavations of Cave One in 1949, Father Roland de Vaux and G. L. Harding searched for evidence of previous human habitation which might explain the deposit of the scrolls in the cave.

    a. About 1,000 yards to the southeast of the first cave they discovered the ruins of a building standing on a plateau midway between the sea and the cliffs.
    b. This khirbet (or ruin) had been seen before by travelers and mentioned in their reports.
       (1) F. De Saulcy in 1851 suggested it might be the ruins of the biblical Gomorrah.
       (2) C. Clermont-Ganneau in 1873 gave the first valuable description.
       (3) Dolman correctly recognized Roman remains on the spot in his report of 1920.
       (4) Martin Noth has recently suggested with much plausibility that the site and general area represent the ancient "city of salt" mentioned in Joshua 15 : 62.

2. Excavations at Khirbet Qumran began in 1951 and continued until 1956.

    a. The first campaign in 1951 led to the discovery of pottery and cloths as well as hundreds of tiny manuscript fragments.
       (1) The pottery finds, according to the archaeologists, were of two main groupings:
           (a) Hellenistic sherds of about fifty jars, corresponding lids, and two lamps
           (b) A handful of Roman sherds, including the fragments of two lamps and a pot
       (2) The cloths found in the cave were obviously used as envelopes for the scrolls.
    b. In 1949 two tombs were dug out of an adjacent cemetery. (For more about the cemetery, see C below.)
       (1) The graves were oriented north and south, unusual in a Moslem country.
       (2) Clermont-Ganneau had commented on this peculiarity and suggested that the graves must date from pre-Islamic times.

c. In the following year the rubble was cleared from the walls and the main outlines of the building stood out.
   (1) It was seen that this was not a dwelling house, but a community center.
      (a) There were large meeting rooms with plaster benches running around the walls.
      (b) A water cistern, far larger than an ordinary family would need, was discovered outside the main building.
   (2) One of the most important objects found amid the ruins was a jar, still intact, of exactly the same shape as those found in the first cave, thus linking quite certainly the cave with the ruins and the scrolls with the people who had inhabited the settlement and had been buried in the cemetery.
   (3) Three occupation levels covering a period of some 250 years were found.
      (a) The lowest stratum is the oldest (about 135 B.C.).
      (b) There is also evidence of occupation in the eighth and seventh centuries B.C.

B. *The history of the occupation of the building*

1. At a very low level remains of walls and pottery were found which belonged to Iron Age II (eighth to seventh centuries B.C.).
   a. One of the potsherds found at this level was inscribed with Phoenician characters of the kinds used for writing Hebrew at the time.
   b. Also found from this period was a fragmentary ostracon, a royal seal stamped on a jar handle.
2. One suggestion is that this building from the period of the Hebrew monarchy illustrates a statement made about King Uzziah of Judah (ca. 780-740 B.C.) in II Chronicles 26 : 10, that "he built towers in the wilderness."

However, the chief interest in the occupation attaches to the 250 years covering the Greco-Roman period. Abundant evidence of occupation of the site in that period has been found and there is evidence of three stages of occupation:

Occupation by a religious community from the end of the second century B.C. to A.D. 68.

Occupation by a Roman garrison between A.D. 68 and 86.

Occupation by Jewish insurgents in the second war against Rome
—A.D. 132-135.
a. The first stage is divided into two parts:
   (1) The community appears to have left the building for thirty to forty years at the end of the first century B.C.
   (2) Not long after that, the building was severely damaged by an earthquake and extensive reconstruction was necessary when the sect returned to occupy it again.
      (a) The earthquake can be accurately dated. From the hisstorian Flavius Josephus writing in the first century A.D. we learn that in the spring of 31 B.C. a terrible earthquake shook Judea, devastating its towns and killing thousands of men and beasts.
      (b) Evidence in the ruins of the earthquake:
         (i) One of the cisterns is cracked.
         (ii) The eastern wall of the northwest tower is split and part of the door between two of the rooms is broken, which caused the ceiling to collapse.
         (iii) The plaster on the south and east walls of the room is cracked in two lines converging on the southeast corner.
      (c) The question of whether the earthquake drove out the inhabitants or whether they had already left when it occurred has not yet been answered.
      (d) The sectarians apparently returned some thirty years after the earthquake. They cleared the rubble from the buildings and rebuilt the walls. This second phase of the first period of the occupation of the site lasted until the fall of the monastery in A.D. 68.
b. The period of occupation by a Roman garrison was between A.D. 68 and 86.
   (1) Josephus tells us that in the late spring of A.D. 68, the Emperor Vespasian brought his Tenth Legion down the Jordan Valley to Jericho. We are told that Vespasian left a garrison at Jericho and in the following year Titus led the Legion against Jerusalem to raze that city to the ground.
      (a) Josephus tells us that the Roman approach was heralded by a general panic, when the mass of the population fled into "those mountainous parts which lay over against Jerusalem."

(b) The presence of arrowheads among the debris points to some resistance from the buildings.

(2) The Roman victors did not leave immediately and this period in the life of the buildings is marked by a re-utilization of its defense works, the leveling of the debris to some extent, and the division of the larger meetings rooms into small living quarters.

   (a) The occupants enlarged the bread oven which had been built toward the end of the last sectarian occupation and made changes in the water conduits to serve their less demanding needs.

   (b) The fact that the large cistern was no longer used points to a much smaller group of inhabitants without the ritualistic requirements of the sect.

   (c) The Romans built a few rooms over the ruins and remained in occupation for ten or twenty years.

c. Following the Roman occupation the building remained empty until A.D. 132, when a second Jewish revolt against Rome broke out in Judea, and was put down only after three years of bitter and costly guerilla fighting. The Jewish guerilla forces made use of the monastery's excellent strategic position as a stronghold to protect the Dead Sea route to their southern posts.

d. This brief occupation was followed by complete demolition by the Romans of the fortifications of Khirbet Qumran.

3. Archaeological evidence as to the three main stages of occupation of Khirbet Qumran.

   a. Coins. Several hundred coins found are the most important evidence of the occupation of the building.

   (1) The first important group of coins come from the reign of John Hyrcanus—135-104 B.C.

   (2) The series carries on in an unbroken succession until the time of Herod the Great—37-4 B.C.—which is represented by only one coin. (The evidence of these coins fits in well with Josephus' earthquake of 31 B.C.)

   (3) The series begins again from Herod Archelaus 4 B.C.-A.D. 6 and continues until the second year of the first revolt, A.D. 68. Some seventy-three bronze coins were found for this year.

(4) There are a handful of coins after this. One of them is countermarked with "X" on the reverse, probably indicating possession by the Roman Tenth Legion. The military occupation of Khirbet Qumran by the Romans is also represented by a few coins ranging in date from the last two years of Nero's reign to the reign of Titus (A.D. 79-81). A coin of Herod Agrippa II, dated A.D. 86, was found outside the building.

(5) The next large batch of coins is from the time of the second Jewish revolt of A.D. 132-135. Three coins of the Emperor Trajan (A.D. 98-117) were found in addition to one coin of a type struck by the insurgent leaders during the revolt.

b. Pottery remains.

(1) The pottery ascribed to the first period of occupation was found either in the rooms which were no longer used after the earthquake or in a trench some 30 meters north of the building which served, in Father de Vaux's opinion, to receive the rubble while the repairs after the earthquake were carried on. The sherds are of the same pattern as those found in Bethsur and in Jerusalem citadel of the Hasmonean period; they may thus be dated from the end of the Hellenistic period.

(2) The ceramics of the second period of occupation in level II are related to those of the Jewish tombs of the Herodian period. That level is particularly rich both in sherds and coins.

(3) In the last level, the level of the third period of occupation, there is not very much pottery, but the pottery that was found dates from the Roman period.

(4) Father de Vaux suggests that the ceramics indicate the following dates:

(a) Level I, the end of the Hellenistic period.

(b) Level II, from the beginning of the Roman period.

(c) Level III, only slightly more recent.

(d) The use of the caves was contemporary to that of the Khirbet at periods I and II; the material corresponding to period II is preponderant.

C. *The cemetery (the Necropolis)*

1. The cemetery is situated to the east of the building on a plateau and four small hills; its tidily arranged eleven hundred tombs are not artistic monuments but humble pebble heaps which are, with a few exceptions, directed southward.
2. Father de Vaux and Harding, as mentioned before, explored two tombs in 1949. They explored nine others in 1951 and nine in 1953.
   a. The skeletons were lying on their backs, with their heads, in most cases, to the south.
   b. Contrary to the Jewish custom at the time, no funeral offerings were found—no jewels and no sign of any garment. This confirmed the impression of strict discipline and communal living. The raw bricks and earth trash of the tombs yielded nothing but a few pottery sherds apparently contemporary with the pottery fragments found in the building.
   c. A jar found in one tomb might be dated from the last century B.C.
3. Nine skeletons have been unearthed, several of women.
   a. Professor H. V. Vallois, Director of the Paris Musée de l'Homme, proposes these approximate ages: two individuals from twenty to thirty, four of about forty, two over fifty years old. The ninth skeleton is not mentioned in his report nor is the number of women given.
   b. No child's skeleton has so far been traced.

D. *Description of the buildings*

1. The buildings cover a total area of 80 by 80 meters.
2. They form a rectangular enclosure with an impressive tower at the northwest, and behind it, to the west, some less imposing installations.
3. The main entrance pierces a wall running out of the north face of the tower.
4. To one passing through this gate, the most noticeable feature is a solidly built canal supplied by an aqueduct leading from a small dam at the foot of a waterfall in the Wadi Qumran. This canal brings water to seven large cisterns, scattered all over the settlement. The first cistern to which the canal comes is circular; all the others are rectangular, and have steps inside them enabling one to reach down to the level of the water in the dry season.

5. The western part of the settlement consists of various rooms used either as storerooms or as workshops; we find a cornmill, a baker's oven, silos for storing fruits, and rooms for storing grain. In the southwest corner of this part is a stable with stalls for about eight pack animals.
6. The entrance to the main building itself lies at the southwest corner of the tower. This tower had three floors, the third being built of bricks. A strong belt of stones was at one time put around the lower courses of the tower, and this considerably narrows the short corridor which leads from the entrance along the south of the tower into the center of the main building.
7. A small courtyard to the east of this corridor opens into two rooms, in the first of which a low plastered bench runs along the walls. A staircase from the courtyard leads to an upper floor which runs above these two rooms and over a third long room to the east of them. Above this long room was a sort of veranda, well lightened and airy. Here was the *scriptorium*. The excavators found broken structures in the debris which, reconstructed, were found to constitute the following:
    a. A narrow table, some 17 feet long and 20 inches high, and one or two shorter tables. These structures are associated with plaster benches which ran around the walls.
    b. A desk top, divided by a longitudinal ridge into two sections, each with a small basin hollowed out at the top. Three inkwells, one of brass, the others of baked clay, and all containing remains of a carbon ink of the type used on the scrolls, were also found.
    c. The hand basins, explained as basins where the scribes might perform the ritual of washing their hands when the name of God had to be written.
    d. The writing and copying of the scrolls were, Milik feels, done as follows:
        (1) The scribes sat squatting before the long, narrow tables.
        (2) In addition to his sheet of papyrus or leather, each scribe shared with his neighbor a small table on which was kept a supply of reed pens and cylindrical inkstands.
8. To the east of the tower is the kitchen with well-preserved, rather rudimentary fireplaces, and in the southeast corner of the main building are the laundry and a dump for dirty water.

9. The largest room of all—22 by 4.5 meters in size—lies outside on the south of the main block, its eastern end covered by a roof supported by four central pillars. Here the liturgical gatherings of the Essenes were probably held: their reading of and commenting on the Scriptures, and their prayers and sacred meals. In the southeast corner of this room more than a hundred pieces of pottery were found, which had probably served for the last meals that the community took just before monastery was destroyed. Near this is a circular paved area of the floor which probably was the base of a pulpit or lectern.
10. An adjacent room served as a pantry, in which were found what had once been neat stacks of over a thousand pieces of pottery.
11. To the southwest there is a complete potter's shop, with the basin where the clay was kneaded, the tank in which it was kept, a hollow where the wheel once stood, and two conical kilns—one for baking jars and the other for smaller pieces.
12. In normal times these buildings did not house many occupants, and a good part of the community must have lived nearby in huts and caves. About thirty caves in the limestone cliffs were occupied, as is shown by the evidence of the pottery and manuscripts found in them. Some others were even cut out of the marly slopes of the plateau itself.

E. *The buildings in the different phases of occupation*

1. As has been mentioned, articles from the seventh and eighth centuries B.C. have been found at the ruins, and so it is certain that when the sect first came to establish itself on the shore of the Dead Sea it did not choose a virgin site.
2. The plan of the buildings in the early centuries, somewhat obscured by later Essene constructions, can be restored as follows:
   a. The buildings consisted of a rectangular enclosure built of roughly dressed stones.
   b. Along the inside of one, two, or four of these were small rooms, called "casemates" by archaeologists.
   c. To the west of the four walls there is a deep, round cistern.
   d. To the south of Khirbet Qumran, there is another Iron Age II enclosure, bigger than that of the Khirbet but with flimsy walls. It may have been nothing more than a pen for flocks and herds. A very long retaining wall, running from north to south, kept the

cultivated fields to the east from being harmed either by violent mountain floods or by animals.

e. From the detailed list of place names in Joshua 15, it is possible to trace the Israelitish names of these settlements. The district of "the Desert" described in Joshua 15 : 61 contains six villages: Bet Ha'arabah (near Jericho), 'Ein Gedi, and four others between them.
  (1) One of these is called *Ir Hammelaḥ*, that is, the city of salt. Its identification with Qumran is now certain, since the remaining three names can be assigned to three other sites.
  (2) The identification of the four sites depends partly on the fact that no other Iron Age II sites were found in the region.

3. When the Essenes left Jerusalem to settle in the ruins of the city of salt, they cleaned out the round cistern and built two other rectangular cisterns nearby, all of which collected the rain water from the flat surface around.
   a. They built some modest rooms around these, perhaps cleared and re-utilized some of the Iron Age II casemates and installed a new potter's kiln inside the old enclosure.
   b. When the sect completed their latter-scale installation, most traces of the earlier occupation were obliterated.

4. Some time in Hyrcanus' reign (135-104 B.C.) the site entered into its most flourishing stage, and there was a radical rebuilding on the site.
   a. An impressive and well-planned structure of two and three floors filled in the older enclosure. The settlement expanded beyond these walls to the west and south.
   b. The increased number of inhabitants could no longer rely on a haphazard supply of rainwater, and the extensive and complicated network of canals and cisterns was installed at this time. A dam was built to catch the water which, once or twice each spring, runs down the Wadi Qumran.
   c. An aqueduct was cut out of the rocks and a trench dug through the marl to bring all this water to the settlement, where it was stored in cisterns. The whole system was carefully coated with impermeable plaster.
   d. The fact that so large an area was built over and the water storage capacity so enlarged suggests that the occupants of the settlement had become more numerous during the reign of John Hyrcanus.

EXCAVATIONS AT KHIRBET QUMRAN 21

e. The closing years of this phase were marked by two disasters—an earthquake which we have already discussed and a fire which ravaged the settlement from north to south.
5. No major rebuilding of the damaged settlement took place for some years until the beginning of the reign of Archelaus in 4 B.C.
   a. Several indications of a long interval can be seen in the ruins of the settlement.
      (1) On top of the thick layer of ashes in the northwest corner there is a layer of mud which settled there because the aqueduct overflowed; this presupposes a period when the system of canals and cisterns was not being properly supervised.
      (2) During the work of reconstruction by the sect, the collapsed buildings were thoroughly cleaned out and swept, and the debris was thrown away in a small ravine to the north of the settlement. In 1953 a large trench was dug into the slope of the ravine and yielded pottery, an inscribed ostracon, plaster, and numerous coins; there is no coin of Herod's reign, and only one from the reign of Archelaus.
   b. In spite of the archaeological evidence that there was no rebuilding during this period, it is still possible that the building was occupied during this time. It seems plausible to assume that a small number of the sect members continued to live in the ruins in the interval before rebuilding.
6. The death of Herod (4 B.C.) marks a major rebuilding at Qumran and this major rebuilding followed the lines of the old settlement fairly closely.
   a. Because of a fear of damage from another earthquake, the upper parts of the structure were strengthened, belts of stone were put around the base of the northwest tower, the western building, and the pantry.
   b. Some parts were abandoned such as the cistern that had been split by the earthquake—a fact which might suggest a slightly reduced number of inhabitants.
   c. Some new areas were enclosed such, as the north side of the main building, but the purpose of this was probably to reduce the number of secondary entrances and so increase the building's defensibility.
7. The Roman garrison stationed at Qumran did the following building:
   a. They leveled the thick layer of fallen stones and beams and built a few modest barracks inside the ruins.

EXCAVATIONS AT KHIRBET QUMRAN

b. The main group of rooms of this period was found above the southwest corner of the central Essene building, where the scriptorium and the council chamber had been.

8. As mentioned before, the buildings served as a refuge in A.D. 132-135 for the partisans of Bar Kochba, and the second Jewish revolt.

9. In the centuries following that, dust covered the ruins more and more, and only some transient monks and shepherds left traces of their passage.

Topics for Study and Discussion

A. Discuss the following aspects of the excavations at Qumran:
   1. Factors that prompted the excavations.
   2. The beginning and duration of the excavations and some of the things found and their importance.
   3. Earlier reports of the Khirbet Qumran site.

B. Summarize the history of the Qumran ruins—that is, the four stages of occupation—and discuss the three stages of occupation in the Greco-Roman period.

C. Discuss the archaeological evidence which has enabled scholars to reconstruct the history of Khirbet Qumran.

D. Discuss some of the buildings or places reconstructed at the site, the importance of the reconstructed area and its relevance to the study of the Dead Sea Scrolls.

E. Discuss the importance and relevance of the excavations at Khirbet Qumran to further knowledge of the Dead Sea Scrolls and the the sect that wrote them.

IV

THE DATING OF THE SCROLLS

Dating the scrolls was a fundamental problem which the scholars had to study and about which they had to reach a generally accepted solution. It was important to determine whether the scrolls are pre-Christian or medieval. At the very first announcement of the discovery in 1947, sharp controversy broke out on the question of the age of the texts. This battle raged for nearly a decade following the discovery. For several years almost everyone who wrote about the scrolls suggested a different date. The range was from the third century B.C. to the twelfth century A.D. Back of the most extreme of the "wars" on the scrolls was Solomon Zeitlin of Dropsie College. From the very beginning he questioned the date of the scrolls—even before seeing them—and violently branded the entire find as a hoax of the twentieth century. Several years later he suggested that the scrolls belonged to a Jewish medieval sect known as the Karaites—a sect which believed in the Old Testament books but not in postbiblical and rabbinical books.

Archaeology played an important role in dating these documents, a fact to which some scholars attribute the bitter controversy and difference of opinion. They claim that archaeology is an inexact science, a notion strongly rejected by such eminent scholars as W. F. Albright, F. M. Cross, Jr., and others.

In view of the archaeological, linguistic, paleographical, and other evidence, it is now generally agreed that the date of the scrolls is between the second century B.C. and the first century A.D. With few exceptions, there have been no challengers of this date.

RECOMMENDED READING

You are required to read at least TWO of the following:
Allegro, J. M. *The Dead Sea Scrolls*, pages 75-93
Burrows, M., *The Dead Sea Scrolls*, pages 73-122
Burrows, M., *More Light on the Dead Sea Scrolls*, pages 10-11 and pages 191-203

24 THE DATING OF THE SCROLLS

Mansoor, M., *The Thanksgiving Hymns*, chapter on the "Dating of the Scrolls," pages 7-10
Van der Ploeg, J., *The Excavations at Qumran*, pages 29-52
Vermes, G., *Discovery in the Judean Desert*, pages 30-35
Yadin, Y., *The Message of the Scrolls*, pages 160-173

Read the material carefully and note the various methods adopted to reach the date of the scrolls.

If you wish to study the subject further, consult the bibliography given in W. S. La Sor, *Bibliography of the Dead Sea Scrolls*, 1948-1957, pages 44-46. For a discussion and summary of the dating of the scrolls, see also the chapter on the age of the scrolls in Menahem Mansoor, *The Thanksgiving Hymns*. Your instructor will be glad to recommend additional bibliographical material to you.

DATING THE SCROLLS

A. *Battle of the dating*

1. A whole series of dates—from the second and third century B.C. to the Middle Ages and even to the twentieth century—was offered when the scrolls were found.
   a. Solomon Zeitlin remains one of the few scholars who will not accept the antiquity of the scrolls. He claims they are Karaite writings of the Middle Ages. At the beginning he even thought the scrolls to be a hoax.
   b. Most scholars are now generally agreed in dating the manuscripts between the second century B.C. and the first century A.D.
2. Two questions are considered in the dating: (1) when were the scrolls composed or copied? and (2) when were they placed in the caves?
   a. It is generally agreed that all the scrolls were written before A.D. 68 because the cave in which they were found showed no evidence of habitation after that date.
   b. It is possible that the scrolls might have been deposited on two occasions: before A.D. 68 and between A.D. 68 and A.D. 135, when Jerusalem was completely destroyed. This possibility is supported by coins found in the area.
3. Two factors contributed to the long preservation of the scrolls:
   a. The climate of the Dead Sea Region, which is more than 1,200 feet below Mediterranean sea level, is extremely dry.

b. The sealed jars in which the scrolls were placed. (Refer to Jeremiah 32 : 14.)

B. Four factors determining the dating

1. Archaeological context. Three main elements are included in the archaeological context in which the manuscripts were found.
   a. *Pottery.* Archaeologists concluded that the pottery, though fragmentary, is clearly Roman of approximately the second century B.C. to the first century A.D.
   b. *Coins.* Scores of coins found in the Qumran ruins and the caves were from the second century B.C. to the second century A.D.
      (1) Coins found in the ruins suggest the main periods of occupation of Qumran as ranging from shortly after the reign of John Hyrcanus (135-104 B.C.) to the second year of the first revolt (A.D. 68).
      (2) It is probable that in A.D. 68, Roman legions advancing on Jerusalem destroyed the settlement. The community deposited the library in caves and specially constructed places. Hence the scrolls must be earlier than A.D. 68.
   c. *Linen.* Evidence provided by the "carbon 14" test on fragments of linen textiles in which the scrolls were wrapped supports the A.D. 68 date.
      (1) W. F. Libby, the atomic energy expert, carried out the "carbon 14" test in 1950 in the laboratories of the Institute of Nuclear Studies of the University of Chicago to determine the age of the linen.
         (a) As a result of this test, Libby announced the date to be A.D. 33, with a margin of error of plus or minus two hundred years.
         (b) This places the date of the linen wrappings roughly between 200 B.C. and A.D. 200.
      (2) G.M. Crowfoot, who conducted a detailed study of the linen, suggested that the scrolls were deposited in the caves toward the end of the first century A.D.
      (3) The half-life of carbon 14 has recently been revised, placing the age of the scrolls at 1983 years, that is, back to 20 B.C.
2. Paleography. The London University scholar, S. Birnbaum, on paleographical grounds, reached the conclusion that the scrolls were composed before the Roman period.
   a. Methods employed in paleography

(1) The basic technique is measuring—the proportion between the height and the width of a letter, the relation between the letter and the line, and the relative thickness of the strokes.

(2) The method is to examine a large number of letters from documents whose date is known, assemble and tabulate systematically the features characteristic of various periods, and thus have a framework into which to fit the forms of letters appearing in undated manuscripts.

b. Material available for comparison

(1) There are a number of dated papyri, ostraca, parchments, and inscriptions previously discovered.

(2) The letters of the alphabet in the scrolls were compared with the corresponding forms in the dated material, such as the Nash Papyrus.

(3) A good example is the material found in the excavations at Masada—about the date of which there is no doubt. A piece of pottery and a papyrus fragment were found, both inscribed in black ink and Hebrew letters very similar to those in which the Dead Sea Scrolls were written.

c. Paleographic findings

(1) The Qumran manuscripts do not all emanate from the same date. Those in square script were written within a period of about two and a half centuries.

(2) The date when the manuscript was written is not necessarily the same as the date when the text was composed. However, by determining the script, paleography established the latest possible time that the text could have been written.

3. Orthography and language
   a. The language of the scrolls, solidly based on biblical Hebrew, is strongly flavored with pre-Christian Aramaic, late Hebrew, and, to some extent, Samaritan.
   b. The spelling and other linguistic features of the text support a date between 200 B.C. and A.D. 100.

4. Historical allusions
   a. The sect of the scrolls has been equated by some with the Essenes, a pre-Christian Jewish community which lived in that region from the second century B.C. to the first century A.D.
   b. One important fragmentary scroll, the *Nahum Commentary*, contains actual historical names, those of Antiochus and Deme-

trius, who ruled over Palestine during the first century B.C. and earlier.

c. There is, besides the *Nahum Commentary*, a liturgical calendar in which a series of kings is named.

d. Another proof is the existence among the scrolls of a type of biblical commentary which we know conclusively cannot have existed later than the second century B.C.

TOPICS FOR STUDY AND DISCUSSION

A. Discuss the battle of dating the scrolls and the date now generally accepted by most scholars.

B. Write a brief account of the coins discovered in the Qumran area.

C. Give the views of TWO of the following scholars on the date of the scrolls:

   1. William F. Albright
   2. Millar Burrows
   3. Solomon Birnbaum
   4. Solomon Zeitlin

D. Cite the evidence which determines the date of the scrolls.

E. Give Zeitlin's main arguments on the age of the scrolls.

F. Discuss the (1) archaeological, (2) paleographical, (3) linguistic, and (4) historical evidence relevant to the dating of the scrolls.

V

DISCOVERIES AT WADI MURABBAAT

In 1951 the first discoveries were made in the caves at Wadi Murabbaat, south of Qumran, and at a location in the same region which has never been identified. These caves show a long history of occupation—from the Chalcolithic period (fourth millenium B.C.) to the tenth century A.D. Most of the documents found, however, date from the second Jewish revolt (A.D. 132-135). Pieces of second century letters, contracts, and deeds were found in addition to manuscripts of the books of the Old Testament. (See Units 20, 21, and 22 for discoveries pertaining to Bar Kochba, made in 1960 and 1961.)

The biblical manuscripts found at Wadi Murabbaat are important in that, unlike the Qumran manuscripts, they uniformly exhibit a text coinciding with the Massoretic text. Thus these manuscripts provide us with definite evidence as to the time when the process of standardization of the Hebrew Bible had reached its goal and only the officially approved text continued in use. Such unorthodox writings as Qumran affords in abundance were not found in the Murabbaat caves, and the text of the Scriptures, still fluid at Qumran, was now set. Thus we know that by the end of the first one-third of the second century A.D. the text which was to prevail from then on to the present day had practically achieved its final form.

Most of the documents, however, are from the second Jewish revolt in A.D. 135 and are of historical importance, providing us with new and precise information about this revolt. Especially interesting historically is the discovery of two letters sent by Simeon Bar Kochba, the leader of the revolt, and one letter sent to him. The documents from the second revolt also provide us with new information concerning the development of the Hebrew and Aramaic languages as used in Palestine in the Greek and Roman periods. In addition, the discoveries at Wadi Murabbaat have increased our knowledge of the toponymy in the Roman-Byzantine period and finally, from the legal point of view, the contracts found—the first such discoveries made in Palestine—give us striking information. Through these documents we now have direct contact with the legal institutions and customs of the Roman period, matters which up to now we had to deduce indirectly from rabbinic texts. Included among these documents are a bill of divorce, a marriage contract, real estate transactions, and contracts dealing with the renting of fields, all composed in Mishnaic Hebrew.

RECOMMENDED READING

You are required to read TWO of the following:
Allegro, J., *The Dead Sea Scrolls*, pages 168-179
Burrows, M., *More Light on the Dead Sea Scrolls*, pages 16-19 and 31-33
Cross, F. M., Jr., *The Ancient Library of Qumran*, pages 9-23 and 120-145
Milik, J. T., *Ten Years of Discovery in the Wilderness of Judaea*, pages 135-141
Van der Ploeg, J., *The Excavations at Qumran*, pages 26-28
Vermes, G., *Discovery in the Judean Desert*, pages 20-22
Yadin, Y, *The Message of the Scrolls*, pages 68-72

THE DISCOVERIES AT WADI MURABBAAT AND THE UNIDENTIFIED SITE NEARBY

A. *The location of Wadi Murabbaat*

1. Wadi Murabbaat rarely figures in Palestinian maps.
2. It is the name given to a section of the great Wadi which begins south of Bethlehem, where it is called Wadi Taamre, and falls into the Dead Sea some 12 kilometers south of Ein Geddi, under the name of Wadi Daraje.
3. The caves are situated 25 kilometers southeast of Jerusalem (about 15 miles) and 18 kilometers south of Qumran (about 10 miles) from the Dead Sea.
4. The Wadi Murabbaat caves are situated at about sea level, while the Qumran caves are 1,000 feet lower.

B. *Excavations at Wadi Murabbaat*

1. Between January 21 and March 3 of 1952 the Jordanian Department of Antiquities, the Ecole Biblique et Archéologique Française de Jérusalem and the Palestine Archeological Museum excavated these caves.

2. Four large caves were successfully explored. The documents and objects recovered enabled the archaeologists to establish that there had been five phases of occupation, although often the occupants of one period destroyed what remained of a previous occupation.
   a. Severe damage had been caused by falling stones.
   b. Damage had also been caused by Bedouins who had been doing clandestine digging.
3. The five phases of occupation
   a. The Chalcolithic period (4000-3000 B.C.) is well represented by pottery fragments, silex, carved stones, and—what is less common —articles of wood and leather, remains of a fish net, and several fragments of basketwork. This is the first time that ancient objects found in perishable materials, such as the wooden vessels and the remains of rush nets, have been discovered in Palestine.
   b. The Middle Bronze Age (2000-1600 B.C.) is represented by some sherds of pottery, two bronze pins, a small alabaster vase, and a Hyksos scarab.
   c. Iron Age II (eighth and seventh centuries B.C.) is represented only by some fragments of Judean pottery.
   d. The Greco-Roman period is well represented, especially the Roman period. The following have been found:
      (1) Pottery similar in many respects to that of Qumran.
      (2) Weapons, bronze spearheads, iron arrowheads and tools (knives, including one with a wooden handle, nails and a sickle).
      (3) Wooden objects—plates, spoons, bowls, combs, studs.
      (4) Fabrics, some of them embroidered, and remains of sandals and of leather outfits.
      (5) About twenty coins—three of the procurators under Nero (d. 68 A.D.) and nine from the second revolt in A.D. 132-135. Two worn Roman coins are countermarked with a galley, one of the *Decima Legia Fretensi's* emblems (that legion was stationed in Judea from Titus' victory on).
   e. The Arab period left the sherds of a bowl, a piece of fabric, and two coins—one from the Omayyad period. We also have a few fragments in Arabic written on cotton paper which are as late as the tenth century.

C. *Documents found at Murabbaat*

1. Murabbaat has provided us with one of the earliest manuscripts found in Palestine—a palimpsest papyrus. (A palimpsest is a new text which was written over an older one.)
   a. The older text is too faint to be deciphered fully, but it is believed that the text can be dated by the script in the eighth century B.C., the time of the prophets Amos, Hosea, Micah, and Isaiah.
   b. The newer text has been dated as sixth century B.C.—the time of the prophet Jeremiah and the Babylonian exile. A list of four personal names with symbols and figures can be made out.
   c. The language of both earlier and later texts is Hebrew and the script is Phoenician.
   d. The above datings have not been confirmed.
   e. No older Semitic papyrus is known and only Egyptian hieroglyphic and hieratic papyri antedate it.

2. From the same time as some of the Qumran manuscripts are two ostraca (inscribed potsherds).
   a. Their script indicates a date near the end of the second century B.C.
   b. One of them bears only a few letters but the other lines of text are in a very old form of Aramaic.
   c. At the other end of the period covered by the Qumran texts there is a contract in Aramaic dated *in the second year of the reign of Nero*, A.D. 56, just two years before the destruction of Khirbet Qumran.

3. Biblical fragments dating from the first and second centuries A.D. were found. The fragments from the Murabbaat caves provide a text identical with that of the Massoretes in the texts of the Pentateuch, Isaiah, Minor Prophets, and Psalms, whereas this is not true of the biblical texts found at Qumran.

4. A complete phylactery was found. It consisted of a bag containing a thin band of rolled parchment inscribed with the following three passages: Exodus 13 : 1-16, Deuteronomy 11 : 13-21 and 6 : 4-9. This last passage which appears on the extreme right of the leather is the text known as the *Shema*.

5. With the exception of the manuscripts described in 1 and 2 above, the material from Wadi Murabbaat dates from the time just before and during the second Jewish revolt against Rome (A.D. 132-135) and consists mostly of contracts and letters.

a. Several contracts are written in Greek. Two concern matrimonial matters. One of these, which dates back to the seventh year of the Emperor Hadrian, corresponding to A.D. 124, deals with the reconciliation of husband and wife, Eleos and Salome. Another Greek papyrus is a debt acknowledgement dating from A.D. 171.

b. Other Greek documents
   (1) A text mentioning the Emperor Commodus (A.D. 180-192).
   (2) Two literary fragments: one might be a part of some religious text, the other is historical, judging by the name of Salome and Marianne, possibly the sister and the second or third wife of Herod the Great.

c. Of the nonbiblical manuscripts in Hebrew, one is a hymn-like composition. Most of the texts, however, are of more historical than literary interest.
   (1) Bill of divorce dated in "the sixth year" (probably A.D. 111).
   (2) A marriage contract dated five years later.
   (3) A fragment coming from the eve of the second revolt (A.D. 131).
   (4) A tiny scrap of papyrus dealing with the sale of real estate bearing the date "Year 1 of of Redemption of Israel," that is, A.D. 132-133, the beginning of the second revolt.
   (5) Twelve contracts dated in the following year concerning the renting of fields and guaranteed by the authority of the leader of the revolt, Simeon ben Kosiba (also spelled Koseba, Kosebah, Kosibah, Kozibah, or Kozba).
   (6) Four fragmentary documents dealing with real estate transactions, one of which is dated "Year three of the freedom of Jerusalem," that is, A.D. 134-135, the third year of the revolt; still another real estate contract is dated "Year three of the freedom of Israel."
   (7) An unusual document from the same year, a bill of divorce given by a woman to her husband.
   (8) Several contracts not dated, or in which the dates are not preserved.

d. Some of the most interesting texts from Wadi Murabbaat are letters. There are two letters addressed by Simeon ben Kosiba (Bar Kochba) to Yeshua ben Galgola, believed to be original letters from Bar Kochba in person. There was also a letter to Bar Kochba from two officials of the Jewish community, and there is a letter addressed to ben Galgola who is here described as the Head of the Camp, that is, commander of the army, and is written by several leaders of the community in a village called Beth Mashko.

(1) One of the letters to ben Galgola is an order.

(2) There are many lacunae, but it shows us that ben Kosiba was in the habit of issuing direct and short orders to his subcommanders, that he was ruthless towards those who disobeyed him, and that he demanded absolute discipline.

(3) The letter also mentions the fact that ben Galgola must mobilize "from the Galileans," and there is speculation as to who the Galileans were—Christians, or members of a Galilean sect that lived in the neighborhood of Khirbet Qumran itself.

(4) The letter from Beth Mashko to ben Galgola contains a complaint about a cow that was carried off and explains that the people put the complaint about the cow in writing "because the gentiles (Romans) are approaching us" or "are in our vicinity."

e. Other finds include a few small fragments in Latin, administrative registers written on skins or parchments, and a complete phylactery.

f. The Latin fragments in addition to the Greek fragments dated after the Jewish revolt suggest that after the suppression of the revolt a Roman garrison held the place for some time.

6. Material found in unidentified site.
   a. A few fragments of Genesis, Numbers, and Psalms.
   b. A phylactery.
   c. A letter addressed to Simeon ben Kosiba.
   d. Two Aramaic contracts dated in the third year of "the liberation of Israel" by ben Kosiba (Bar Kochba).
   e. Two other Aramaic documents and two in Greek, dated according to the era of the Roman province of Arabia.
   f. A group of papyri in the Nabatean dialect, important matter for the study of the Semitic languages, particularly Aramaic, since these papyri provide more extensive and continuous texts than the inscriptions on which our knowledge of this dialect has depended hitherto.
   g. A fragmentary column from a Greek manuscript of the book of Habakkuk, affording what Barthélemy has called a missing link in the history of the Septuagint.

7. Both the archaeological and epigraphical documents point to the caves as having provided a shelter during the Bar Kochba war for a Jewish military outpost, probably under the command of Yeshua ben Galgola. The Romans apparently succeeded in dislodging him, and sacked the place. As mentioned above (in section 5) the Romans established a post there, probably to control the road to Ein Geddi.

D. *Importance of the finds at Wadi Murabbaat and the unidentified site*
1. Language and script
    a. The eight languages represented among the scrolls from the Dead Sea area are biblical Hebrew, Mishnaic Hebrew, Palestinian Aramaic, Nabatean, Palestinian Christian Aramaic, Greek, Latin, and Arabic. The last five mainly appear in the texts of Khirbet Mird, from the Byzantine period. The other three may be reduced to Hebrew and Aramaic.
        (1) It is clear that Hebrew and Aramaic were used together by the Qumran community and also by the second century A.D. revolutionaries who left the manuscripts of the Wadi Murabbaat.
        (2) Mishnaic Hebrew and Aramaic were the two languages in use at Murabbaat.
        (3) The Aramaic texts of the Qumran and Murabbaat caves fill a gap in our sources for the knowledge of that language as used in Palestine in the Greco-Roman periods.
        (4) Later forms of Aramaic are exemplified by the texts of Murabbaat and Khirbet Mird.
        (5) The dialect of the Nabatean kingdom across the Jordan appears in papyrus documents from the unidentified site and teaches us much about that dialect.
    b. The type of script in the biblical as well as nonbiblical manuscripts is the type known as *ornamental* script.
        (1) It is the script used after the first half of the first century A.D.
        (2) This is the script the rabbis at the Synod of Jamnia used for copying the Scriptures, and its presence in the Murabbaat documents confirms the fact that prescriptions concerning transmission of the Bible had already attained final form by the second century A.D.
        (3) This script is characterized by uniformity in the size and shape of the letters and by florid curves and titles.

2. Historical importance of the Murabbaat documents
   a. The texts found at Murabbaat provide several precise details about the second Jewish revolt.
   b. Hitherto scholars have had to rely on sparse allusions in the classical historians and in the Talmud and on a few inscriptions on coins for their information of the second Jewish revolt.
   c. Though the discoveries do not help us to know more exactly the course of the principal events of the war, they do show how the rebels organized the civil and military government of the country and what motives inspired them.
   d. We now have more information about the leader of the revolt as a result of the discovery of two letters sent by him and one sent to him.
      (1) One of the letters was possibly written in his own hand, as there is a resemblance between the script in which the text is written and that of the signature.
      (2) A reference to his headquarters is contained in a legal contract found.
   e. The letters have also revived discussion among scholars concerning the original form and meaning of the name *Bar Kochba*. In the Wadi Murabbaat texts he is called Simeon ben Kosiba. He is commonly known as Simeon Bar Kochba, that is, "son of the Star," who was believed by some of his contemporaries to be the "star of Jacob" predicted in Numbers 24 : 17. (For details see Units 20, 21, and 22.)
3. These documents have also increased our knowledge of the toponymy of Palestine in the Romano-Byzantine period.
   a. For example, a contract from Murabbaat mentions the village of Hnblt', probably to be identified with the Anablata which, according to a letter of St. Epiphanius, lies on the road from Jerusalem to Bethel and is therefore the present-day Bir Nabalah, about five miles northwest of Jerusalem.
   b. In a fragmentary marriage contract from Murabbaat there is mention of a village called Hrdwn', where some member of the priestly family of Elyašib was living. In the uncertain manuscript transmission of the Talmud we sometimes find Bet Harôdôn as the place to which the scapegoat was led; the name seems to have survived in Hirbet Haredân, a hill in the Judean wilderness some three miles from Jerusalem.
4. From the legal point of view it is the contracts from Murabbaat and

the similar unidentified site which give us the most striking information.

a. They are the first such discoveries made in Palestine. Four languages are represented in them: Mishnaic Hebrew, Palestinian Aramaic, Nabatean, and Greek.

b. Through these documents we have direct contact with the legal institutions and customs of the Roman period and their appropriate formulas, matters which up to now we had to deduce indirectly from rabbinical texts (and these are more concerned with Jewish jurisprudence of a slightly later period).

c. At the present early stage in the study of these documents it is becoming apparent that there are points of contact with the forms we find in Babylonian contracts and in Aramaic contracts from Elephantine and Greek papyri in Egypt as well as with later Talmudic legal practice.

E. *Conclusions*

1. The discoveries at Wadi Murabbaat have lost some of their drama because they were discovered at the same time as the manuscripts at Qumran.

2. These discoveries throw additional light on the Qumran finds and prove beyond a doubt that even after the destruction of the main building of the Dead Sea sect at the end of the first Jewish revolt, the Judean desert continued to serve as an asylum for victims of persecution and for rebels.

3. The Bar Kochba letters form a unique treasure in that they provide us with the only original archive known from the period of the end of the Second Temple and the revolt. (See Units 20, 21, and 22 which are devoted to recent discoveries of Bar Kochba texts).

TOPICS FOR STUDY AND DISCUSSION

A. Discuss each of the following:

1. The location of Wadi Murabbaat

2. The excavations at Wadi Murabbaat

3. The five phases of occupation at Wadi Murabbaat, and the archaeological evidence of these phases.

B. Discuss the phylactery and the biblical fragments found in Murabbaat. Explain the significance of these finds.

C. Discuss the manuscripts found which date from the time of the second Jewish revolt. Make reference to the Bar Kochba materials.

D. Discuss the importance of the manuscripts found at Wadi Murabbaat for further knowledge in two of the following areas of study and research:

1. Language and script of the first to second centuries A.D.
2. History of the first to second centuries A.D.
3. Jurisprudence in the first to second centuries A.D.

VI

DISCOVERIES AT KHIRBET MIRD AND LATER DISCOVERIES

The discoveries at Khirbet Mird are not related to the Qumran or Murabbaat finds but will be of interest to students of later periods. The biblical fragments from this site are of Christian origin, whereas those from Qumran and Murabbaat relate to the Jews. This unit also briefly reviews later discoveries in the Judean desert, that is, the caves found after the discovery of Cave One in 1947. Very little has been written on the Khirbet Mird discovery. (See also Units 20, 21, and 22 for the 1960-1961 discoveries in Israel.)

RECOMMENDED READING

Read at least THREE of the following:

Allegro, J., *The Dead Sea Scrolls*, pages 35-49 and 179-180
Burrows, M., *The Dead Sea Scrolls*, pages 54-69
Cross, F. M., Jr., *The Ancient Library of Qumran*, pages 9-36
Milik, J. T., *Ten Years of Discovery in the Wilderness of Judaea*, pages 15-19 and 129-132
Van der Ploeg, J., *The Excavations at Qumran*, pages 21-28
Vermes, G., *Discovery in the Judean Desert*. pages 23-25

DISCOVERIES AT KHIRBET MIRD

A. *History of Khirbet Mird*

1. Khirbet Mird is the site of the ancient fortress Hyrcania, built by John (Jonathan) Hyrcanus, high priest and prince of the Hasmonean family, who was born about 175 B.C. and died about 104 B.C.

2. Khirbet Mird is located about nine miles southeast of Jerusalem. Bedouins discovered manuscripts here in 1952.

3. In A.D. 492 a Castellion monastery was founded on this site by Mar

Saba (Saint Sabas). This monastery flourished until the ninth century.
4. The monastery is called in Byzantine writings *Castellion* or *Marda*. The latter is Aramaic and means the same as the first, that is, "fortress".
5. The region of Khirbet Mird knew its greatest days in the fifth and sixth centuries A.D.; the site has produced a series of texts dating from the fifth to eighth centuries A.D.
6. The remains of the library of Khirbet Mird were discovered in an underground chamber.
7. A Belgian archaeological mission conducted by Prof. R. de Langhe of the University of Louvain explored Khirbet Mird from February to April of 1953.

B. *The texts*

1. The manuscripts found were in three languages: Arabic, Greek, and Christian Palestinian Aramaic, the dialect used by the Christians of Palestine in the Byzantine period and during the first centuries of Arab domination.
2. Paleographical criteria lead one to date all these texts towards the end of the Byzantine and the beginning of the Arab periods. An Arabic contract contains a date in the second century of the Hegira (eighth century A.D.).
3. Texts include fragments of *codices* written on both sides from the Book of Wisdom, the Gospels of Mark and John, and Acts of the Apostles; they are written in Greek uncial and may be dated from between the fifth to eighth centuries A.D.
4. Biblical fragments range from Joshua to the Gospels of Matthew and Luke, the Acts, and the Epistle to the Colossians, all of them written in Syro-Palestinian tongue and script. Greek fragments of non-biblical works, documents in cursive script, and Arabic and Syriac papyri are also included in the texts found.
5. Deciphering work is only beginning, but a fragment of Euripides' *Andromache* has already been identified. It dates from the sixth century A.D., making it a thousand years older than the most ancient manuscript on parchment hitherto known. The field of classical literature brings us into a world very different from that of Qumran.
6. One of the texts that has been deciphered is a complete letter on papyrus, written by a monk called Gabriel to the superior of the Monastery of Marda-Castellion.

C. *Significance of discoveries at Khirbet Mird*

1. It is hoped the documents from Khirbet Mird will improve our knowledge of monastic life in Judea in several details.
2. There are many manuscripts in Christian Palestinian Aramaic in the Khirbet Mird find. Other manuscripts written in this language are known but the Khirbet Mird manuscripts give us for the first time literary texts found in Palestine itself, and nonliterary texts composed in that language.
3. The Greek biblical texts come from the library of the sacred books which the monks used in church and cloister. We see that Syro-Palestinian is the language they spoke and which they used in the liturgy along with the Greek, until it was eliminated by Arabic.
4. The finds from Khirbet Mird appear so far to be relevant above all to the study of the history of Greek Bible translations.

CHRONOLOGICAL SUMMARY OF THE LATER DISCOVERIES IN THE JUDEAN DESERT

(By "later discoveries" we mean all the caves and documents found after the first cave was discovered in 1947.)

A. *Discoveries in* 1951

1. Khirbet Qumran, the headquarters of the Jewish community that produced the Qumran manuscripts, was discovered in 1949, but excavations were not begun until 1951. These excavations continued until 1956.
2. In 1951 Bedouins found separate collections of manuscripts from the second century in Wadi Murabbaat, a few miles farther south than Wadi Qumran.
3. Other fragments from the same period were brought in by Bedouins from a place in the same region which has never been definitely relocated.

B. *Discoveries in* 1952

1. In 1952 four caves in Wadi Murabbaat were excavated.
2. While excavations at Wadi Murabbaat were going on, Bedouins found another cave containing remnants of manuscripts, north of Wadi Qumran near Cave One. Many caves were explored in 1952. In one of them, Cave Three, the copper rolls were found.

3. In the summer of 1952 manuscripts were found at Khirbet Mird, about three miles northwest of Khirbet Qumran.
4. Also in 1952, Bedouins found a fourth cave in the Wadi Qumran, very close to Khirbet Qumran, and shortly thereafter two other caves were discovered. The richest of all the caves in manuscript fragments was Cave Four.

C. *Discoveries in* 1955

1. Four more caves with scraps of manuscripts were discovered during the 1955 excavations at Khirbet Qumran.
2. At about the same time a badly damaged scroll of the minor prophets from the second century A.D. was found by Bedouins in a cave of Wadi Murabbaat.

D. *Discoveries in* 1956

1. In 1956, Bedouins found another cave in the Qumran area, a little north of Cave one, the eleventh cave found in that area.
2. In the importance of its contents, Cave Eleven rivals Cave One and Cave Four.
3. Contents of Cave Eleven.
   a. Four relatively complete scrolls similar to those of Cave One.
   b. Part of the Book of Leviticus and parts of an Apocalypse of the New Testament.
   c. A scroll of Psalms and an Aramaic Targum of Job.

E. *Seasons of excavations*

1. First three seasons of excavation at Khirbet Qumran:
   a. November 24-December 12, 1951.
   b. February 9-April 24, 1953.
   c. February 13-April 14, 1954.
2. Fourth season: February 2-April 6, 1955.
3. Fifth season: February 18-March 28, 1956.

F. *The material found in the desert of Judea falls into three general groups:*

1. Manuscripts coming from caves in the Qumran area in the vicinity of the community settlement at Khirbet Qumran, dating broadly speaking from the second century B.C. to the first century A.D.
2. Documents from Wadi Murabbaat and the unidentified site, found in caves and wadis that are difficult of access and remote from all centers of habitation in the southern part of the Judean desert. These caves

served as a refuge in all periods but were especially used so during the second Jewish revolt.
3. Manuscripts found in the ruins of the Byzantine monastery, Khirbet Mird. This lay not far from Jerusalem, in the middle of the monk's desert, which knew its greatest days in the fifth and sixth centuries A.D.

Topics for Study and Discussion

A. Describe the history and location of the site known as Khirbet Mird and the manuscripts found there.
B. Describe the later discoveries in the Judean desert and the general groupings into which we can place the material from the Judean desert.
C. Discuss the texts found at Khirbet Mird and their significance.

VII

THE COPPER SCROLLS

This unit outlines the interesting discovery of two copper rolls in one of the caves. These two rolls actually form a single copper scroll which contains a long list of hidden treasure to the amount of some six thousand gold and silver talents. It is advisable that you read Allegro's writings on the copper scrolls, since he had actually prepared the transcription of the text of these scrolls. Another good description is that of Yadin.

RECOMMENDED READING

Allegro, J. M., *The Dead Sea Scrolls*, pages 181-184
———, *The Treasure of the Copper Scrolls*, pages 33-55, the text and the scroll and a translation
Van der Ploeg, J., *The Excavations at Qumran*, pages 182-183
Vermes, G., *The Dead Sea Scrolls in English*, pp. 248-251
Yadin, Y., *The Message of the Scrolls*, pages 156-159.

Read at least two of the books listed above. Make your own notes as you read. The work by Allegro on this scroll is of importance, since he has actually assisted Professor Wright-Baker of Manchester University in unrolling the scroll and has transcribed the Hebrew text.

THE COPPER SCROLLS

A. *Discovery and description*

1. On March 14, 1952, two badly corroded copper scrolls were found in a cave (now known as Cave Three) whose roof had collapsed in antiquity.

2. Originally, these two copper scrolls belonged to a single plaque, 8 feet long and 11 inches high, composed of three sheets of thin copper each about 12 by 30 inches riveted at the edges.

3. The copper scrolls had been made as a replica of a normal leather scroll, with riveting instead of stitching.

4. The writing in these metal scrolls had been beaten out by a sharp instrument, probably a stylus with a point one-eighth of an inch wide.
5. Due to centuries of oxidization the scrolls were extremely brittle and crumbled to dust at any manipulation of the edges. It was impossible to unwind them in this form to read the text. Early attempts between 1952 and 1956 to unroll the copper scrolls failed.

B. *Unrolling the scrolls*

1. The strips were coated with a paraffin wax and taken to the Palestine Archaeological Museum, where they rested for three years until the problem of opening them without damaging the inscription was solved.
2. In 1955 the scrolls were taken to the Manchester College of Technology in England where Mr. Wright-Baker, professor of mechanical engineering, had designed and constructed a sawing machine which could cut the rolls into strips.
3. The cutting process involved three steps:
   a. The dust was removed from the center of the scroll and a spindle was inserted through the hollow and tightened with dental plaster. The scrolls were mounted on a spindle in this way to avoid direct and unnecessary handling.
   b. The roll was coated with a chemical solution to strengthen the decomposed metal.
4. The cutting was done by a sawing machine with a diamond cutter six-thousandth of an inch thick, which cut the scrolls into strips with little damage to the letters.

C. *Contents*

1. Originally the scrolls contained some three thousand letters, but one hundred fifty have been lost through breakage. The remaining are clear and easily read, although they contain twelve columns of writing.
2. The treasure recorded in these scrolls includes gold and silver in bullion, coins, and sacred vessels.
3. The language used is Mishnaic (postbiblical) Hebrew.
4. The scrolls contain a list of some sixty hiding places of treasures amounting to two hundred tons each of gold and silver. Sites over all of Palestine, but most centering around Jerusalem, are mentioned.

a. The treasures were hidden in wells and tombs near conspicuous objects, such as trees and springs.
   b. The description of the localities of the caches follows a definite pattern:
      (1) The place name in Palestine is given.
      (2) Details describing the geographical and topographical location are mentioned.
      (3) The depth of the treasure below the surface is recorded in cubits.
      (4) Details of the treasure are enumerated.
5. At first sight, the amounts of treasure recorded in the copper scrolls might seem fantastic. Totals of precious metals concerned (as far as the text can now be read) are as follows:

   Gold: 1,280 talents
   Gold Bars: 65 plus
   Pitchers containing silver: 608
   Vessels made of silver and gold: 619

6. Whether these amounts are abnormally large depends on the weight we accord the talent of this period.
   a. We have no certain knowledge of the values accorded the talent and its factors in Judean common speech of the first century.
   b. Allegro suggests that we come nearer to the truth in the scroll if we downgrade the official "talent" to the value of the next denomination, the *maneh* (Greek *mina*), the sixtieth part of a talent, and the *maneh* to the shekel, a fiftieth part of the *maneh*.
   c. Allegro feels that there is other evidence for a similar regionalization of monetary values at the time, for we read that the Galilean *sela'* was reckoned as only half the Judean value for this coin. He feels that we may compare the English slang "dollar" for five shillings, or the semijocular substitution of "pound" for "shilling" and "shilling" for "penny" among British tradesmen, omnibus conductors, and the like.
   d. As Allegro puts it, "All one can say for certain is that this supposition gives very reasonable amounts for the treasure deposits of our scroll."
7. An interesting confirmation of Allegro's theory may be found in an actual treasure deposit within the Qumran monastery.

a. Under the plaster floor of one of the rooms was found a treasure hoard of 558 Tyrian tetradrachmae whose weight must be something in the region of twenty pounds. The coins had been carefully hidden away in three small juglets, sealed with fibre stoppers. The size of this cache coincides rather well with the average of the scroll items.
b. In view of this, Allegro suggests that we understand the "talent" of the scroll to be a *maneh* of twelve ounces.
  (1) The totals may then be estimated as follows:
      Silver: 21 1/2 cwt
      Gold: 8 1/2 cwt
  (2) The present-day value would be about a million U.S. dollars.
8. Great as this wealth was, there is reason to believe that it was not for its monetary value alone that the treasure was hidden away.
  a. Many of the hidden items had been collected as "tithes" for the Temple and its priests from the people.
  b. These "tithe" items were holy and were not to be used by any but the priests. To use the tithes and the "tithe vessels" for nonreligious purposes was a heinous sin.
9. Allegro feels, therefore, that the main purpose of the copper scrolls was as follows:
  a. They are a record of such deposits of sacred material, tithe and tithe vessels as well as silver and gold and precious vessels, sanctified by dedication or actual use in God's service.
  b. The copper scrolls and their copy (or copies) were intended to tell the Jewish survivors of the war then raging where this sacred material lay buried, so that if any should be found, it would never be desecrated by profane use. The scrolls would also act as a guide to the recovery of the treasure, should it be needed to carry on the war.
10. Allegro offers the following explanations for the use of a comparatively expensive and certainly unusual writing material like copper for these scrolls.
  a. It may have been simply a desire to ensure their preservation longer than could be expected of parchment or papyrus.
  b. It could also have a ritual significance, since it is decreed that articles made of sheet metal are not susceptible to ritual uncleanness. That would mean that if the copper scrolls were in any way ritually defiled during interment in the cave, they would, on rediscovery, be washed clean again and be fit for priestly handling.

THE COPPER SCROLL 47

D. *Places mentioned in the scroll as hiding places for the treasure, and the problem of identification*
 1. Identification of biblical place names is notoriously uncertain. Towns and villages, well known in their day, have often disappeared without trace. Sometimes their sites have been reused by subsequent generations and renamed, and even when the ancient names have been preserved in more or less recognizable forms, they may now apply to a village nearby and not to the ancient site itself.
 2. The problem of identifying biblical place names is relevant to our study, as the scrolls often locate their treasure by biblical names, and we could learn much about the topography of ancient Palestine if we could identify the places mentioned in the scroll.
 3. The locations covered by the treasure inventory seem to fall into three main areas:
    a. Sites about the Dead Sea (including Qumran)
    b. The environs of Jericho
    c. Jerusalem
 4. The problem in identifying the places mentioned in these three areas, we can be sure, often hinges upon the fact that the scribe of the copper scrolls used alternative names, often synonyms, for locating his treasure deposits, doubtless for secrecy. It is therefore possible that for each location mentioned the first-century name or names was or were different, and if a name mentioned appears nowhere else in the literature or tradition, it is very probably a pseudonym or synonym for a more well-known name.
 5. Once the places mentioned can be identified, they will be of great help in illuminating the history of the sect, the history of the sect in relation to other Jewish groups and to the foreign invaders, and the history of the people as a whole at the time. An example of this is the problem of the identification of the city of Secacah.
    a. According to the evidence in the scrolls, Secacah seems to be Khirbet Qumran itself, the site of the Essene monastery.
    b. Following the principle of suspecting the existence of an alternative for any proper name given by the scribe, we may doubt that Secacah was the name most commonly used for Khirbet Qumran in the first century A.D.
    c. Its verbal root SKK is common enough in the Old Testament, meaning "overshadow," "screen," or "cover" and it has a very close synonym in SLL, "shade" or "screen," which lies behind

a place name which can be identified without much difficulty as the alternative we are seeking and which occurs in the book of Zechariah: "I saw in the night, and behold, a man riding upon a red horse. He was standing among the myrtle trees in Meṣullah (shady place)."

d. The Aramaic word for "healer-physician" is ʿasyā, plural āsayyā, which is sufficiently close to the Greek of "Essenes" (*Essaioi, Essenoi*) to lead many scholars to think this is its derivation. The hypothesis on the origin of the name "Essenes" has strong support. We note that the Aramaic word for "myrtle" (famed in antiquity for its medicinal properties) is almost exactly the same—ʿasaʿ, plural *asayya*—and that the myrtles among which the man on the red horse stood in Meṣullah were interpreted homiletically as "the righteous ones," a title claimed by the Essenes for themselves.

6. The identification of Secacah is an example of garnering additional historical information through the identification of the places in the copper scroll.
    a. If Secacah is the Meṣullah mentioned in Zechariah, it might also be the same place as that spoken of by Josephus under the Graecized form Bemeselis (that is, *Beth*, "house or place of," plus *Meṣullah*): *JW* I iv 6, parag. 96 with an alternative *Bethome* (that is, *Beth* plus *omi*, "shade"): *JA* XIII xiv 2, parag. 380.
    b. It was to this place that Alexander Jannaeus, the Jewish priest-king (103-76 B.C.) pursued the ringleaders of the revolt against him after their defeat in battle. After besieging the settlement, he dragged them out to be crucified in Jerusalem along with eight hundred of their fellow rebels.
    c. There is good reason for connecting this revolt against Jannaeus with the Essenes and their history. It is therefore possible that the remaining ringleaders of the revolt fled to this sanctuary in the desert. It is also possible that, when Jannaeus followed them and killed them, he also killed the Teacher of Righteousness with whom he might have been involved earlier if we may identify him as the Wicked Priest of the scrolls.
7. It is hoped that these scrolls will shed much needed light on the topography of first-century Jerusalem, for it is in and around Jerusalem that the greater part of the scrolls' treasure was deposited. The scrolls also will help in further archaeological excavations in Jerussalem, which in turn will give us more historical information about

the city—its buildings and the life and events that took place in those ancient buildings.
8. Allegro feels that some two dozen of the scrolls' locations are situated within the Temple area, one of the few undisputed features of the topography of first-century Jerusalem. However, only persons having an intimate knowledge of the Temple courts and chambers and their private names and functions would be able to recognize many of the places mentioned. Nevertheless, with the help of Josephus and rabbinic tradition (mainly in the Mishnah) it is hoped that the locations and functions of the various places will be found, along with the original names underlying the scribes' pseudonyms.
9. The problem arises of who hid the treasure and the scrolls.
   a. Allegro feels the Zealots engraved and hid the copper scrolls, which they compiled largely from reports sent in from Jerusalem and other garrisons.
   b. He feels that this is possible if the last defenders of the community center at Qumran were not the pacifist-minded Essenes but their more warlike compatriots, the Zealots.
   c. In sum, Allegro feels that the copper scrolls are an inventory of sacred treasure hidden away by the Zealots most probably during the spring of A.D. 68. He also feels that the treasure, which comprises dedicated produce and its containers as well as gold and silver in coin and bullion, comes mostly from the Jerusalem Temple, but may also include the fruits of raids made upon settlements in the Judean desert, among them the Essene community center of Qumran.
10. The questions surrounding the copper scrolls—Who hid the treasure? Where did it come from? At which places was it hidden? Did the treasure actually exist and was it actually hidden?—all await further study of the scrolls and further archaeological excavations.
    a. The difficulties in deciphering the texts are great, partly due to problems inherent in reading a unique work written in insufficiently voweled script and in a dialect not fully understood.
    b. Further difficulties ensue from the cryptic nature of the document and the idiosyncrasies of the scribe.

E. *The first announcement of the contents of the copper scrolls, June 1, 1956. The following is the only text from the scrolls published in English at the time*

1. "In the cistern which is below the rampart, on the east side, in a

place hollowed out of the rock, there are six hundred bars of silver..."
2. "Close by, below the southern corner of the portico, at Zadok's tomb, there is a vessel of incense in pine wood and a vessel of incense in cassia wood..."
3. "Nearby, in the pit, facing north near the grave, in the hole opening to the north there is a copy of a book with explanation, measurements, and all details."

According to Cross, the scrolls are scheduled to be published in the third volume of *Discoveries in the Judean Desert*, by D. Barthélemy, J. T. Milik, *et al.* The Hebrew text of this scroll with a French translation by J. T. Milik was published in the French journal *Revue Biblique* I (July, 1959), pages 321-357, and the Hebrew text with an English translation in Allegro's book, *The Treasure of the Copper Scrolls*.

F. *Theories and arguments advanced about the existence of the treasure*

1. The fabulous size of the treasures and the vague or traditional character of their hiding places are sufficient evidence of the folkloristic character of the document, which has no real significance.
   a. Lists of secret caches are not generally inscribed on metal plates difficult to conceal.
   b. The engraver's hand is not very expert.
2. These are lists of the Temple's treasures, hidden about the time of the siege. Proponents of this theory point out:
   a. Stories about hiding temple treasures during the war between the Jews and Romans, A.D. 66-70, have been recorded and translated.
   b. An expensive roll of pure copper is not the proper material on which to inscribe fairy tales.
   c. Durable and unusual material was purposefully used to write up these lists of hiding places.
3. These are lists of the treasures of a sect, hidden by one of its members, perhaps the treasurer, before their escape from the Romans, and engraved into a copper sheet in hopes of finding it on their eventual return.
4. The copper plates were originally designed for something else, and someone engraved the present text on them as the Romans closed in on Jerusalem, in hopes of misleading the Romans when and if they found the scrolls.

G. *Importance*

1. These are the first ancient documents discovered giving clues to buried treasures.
2. They are the earliest known extensive texts in Mishnaic Hebrew.
3. Their contents may add to our knowledge of Palestinian topography.

TOPICS FOR STUDY AND DISCUSSION

A. Give an account of the discovery and describe the copper scrolls.

B. Describe the unrolling of the copper scrolls at the University of Manchester, England.

C. Discuss in detail the different theories on the treasures described in these scrolls.

D. Write at least one page on the significance of these scrolls.

VIII

THE GENESIS APOCRYPHON

The *Genesis Apocryphon* is one of the last scrolls from Cave One to be deciphered. Essentially it is an apocryphal collection of stories (that is, writings not included in the Canon of the Hebrew Bible) written in Aramaic—a language spoken in Palestine at the time of the rise of Christianity. New and fascinating stories concerning the lives of several patriarchs in the Book of Genesis, such as Lamech, Enoch, Methuselah, Noah, Abraham, and Sarah, are included in this ancient document.

The style and contents of this scroll are similar to those found in the nonlegal portions of the Talmud and the Midrash—the homiletic interpretation of the Scriptures. A large number of homilies, traditions, legends, and other folkloristic material had been circulating among the Jewish people for over two thousand years. These are scattered in the gigantic postbiblical Jewish work known as the Talmud but especially in the Midrash. You see, from the time that the institution of the synagogue was first created, rabbis have delivered sermons in the synagogue, especially during the divine services on Sabbaths and holidays. Philo, a Jewish scholar of the first century A.D., describes one of these services, remarking that some priest or leader read several verses from the Pentateuch to the congregation in the synagogue and expounded upon them point by point. To do so, he often made use of parables, legends, traditions, or words of wisdom. Most of these rabbinical interpretations were based on scriptural passages, usually drawn from the Pentateuch. These interpretations were first transmitted orally from one generation to another and circulated in academic rabbinical schools. At a later date from about the fifth century A.D. this vast material was committed to writing, and these have been preserved to us. The most important works on this material are known by the Hebrew word *Midrash*, or by its plural form, *Midrashim*. There is no doubt that there were also several traditions and legends about Noah's birth and Sarah's beauty, and the *Genesis Apocryphon* discussed above is probably one of these works. Fascinating legends about these Patriarchs are also to be found in the English translation of the Midrashim, in a book entitled *The Legends of the Jews* by a great scholar, Louis Ginzberg.

Recommended Reading

It is important that you read Yigael Yadin's chapter on the Genesis Apocryphon in his book, *The Message of the Scrolls*. Yadin was one of the translators of this important scroll, and the best account is given in his book on pages 144-155. You should constantly consult the Book of Genesis in the Bible. It is interesting to compare the account in both books and to note the additional details given in the scroll.

If you wish to read a partial translation of the text so far published, turn to N. Avigad and Y. Yadin, *A Genesis Apocryphon*, pages 43-48. It is fascinating reading. You are also strongly advised to read the articles on the (a) Apocrypha, (b) Talmud, and (c) Midrash in any of the encyclopedias or other reference books. The following is assigned for this unit:

Avigad, N., and Y. Yadin, *A Genesis Apochryphon*, pages 12-15 and 43-48.
Vermes, G., *The Dead Sea Scrolls in English*, pp. 214-224.
Yadin, Y., *The Message of the Scrolls*, pages 144-155.

The Genesis Apocryphon

A. *Discovery*

1. This scroll is one of the seven original scrolls found in Cave One in 1947 and the last to be deciphered, in 1956.
2. It is written in Aramaic.

B. *Description*

1. Of the seven scrolls found in Cave One, this scroll was in the worst state of preservation.
2. The scroll was very brittle and fragile and difficult to unroll.
3. About half of the pages of the scroll—the beginning and the end parts—are missing.
   a. It appears that the end part was cut off in antiquity for some unknown reason; the text stops in the middle of a sentence.
   b. Of the scroll's twenty-two original columns, four complete columns each with thirty-four lines of writing, were preserved.
   c. In addition to these columns, there were large sections of decipher-

able writing on five columns and several legible lines and words in other additional columns.

C. *Name of the scroll*

1. It was first called the *Lamech Scroll* for these reasons:
   a. The first fragment unrolled from this scroll contained a speech by Lamech using the first person.
   b. Scholars assumed they had found the apocryphal Book of Lamech mentioned in a Greek list of apocryphal books.
2. When the scroll was unrolled and partly deciphered, the scholars realized:
   a. The Lamech story constitutes only a small part of the scroll.
   b. The scroll contains apocryphal stories about Lamech, Enoch, Methuselah, Sarah, and Abraham. These stories enlarge on the accounts of the patriarchal personalities as given in the Book of Genesis with additional details and hitherto unknown names.
3. This scroll was thus renamed the *Genesis Apocryphon* by its editors N. Avigad and Y. Yadin. The editors published several columns of the text with an English translation.

D. *Date of the scroll*

N. Avigad and Y. Yadin believe that, on linguistic grounds, the scroll was written at the end of the first century B.C. or during the first century A.D.

E. *Literary evaluation*

1. The *Genesis Apocryphon* is a collection of stories, written in the first person, about some biblical patriarchs.
2. Each patriarch relates his own story, adding to the material in Genesis.
3. This work presents many parallels with the apocryphal Book of Jubilees and the Book of Enoch.

F. *Contents*

1. Column II, which is moderately well preserved, contains Lamech's story about the odd birth of Noah (Genesis, Chapter 5). It contains:
   a. The doubts of Lamech as to the faithfulness of his wife Bat-Enosh.
   b. Bat-Enosh's statement that Noah is Lamech's son and not the fruit of alliance with angels or any other mortal.
   c. Lamech's consultation with his father, Methuselah, who in turn consults Enoch as to the true circumstances of Noah's birth.

2. Of Columns III and IV very few words remain.
3. Columns V-XVIII are poorly preserved but seem to cover Genesis 6-11.
4. Columns XIX and XX are on Genesis, Chapter 12.
   a. Abraham goes to Hebron and then to Egypt to escape the famine.
   b. Abraham tells of the dream of the cedar and the palm, which he interprets as God's counsel for Sarah to hide her true identity in Egypt by claiming that Abraham is her brother.
   c. Detailed description of Sarah's beauty, lacking in Genesis, is given in this scroll.
   d. Sarah is carried off by a Pharoah named Zoan to be one of his wives.
   e. Plague sets upon Pharoah and his household and prevents the consummation of his marriage with Sarah.
   f. Abraham, Sarah, Lot, and Hagar leave Egypt.
5. In Column XXI, which covers Genesis, Chapter 13, Abraham describes how he walked the length and breadth of the country, after he had come to Beth-El.
   a. He enumerates the names and the places he passed.
   b. These names are interesting topographically, as they resemble the names in the Book of Jubilees, but in some details they add new material.
   c. The war of the four kings against the five kings of Sodom and Gomorrah described in Genesis 14 is also mentioned here.
      (1) The version of this chapter in the scroll enriches our knowledge of place-names, some of which were unknown up to now.
      (2) The second part of this chapter, dealing with Lot's captivity, is almost identical with Genesis, except for a few topographical details.
6. Column XXII relates to the freeing of Lot from the hands of the Sodomites and the meeting of the King of Sodom and Abraham. This follows, in general terms, the account of Genesis.
   a. The rest of this column is probably from Chapter 15 of Genesis, and is only partly preserved. Here Abraham asks God to give him a son and heir.
   b. It is possible that those sheets not yet discovered contain the remaining chapters of Genesis from Chapter 15 onward.

G. *Significance*

1. This scroll is the only one of seven *original* scrolls written in Aramaic.
2. It has preserved contemporary Aramaic texts (second century B.C. to first century A.D.) which increase our understanding and knowledge of the language.
3. It contains topographical details of Palestine of significance to biblical studies.
4. It has important bearing on Talmudic and Midrashic lore.

Topics for Study and Discussion

A. Write briefly on each of the following.
   1. Apocrypha
   2. Talmud
   3. Midrash (Consult the Encyclopedia, if necessary.)
B. Give the contents of the *Genesis Apocryphon* with reference to the corresponding material in the Book of Genesis.
C. What is the significance of this scroll to the study of (1) the Aramaic language, (2) the topography of Palestine, and (3) Talmudic and Midrashim lore?
D. Make a comparative study of the *Genesis Apocryphon* and the corresponding material in the Book of Genesis.

IX

THE WAR SCROLL

The *War Scroll*, whose full title is *The Scroll of the War of the Sons of Light against the Sons of Darkness*, is one of the seven scrolls found in Cave One in 1947 and was a theretofore unknown work. There is no other work like it in the Jewish or Christian literature of the time of the Second Temple or in the period following, and no work like it has been found among the sect's other books.

The scroll is important for several reasons. It provides the first comprehensive data on military regulations for the Jewish armies during the late period of the Second Temple. The material also includes military and technical terms hitherto unknown. Yigael Yadin of the Hebrew University, one of the foremost authorities on the *War Scroll*, says that it contains "the oldest record of Hebrew military craft that we have extant, clearer and more precise than anything on the subject by the best classical historians." Since the sect of the *War Scroll* sought to follow the pattern of organization of the tribes of Israel during their wilderness sojourn (described in the Book of Numbers), we have an opportunity through this scroll to study that organization and to comprehend some of the unclear passages in the biblical account. In addition, the scroll brings to light a number of beautiful prayers to be recited at various stages of the war. Most of these prayers were also previously unknown.

RECOMMENDED READING

Burrows, M., *The Dead Sea Scrolls*, pages 203-208, 260-262 and 390-399
Burrows, M., *More Light on the Dead Sea Scrolls*, pages 195-203, and 283-285
Gaster, T. H., *The Dead Sea Scriptures in English Translation*, pages 281-306
Van der Ploeg, J., *The Excavations at Qumran*, pages 172-175 and 101-105
Vermes, G., *The Dead Sea Scrolls in English*, pages 122-148
Yadin, Y., *The Message of the Scrolls*, pages 128-143

A. Discovery

1. The *War Scroll* is one of seven scrolls found in Cave One in 1947.
2. It is also one of three scrolls purchased for the Hebrew University by Sukenik from the antiquities dealer in Bethlehem.
3. Fragments of four manuscripts of the *War Scroll* were found in Cave Four, making it possible to fill some of the numerous gaps in the scroll with many variations in text. Fragments were also found in Cave Two.
4. This scroll is a hitherto unknown work.
    a. No work like it had been found in the Jewish or Christian literature of the time of the Second Temple or in the period following.
    b. No work like it has been found among the sect's other books.
5. The full title given to this scroll by Sukenik is *The Scroll of the War of the Sons of Light against the Sons of Darkness*.

B. Description

1. The scroll consists of nineteen pages written on five sheets.
2. There are four pages on the first sheet, six on the second, five on the third, and three on the fourth.
3. Of the fifth sheet only one page was left, and it is difficult to determine its original place on the sheet. However, among some small fragments discovered later in the cave, one fits nicely into page 19; on this fragment, it is also possible to decipher a few letters of the following page. Some scholars therefore feel that this shows the scroll originally had at least twenty pages.
4. The end of the scroll is missing but its beginning is intact.
    a. This scroll, like the others, is worn at the bottom.
    b. The damaged edge is wavelike in shape; thus one page has more lines than another.
    c. It is estimated that each page originally had an average of twenty lines.
5. The writing
    a. The writing of the scribe was excellent.
    b. Like some of the others, this scribe, using some sharp-edged instrument, ruled his pages horizontally for the lines, and vertically between the columns where he also left a margin. Between

paragraphs he left a space of a line or more.
  c. The letters themselves are written below the lines.
  d. The length of the scroll in its present state of preservation is 2.90 meters, or 9 feet, 8 inches.

C. *General summary of contents*

1. The sect believed in the division of all human creatures into the Sons of Light and the Sons of Darkness—members of the sect belonged to the former, enemies of the sect to the latter.
2. The author feels that the day of victory over the Sons of Darkness is near:
   a. The victory will be caused by God on a day appointed in advance by Him.
   b. The Sons of Light will participate actively in the fight.
   c. Since the Sons of Light are to participate in the war, they must be taught the rules of battle—both those specified in the Bible and those prevalent at the time.
   d. If the Sons of Light keep the rules as specified in the Bible and as understood by them, God will make them victorious in the end.
3. The author warns that the final battle in which both men and angels will participate will not be easy, but it will bring victory for the people of God and annihilation for all the lot of Belial.
4. The war will last forty years altogether; but with no fighting on Sabbatical years, there will be only thirty-five fighting years.

D. *Description of future war*

1. First stage of future war
   a. This is a war against the Edomites, Ammonites, Moabites, and Philistines (peoples immediately surrounding Israel), against the Kittim of Ashur (who remain undefined), and against the enemies in Israel.
   b. The first stage will take place "when the exiles of the Sons of Light return from the wilderness of the peoples (which seems to refer to all the other members of the sect living in countries outside Palestine and especially in Syria) to encamp in the wilderness of Jerusalem."
   c. This first group of enemies are the most dangerous, as they are the nearest geographically—hence they are the first to be fought.
   d. The war of the congregation as a whole against the Kittim and their allies will take six years of fighting.

2. The second stage of the war is against the "Kittim of Egypt."
3. The last stage of the war is against the "Kings of the North."
   a. The congregation as a whole fights the Kittim and their allies, but the war against the "Kings of the North" will be conducted by divisions serving in turn.
   b. The "Kings of the North" are the farthest away and thus are fought last.
   c. The war against the "Kings of the North" will last twenty-nine years. The war plans give exact details of the names of these various enemies and how long the Sons of Light will have to fight each of them individually.
4. The rules of battle begin with rules enumerated in the Bible—those relating to trumpets and standards—based mainly on the Book of Numbers, Chapter 10.
   a. Much space is devoted to the discussion of trumpets in battle.
   (1) For the sect, the priests blow the trumpets. Six priests are specially attired and they move about the units at the front.
   (2) Different trumpets and signals are used for different operations.
   (3) The trumpets described in the *War Scroll* are divided into two groups—ceremonial trumpets and fighting trumpets.
      (a) All bear inscriptions and slogans in keeping with their purpose.
      (b) In the group of ceremonial trumpets are those "for the calling of the congregations" which bear the inscription "The God-summoned" and those "for the calling of the Commanders," which are inscribed "Princes of God." There are "trumpets of the Levites," with the inscription "Band of God"; trumpets of the camps," with the inscription "peace of God in the encampments of His saints"; and "trumpets of the expedition of the camps" with the inscription "Gods mighty deeds to scathe the enemy and to put to flight all opponents of justice and disgraceful retribution to the opponents of God."
      (c) The war trumpets, however, are classified according to the tactical stages of the fighting and the order of the battle. Thus for example the "trumpets of the battle arrays," bearing the inscription "Arrays of God's battalions for His wrathful vengeance upon all Sons of Darkness," serve as a signal to start off the battle. For the assembly

of the "men who fight between the lines," that is the skirmishers, there were special "trumpets for calling the skirmishers" with the inscription "Vengeful remembrance for the appointed time of God."

(d) The sign to commence the fighting proper was given with "trumpets of killing" and their inscription was "The hand of God's might in battle to strike down all sinful slain", and their sound was "highpitched and intermittent."

(e) The trumpets of the ambush were inscribed "Mysteries of God for the perdition of the wicked."

(f) The signal for pursuit of the enemy is given with special "trumpets of pursuit" inscribed: "God has smitten all Sons of Darkness. His wrath shall not cease until they are annihilated." There are also trumpets for withdrawing the fighting forces, entitled "trumpets of withdrawal" with the inscription "God hath gathered."

(4) The above-mentioned trumpets are blown by six priests, but in addition, many horns are used by the Levites and other members of the congregation for the purpose of frightening the enemy. These war cries are given only at the beginning of the battle.

b. The author of the scroll devotes much space to the description of the banners carried by the congregation, both when setting out to war and during the stages of the actual fighting. This description is based mainly on the passage from Numbers 2 : 2.

(1) The banners are carried by the congregation both when setting out to war and during the actual fighting.

(2) Altogether, eight kinds of banners are mentioned; each banner carries the name of the commander and the unit. In addition to these basic inscriptions denoting the nature of the unit, there are three categories of slogans attached to the banners, appropriate to the various stages and progress of the fighting: "When they go to battle," "when they close in for battle," and "when they withdraw from battle."

(3) The above were the inscriptions and slogans of the congregation in general. But the tribe of Levi and its families (the priests), sons of Kohath, Gershon, and Merari, had their own banners, on each of which they wrote the name of the chief of the family (Prince of Kohath etc.) and the names of the commanders of his thousands.

(a) The Levites, too, changed their slogans according to the stages of war. For example, when they went to war the sons of Aaron wrote "Truth of God," when they closed in they wrote "Right hand of God," and when they returned they wrote "Exalt God."

(b) The sons of Kohath carried the following slogans during the three stages: "Justice of God," "Appointed day of God," and "Magnify God."

(c) The sons of Gershon had "Glory of God," "Panic. of God," and 'Praise of God" and the banner of Merari had "Judgment of God","Slain of God", and "Glory of God."

(4) The sub-units of the priest: families, such as the units of a thousand, a hundred, fifty, and ten, had their own inscriptions.

c. The organization of the army and its weapons:

(1) There are two infantry groups: light and heavy infantry.

(a) The heavy infantry is a total force of 21,000 between the ages of forty and fifty, uniformly armed with shields made of copper, spears, and swords.

(b) The light infantry with a force of 7,000 between the ages of thirty and forty-five is not uniformly armed. Their weapons are slings, javelins, lances, and swords.

(2) The cavalry is also composed of two groups: light and heavy cavalry.

(a) The light cavalry had 4,600 riders.

(b) The heavy cavalry had 1,400 riders.

(c) The age range of the riders is the same as that of the light and heavy infantry.

(1) The nonfighting, or service corps has the main tasks of spoiling the slain, collecting the booty, guarding the arms, and preparing the provisions.

(a) The age range of the camp prefects was from fifty to sixty.

(b) The age range of the provosts was from forty to fifty.

(c) The age range of the group that performed other services was from twenty-five to thirty.

d. The method of fighting during the various stages of battle is as follows:

(1) First, all units arrayed themselves in formations for roll call and prayer.

(2) Next, the fighting units deployed themselves in two lines, four formations in the front and three in the rear

(3) Between the formations were intervals to allow the passage of the light infantry.

(4) At certain stages of the battle, if one of the units was defeated, a reserve unit was immediately sent out as a replacement.

e. Further topics in the *War Scroll* include:

(1) Regulations for changing the order of battle and disposition of formations in accordance with the tactical needs of different situations.

   (a) The author starts by saying "This is the disposition of changing the arrays of battle units" which have the following names: "Long rectangle with towers," "Enveloping arms with towers," "Arc with towers," "Flat arc with wings protruding from both sides of the line."

   (b) These technical terms denote the shape of the front line according to the tactics used at each phase of the fighting, and similar terms are known in other armies.

   (c) The "towers", for instance, are explained in detail. They are fighting units organized in square formations moving forward. Their soldiers carry shields some 3 cubits long and spears 8 cubits long. The shields are inscribed with the names of angels. The shields of the first tower carry the name of Michael; of the second, Gabriel; of the third, Sariel; and of the fourth, Raphael—four towers in all.

(2) Mobilization, service exemption, duties of priests at various stages of war, procedure of sacrificing at the Temple during the Sabbatical year.

   (a) On the subject of mobilization and service exemption the author says that no young boy or woman shall enter the encampments from the time the men go to war until they return.

   (b) He states that the following shall not go to war: "anyone halt or blind or lame or a man in whose body there is a permanent defect or a man affected by an impurity of his flesh . . . and any man who is not pure with regard to his sexual organs on the day of battle shall not join them in battle, for holy angels are in common with their hosts."

   (c) Duties of the priest: The priests are divided into twenty-six courses, not twenty-four as was common. Heads of the courses serve according to a roster. After them in service come the chiefs of the Levites, twelve in number, who serve "continually . . . one to each tribe" and keep a definite order of priority amongst themselves. After them come the chiefs of the tribes and the fathers of the congregation "to stand perpetually in the Gates of the Temple." They are followed by the (lay) Israelites who will also serve "on their festivals, on their new moons, and the Sabbaths and on all days of the year."

(3) Different prayers to be said at various stages of the war—prayers said must be appropriate to the action. Examples: prayers at the beginning of battle, prayers of special encouragement after a defeat, and prayers of praise after victory.

(4) Several paragraphs are devoted to the designation of the various priests who supervise the different prayers. Most of the prayers are conducted by the chief priest himself.

(5) The last part of the scroll is devoted to a description of the seven "lots of the battle," and the victory of each lot, with the alternating fortunes of the Sons of Light and the Sons of Darkness. In the final victory of the Sons of Light, a great miracle occurs, like the one in Judah when Sennacherib besieged Jerusalem.

E. *Significance of the scroll*

1. For the first time we find comprehensive data on the military regulations in the Jewish armies during the late period of the Second Temple, containing military terms hitherto unknown. As Yigael Yadin says, the author of the scroll has given us "the oldest record of Hebrew military craft that we have extant, clearer and more precise than anything on the subject by the best classical historians."

2. The scroll brings to light a number of beautiful prayers to be recited at various stages of the war. Most of these prayers were also previously unknown.

3. Since the sect sought to follow the pattern or organization of the tribes of Israel during their sojourn in the wilderness, as described in the Book of Numbers, we have an opportunity through this scroll to study that organization and to interpret more accurately some of the unclear passages in the biblical account.

F. *Controversies surrounding the War Scroll*

1. Dating
   a. Yadin argues that the scroll was written between 50 B.C. and A.D.

THE WAR SCROLL 65

50. He dates the original composition of the work after the Roman conquest (63 B.C.) but before the end of the reign of Herod (4 B.C.).
 b. Del-Medico feels that the text was certainly written after A.D. 70 and possibly as late as A.D. 135.
 c. Del-Medico connects the allusions of all the Dead Sea Scrolls and those of the *Habakkuk Commentary* in particular with the last years before the destruction of the Temple—the years between A.D. 66-70.
 d. Some of the historical allusions in the Habakkuk Commentary are explained by Del-Medico as follows:

   (1) The preacher of the lie is King Agrippa II who made speeches urging peaceful submission to the Romans.

   (2) The "House of Judah" in which all the "doers of the law" will be rescued "from the house of judgment because of their labor and their faith in the Teacher of Righteousness," Del-Medico takes to mean the Zealots, the disciples of Judas the Galilean. For further discussion of the possibility that the sect may be identified with the Zealots see Unit 18, the Essenes and the Identification of the Sect.

   (3) In the reference to fire and brimstone Del-Medico sees a reference to the eruption of Vesuvius in A.D. 79.

 e. Many scholars feel that although Del-Medico's theory shows much erudition and ingenuity it has not sufficient plausibility to outweigh the archaeological evidence for the destruction of the Qumran community in A.D. 68.

   (1) Del-Medico complains that the archaeologists have assumed the earliest possible or median dates established by the Carbon 14 test of linen from Cave One and for the Roman lamps found in the same cave.

   (2) He believes that the latest possible dates should be recognized, which would be A.D. 233 for the linen and about A.D. 300 for the lamps.

   (3) He feels that there is no way of telling when coins of a given date ceased to be used, and the fact that most of the coins are dated before A.D. 68 is no indication that these coins were not used later. However, most scholars feel that when no coins of a later date are found, it is safe to assume that the site was not occupied long after the date in question. In addition, the relative numbers of coins of various dates is also significant. Also,

the stratification of archaeological context in which they are found must be taken into account. The few coins dated later than A.D. 68 which are found at Khirbet Qumran come from later periods of much less extensive occupation when the changes in the character of the buildings indicated use by a different group and for a different purpose.

(4) Del-Medico feels that the Dead Sea Scrolls are not the library of a monastic community which occupied Qumran; they are heretical scrolls committed to the *genizah* in the generation following the destruction of the Temple.

2. Identity of the Kittim
   a. The identity of the Kittim (who are also mentioned in the other scrolls and in several biblical books) has aroused a great deal of controversy and discussion. One theory maintains they were the Romans; another, that they were the Macedonian rulers of the Seleucid Kingdom of Syria, the chief foes of the Jews from about 200-63 B.C.
   b. Most scholars today feel that the name *Kittim* refers to the Romans.
   c. Kittim is the name used for the enemy of the sect. In the *Commentary on Habakkuk* we learn that the Kittim are wild and cruel; they come from the sea; they destroy people, and conquer cities and so forth.
   d. A column from the *Commentary on Nahum* has recently been published in which the commentator refers to "the kings of Greece from Antiochus until the rise of the rulers of the Kittim." The kings of Greece seem to be unquestionably the Seleucids. Antiochus was one of these. Since the rise of the ruler of the Kittim marks the end of the period which begins with Antiochus, the rulers of the Kittim cannot be the same as the kings of Greece; in other words the Seleucid period gives way to the Roman period.
   e. One of the arguments for taking the Kittim to be the Seleucids was the mention of the Kittim of Assyria and the Kittim of Egypt in the *War Scroll*.

      (1) It was difficult to imagine what these might be in the Roman period, but in the Greek period they seemed entirely appropriate for the Macedonian rulers of Egypt and Syria, the Ptolemies and the Seleucids.
      (2) Yigael Yadin however finds a later situation reflected in the *War Scroll*. The Kittim of Assyria and the Kittim in Egypt are explained in terms of the comprehensive plan of war presented

in the scroll. As we mentioned before, the first stage of the war is against the hostile neighbors of Israel, the Kittim of Assyria, and the violators of the covenant within Israel. Of the first group, the Edomites are Israel's neighbors on the south, the Moabites and Ammonites on the east, and the Philistines on the west. The Kittim of Assyria are therefore understood as enemies to the north, the name Assyria being used in a general way for the region of Syria.

(3) In the second phase the war is directed against the Egyptian Kittim. Yadin stresses the fact that they are not called "the Kittim of Egypt" but "the Kittim in Egypt," and he infers from this that they were people of the same ethnic origin as the Kittim of Assyria. Egypt, Yadin notes, was not within the biblical boundaries of Israel, but had to be finished off before the more distant "king of the north" could be attacked, and the name therefore does not necessarily refer to a pre-Roman period.

f. Yadin's most impressive argument that the Kittim are the Romans is based on the details of military equipment and procedure in the *War Scroll*.

(1) He finds these correspond so closely with Roman arms and tactics that the author must have witnessed them himself or consulted contemporary military literature.

(2) Latin terms are not used, as in the later rabbinical literature, but the Hebrew words employed by the author are sometimes transparently "translation Hebrew." The word meaning literally "wing", for example, is used in a way unknown in normal Hebrew for the cavalry unit which the Roman called a wing in Latin (*ala*).

g. Dupont-Sommer adduces another argument for identifying the Kittim of the *War Scroll* with the Romans.

(1) In the third phase of warfare the first year's fighting was to be directed against Aram Naharaim (northern Mesopotamia); the fact that Syria is not mentioned here shows that it had already been conquered in the defeat of the Romans. This agrees with Yadin's identification of the Kittim of Assyria with the Roman rulers of Syria.

(2) Various peoples on Asia Minor and Southern Mesopotamia were to be subjugated in the next four years, the sixth and seventh years were then to be devoted to fighting "all the sons

of Assyria and Persia and the people of the east as far as the great desert." The lumping of these together, Dupont-Sommer contends, implies the existence of the Parthian empire.
3. Description of war
   a. Scholars are faced with the problem of whether the *War Scroll* describes a war that actually took place in the past, a war that was taking place at the time the scroll was being written, or a war that was contemplated for the future.
   b. Scholars are also faced with the problem of whether the war refers to a real or a Messianic war.
   c. Most scholars feel that the *War Scroll* refers to a future war, both real and Messianic.
      (1) The author of the scroll believed that the time was near when his people, the members of the sect, would fight their enemies, "the Sons of Darkness."
      (2) He felt that this battle would take place both on earth and in heaven.
      (3) Although he believed that the Angels of Light and God him-himself would come to the help of the Sons of Light and actually fight for them he also believed that he and his people would actually fight against the enemies with their own hands, and the *War Scroll* is both a description and a manual of this actual future war.
      (4) Yadin believes that one of the purposes of this work was to consider the laws and tactics of warfare as practised by the nations of the world and to determine how they relate to the Torah and how the holy war must be conducted.

TOPICS FOR STUDY AND DISCUSSION

A. Discuss briefly the discovery and general contents of the *War Scroll*.
B. Describe the different stages of the war and the enemies to be fought in the war.
C. Describe the rules of battle and specifically three of the following aspects of the rules of battle:
   1. The role of the trumpets and the different kinds of trumpets
   2. The role of the banners and the different kinds of banners
   3. The organization of the army and its weapons
   4. Methods of fighting, mobilization and service exemption, and the different prayers of the war
D. Discuss the problem of the identity of the Kittim.
E. What controversies surround the scroll?
F. Discuss the significance of the scroll.

X
THE ISAIAH SCROLLS

The text of the *Isaiah Scroll* is, by and large, the same as that of the traditional Book of Isaiah. Most of the deviations from the traditional Hebrew text are in details of spelling and grammar, although in some instances there are very definite variant readings. As far as language is concerned, the complete *Isaiah Scroll* reflects the linguistic situation prevailing in Palestine during the last centuries prior to the Christian era. The most significant fact about this scroll is that it has a few variant readings which are practically nonexistent in the other Hebrew manuscripts or versions of the Old Testament. It has therefore proved helpful in our study of the Hebrew text of Isaiah.

Two manuscripts of the Book of Isaiah have been found at Qumran but only one of these manuscripts is complete. The complete manuscript is known as the *St. Mark's Isaiah* because it was initially owned by the St. Mark's Monastery. It is the largest and oldest of the Dead Sea Scrolls. Although the manuscript is full of minor deviations from the Massoretic text, scholars believe that it is older than the standardized Massoretic version. The *St. Mark's Isaiah* has therefore proved helpful in our studies of the Hebrew text of Isaiah. In a significant number of variant readings, the manuscript gives valuable help in understanding passages that were obscure before. The Revised Standard Version of the Bible in its newest edition has followed, after careful deliberation on the part of a committee of biblical scholars, the *St. Mark's Isaiah* for thirteen variant readings.

On the other hand, the incomplete text of Isaiah, known as the *Hebrew University Isaiah*, is in close agreement with the Massoretic text. The discovery of both versions of the Book of Isaiah in the Qumran caves is important for the textual history of the Old Testament. We know now that several versions of many books of the Old Testament existed simultaneously in Palestine between the second century B.C. and the first century A.D. We also know that the Massoretic text was more or less standardized before its acceptance as the official text in later centuries, since the *Hebrew University Isaiah* is almost identical with the book as we know it today.

RECOMMENDED READING

Allegro, J. M., *The Dead Sea Scrolls*, pages 50-74
Burrows, M., *The Dead Sea Scrolls*, pages 5-8, 12-21, 89-94, 104-107, 110-116, and 303-315
Burrows, M., *More Light on the Dead Sea Scrolls*, pages 17 and 146-153
Milik, J. T., *Ten Years of Discovery in the Wilderness of Judaea*, pages 20-30
Van der Ploeg, J., *The Excavations at Qumran*, pages 158-159
Yadin, Y., *The Message of the Scrolls*, pages 81-89

THE ISAIAH SCROLLS

A. *St. Mark's Manuscript* (1QIs^a)

1. Discovery of the scroll
   a. The St. Mark's manuscript of the Old Testament Book of Isaiah was found in the first discovery of the Dead Sea Scrolls in Cave One, and it is one of the seven original manuscripts found.
   b. The Book of Isaiah is contained in its entirety in this scroll.
   c. This is one of the four scrolls that were originally owned by the St. Mark's Monastery. This scroll and the three others (*Genesis Apocryphon*, *Habakkuk Commentary*, and *Manual of Discipline*), were taken by the Syrian Metropolitan, Mar Athanasius Samuel, to the United States when he left Israel in 1949. The four scrolls were purchased from the Metropolitan by Yigael Yadin in 1954 for $250,000.
2. Dating of the scroll
   a. The manuscript of the *St. Mark's Isaiah* (whose abbreviation is 1QIs^a) is the largest and oldest of the Dead Sea Scrolls.
   b. The earliest known Massoretic text in existence, dating back only to the year A.D. 895, is the "Ben Asher Codex of the Prophets," in the synagogue of the Karaites in Cairo.
   c. Another codex is the manuscript of the whole Bible, preserved, until recently, in the synagogue of the Sephardic Jews in Aleppo, Syria; it dates back to about A.D. 929. This codex, slightly damaged by a fire at the synagogue, is believed to have been brought to Israel.
   d. As for translations of the Bible into other languages, and especial-

ly into Greek, the earliest known translation is the Septuagint, and the earliest Septuagint manuscripts we have are known as the Chester Beatty Papyri, dating in part from the second century A.D. However, the best-known manuscript of the Septuagint (the original Septuagint has not been preserved), and one which is complete, is the *Codex Vaticanus* which dates from about A.D. 350.

e. Thus we know that even from the Septuagint we have no full texts of the Bible earlier than the fourth century A.D. In the light of that fact it is easy to appreciate the great importance of the Isaiah texts discovered at Qumran. They are about a thousand years older than the oldest Hebrew text known to us and about five hundred years older than the earliest Greek version of the Septuagint.

f. The *St. Mark's Isaiah* cannot be dated after 100 B.C. This means that this Isaiah scroll was being copied only about six hundred years after the words were uttered by the prophet himself.

3. Description of the scroll
   a. The scroll is made of leather strips sewed end to end. When unrolled, it is about one foot wide and 24 feet long.
   b. The scroll is remarkably well preserved, though considerably worn by much use. The Hebrew text, written in fifty-four columns, is for the most part still clearly legible.

4. Description of the text
   a. The text does not have our familiar division into chapters and verses. It is divided into sections and paragraphs, indicated by beginning of a new line at the margin when the preceding line has not been filled out, and an indentation when the preceding line is full.
   b. Occasional extra space is left between the lines. Sometimes the larger divisions correspond to our chapters; sometimes they do not.
   c. Within the paragraphs there are often spaces between the sentences, indicating subdivisions which again may or may not correspond to the much later division into verses.
   d. There is a curious system of marks in the margins.
      (1) Sometimes a short horizontal line, with or without a small hook at one end, marks the beginning or end of a passage.
      (2) Sometimes there are very elaborate figures, the meaning of which has not yet been determined. Possibly they have some-

thing to do with a selection of Scripture lesson for use in meetings or services of worship, though the passages between the two consecutive marks often seem too short for such a passage. Or possibly they indicate portions of the text considered especially important by those who used the manuscript.
- e. The scribe of this particular scroll was not one of the best. He made many mistakes, most of which, however, he himself discovered and corrected. Burrows points out that in seven pages he found some forty-nine mistakes which the scribe corrected himself.
- f. Several passages, omitted by this scribe, were later inserted by another, as indicated by a different handwriting.
- g. There are many indications that this manuscript was in use by the sect for a long time and that parts of it which had suffered particularly from wear and tear had already been repaired in those days.

5. Problem of Isaiah I and II
   a. The question whether this ancient manuscript supported or refuted the critical hypothesis of a "Second Isaiah" was raised very soon after the discovery of the scrolls.
   b. Burrows feels that a manuscript made about 100 B.C. could not very well present evidence for or against an editorial process carried out two or three centuries earlier.
   c. Milik, however, has recently called attention to a few facts which he thinks indicate that the two main portions of the book were originally separate.
      (1) The manuscript consists of fifty-four columns and Chapter 33 ends exactly in the middle, at the bottom of column 27. But this is not only the end of a column; it is the end of one of the strips of leather of which the scroll consists, and this strip is a short one; it bears only two columns of text whereas the others usually have four.
      (2) A new strip then begins with Chapter 34.
   d. Bearing in mind the differences in spelling and grammar which have led the scholar Paul Kahle to see two different forms of the Hebrew text in the two halves of the scroll, one may be tempted to infer that the scribe of the St. Mark's manuscript copied the two parts of the book from two different manuscripts. This would to some extent support the idea of two originally separate works.

e. Burrows points out, however, that if the second half of the St. Mark's scroll was taken from a different manuscript, it was one in which Isaiah's authorship of Chapters 34 and 35 at least were already taken for granted, since Chapters 36-39 (taken almost entirely from 2 Kings 18-20) are already present in 1QIs[a]. These chapters have to do with the prophet Isaiah and would surely not have been inserted at this point by a scribe or editor who believed that everything from Chapter 34 on came from a different prophet.

f. The generally accepted conclusion of Old Testament scholars that Chapters 34-35 and 40-66 come from a period two centuries or more later than the time of Isaiah rests securely on the internal evidence of the book itself. The ancient manuscripts do not seem to help us very much in this case, and many scholars feel we do not need their confirmation on this point, since the evidence they present is inconclusive as to a single or double authorship of Isaiah.

6. Language and alphabet
   a. The Hebrew text is written in the square or Aramaic alphabet from which the one still used for printing Hebrew was developed in later times.
   b. The forms of the letters resemble those found in Palestinian inscriptions from about the first century B.C.
   c. Unlike the brief inscriptions found up to now, this manuscript is so extensive that it gives a great many examples of each letter of the alphabet, making possible a comparison that shows many interesting variations and sometimes enables us to see just how the scribe wrote the letters.

7. Corrections in the text
   a. Corrections of a single letter or word appear in the scribe's own hand.
   b. More extensive corrections have been made in another hand.
   c. Letters and words omitted by the copyist are frequently inserted above the line.
   d. When there is not room between the lines for all that has been omitted, the inserted material runs on down the left-hand margin.
   e. There are clear indications also at many points that the copyist left a space for something that was missing or not clear in the manuscript he was copying.
   f. The omitted portions of the text were usually copied in later from another manuscript.

8. Relation of the scroll to the Massoretic text
   a. The text is by and large the same as that of the traditional Book of Isaiah. Most of the deviations from the Massoretic text are in details of spelling and grammar, but in some instances there are very definite variant readings.
   b. Burrows feels that the few conspicuous differences between the St. Mark's manuscript and the Massoretic text make their over-all agreement all the more remarkable. Some scholars, for example Paul Kahle, feel that the most significant fact about the scroll is that it has a large number of variant readings which are practically nonexistent in other Hebrew manuscripts of the Old Testament.
   c. Burrows feels that considering how widely the earliest manuscripts of the New Testament vary, how radically the ancient Greek versions differ from the traditional Hebrew text, and what a long time intervenes between the Dead Sea Scrolls and the oldest of the medieval manuscripts, one might have expected a much larger number of variant readings and a much wider degree of divergence.
   d. The scroll does show, for the first time, what Hebrew manuscripts of the Bible were like before they had been made to conform to a standardized text. Burrows sees three stages in the formation of the standardized text:

   (1) The gradual development of various forms of the text, including that which was later to be accepted as normative. No one manuscript perhaps contained the whole text of any book exactly as the Massoretes adopted it. Their work was presumably eclectic, and perhaps to some extent creative, though not intended to be so. On the whole, however, the text they approved must have had ancient traditions behind it.

   (2) The second stage was the choice among the variant traditions, involving a decision as to what reading was to be accepted for each verse and word.

   (3) The third stage was the elimination of all manuscripts that did not conform to the approved text. Not until after this had been accomplished would the production of new manuscripts containing variant readings cease altogether. Only when new copies were carefully corrected, and all old or new copies that differed from the official norm were destroyed, was the process of standardization complete. That point may not have been reached before the eighth century A.D.

e. Some of the differences between the *St. Mark's Isaiah* scroll and the Massoretic text are merely mistakes in writing—omission or addition of one or more words, the confusion of words and letters, the substitution of one word for another, the transposition of words or of letters within a word, and various errors of other kinds.

(1) Some of these errors are attributable to the seeming carelessness of the scribe.

(2) Skehan points out that this manuscript illustrates the effect of an "exegetical process" in the transmission of the text; that is, the scribe who copied a manuscript was at the same time an interpreter who felt free to expand and modify the text to bring out what he believed to be its meaning. After the text was standardized officially, such exegetical expansions and modifications were no longer permitted; but the fact that they had been common in some quarters before that time is abundantly shown by the Septuagint and the Samaritan Pentateuch. The Qumran sectarians did not feel obliged to preserve any particular form of the text; what seemed to them to convey the meaning, as they understood it, was assumed to be right. Consequently their manuscripts, and especially 1QIs[a], contained many minor additions and modifications. Usually these were derived from passages in the same book or other books. Skehan has listed twenty-seven unique readings of 1QIs[a] which are clearly drawn from other parts of the book or from the other prophetic books.

(3) The mistakes the scribe made may have been due to the fact that he made the scroll from dictation or from memory, or that he was not well educated and his eye skipped and he made errors, or simply that he was careless. The fact that he was careless would seem to be supported by the fact that he himself felt it necessary to correct his text.

f. Some of the differences between 1QIs[a] and the traditional text are due to the orthography of 1QIs[a]. The most conspicuous feature of its orthography is the lavish use of what is known as the *scriptio plena*—that is the use of letters of the alphabet to indicate vowels. The practice of using these vowel letters—technically called *matres lectionis*, began very early, but it was not highly developed until after the Old Testament period. In our printed Hebrew Bibles the vowels are indicated by a system of "pointing" devised in the ninth and tenth centuries A.D. A difference in a vowel can change the entire word, and some of the readings in the traditional Isaiah have been clarified through the *plena* spelling of 1QIs^a.

(1) An example of this is Isaiah 49 : 17. The Massoretic text reads "your sons" whereas the St. Mark's scroll reads "your builders." The latter reading makes better sense in the context and has some support in the other versions of the Bible (Septuagint, Vulgate, etc.). The difference consists only of a vowel, as the same consonants can be read either way. The medieval vowel points of the Massoretic text give the meaning "sons," while the St. Mark's manuscript by inserting a vowel letter gives the reading "builders."

(2) In cases where preferred meanings are secured by assuming different vowels without changing the consonants, the Revised Standard Version was changed, without the insertion of footnotes.

9. The thirteen variant readings recently adopted by the committee for the Revised Standard Version of the Bible
   a. In the places where revisions were adopted, a marginal note cites "One ancient Ms," meaning the *St. Mark's Isaiah* scroll.
   b. Burrows feels that in these thirteen places the superiority of 1QIs^a is not always certain. But several variant readings which were not adopted in the Revised Standard Version have been defended recently by scholars with more or less success.
   c. In eight of the thirteen instances the reading of the scroll is supported to some degree by the ancient versions—that is, the Greek, Aramaic, Syriac, and Latin versions. The most important of these is the Greek version (the Septuagint).
      (1) In three cases the Greek version and two others lend more or less support to the manuscript against the Massoretic text. In Isaiah 60 : 19 the phrase "by night" is omitted in the traditional text, but is attested by 1QIs^a as well as Greek, Old Latin, and Aramaic versions. In Isaiah 51 : 19, the Massoretic text reads in the last line "how may I comfort you?" and the 1QIs^a, Greek, Syriac, and Latin versions read "who will comfort you?" In Isaiah 14 : 4 instead of "insolent fury" previous translations read "the golden city."
      (2) In one passage the Septuagint alone agrees with the scroll. In Isaiah 45 : 2 the traditional text reads "rough places"

instead of "mountains" as found in both the Septuagint and 1QIs ͣ.

(3) Twice where the Greek agrees with the Massoretic text two or three other versions support 1QIs ͣ, such as Isaiah 56 : 12 and Isaiah 49 : 24.

(4) Once the Latin alone agrees with 1QIs ͣ—Isaiah 14 : 30.

(5) In one instance, in Isaiah 15 : 9, the Syriac version gives partial support to the Latin. The name of the city is given in the Massoretic text as Dimon, and in the Latin and 1QIs ͣ it is given as Dibon, a city that is well known.

(6) The remaining five of the thirteen variants that were adopted have no support in any of the ancient versions. In these cases the choice between the Massoretic text and the scroll is governed only by intrinsic probability, as indicated by the context. These variants are Isaiah 3 : 24, 21 : 8, 23 : 2, 33 : 8, and 45 : 8.

d. Burrows points out that the adoption of these thirteen readings by the committee that made the Revised Standard Version does not prove that in these instances and in these alone the St. Mark's scroll is superior to the Massoretic text. Each variant was discussed on its merits by the committee and a decision was taken by vote, but the vote was rarely unanimous. He points out that other scholars and some members of the committee would judge otherwise in some cases.

e. Barthélemy feels that, in some places where the scroll is supported by the ancient versions, the Massoretic reading is a deliberate modification in the interest of a particular group. However, it is also possible that the covenanters altered the text to introduce their own beliefs. This procedure was followed in the scroll known as the *Habakkuk Commentary.*

f. Some of the variant readings are produced by the aforementioned deviations in grammar and spelling: that is, differences in plural and singular forms of a verb or a noun, the use of the active rather than passive voice of a verb, the interchange of letters easily mistaken in Hebrew (such as *dalet* and *resh*), the elimination or addition of a definite article, and the splitting of a word.

g. Some of the differences in orthography and language may be explained in terms of local differences in speech—slightly different dialects or pronunciations existing simultaneously in different parts of Palestine.

h. The question still remains as to how many of the variants were errors on the part of the copyist, how many were the result of an alteration by the copyist to achieve agreement with what he considered a better text, and how many of the variants truly represent the ancient text. There is a possibility that a popular text such as 1QIs[a] would be less subject to correction than a more official text and might therefore preserve ancient readings that were eliminated from official texts.

10. Diametrically opposite inferences have been drawn from the differences that exist between 1QIs[a] and the traditional text.
    a. It has been argued that the *St. Mark's Isaiah* scroll is too full of mistakes to be very ancient.
        (1) If a manuscript is made soon after the composition of the book it contains, it should be relatively free from errors.
        (2) The mistakes naturally accumulate as one copy after another is made.
    b. On the other hand, the very fact that such liberties are taken with the biblical text has been cited as proof that the manuscript must be pre-Massoretic.
        (1) The degree of accuracy in a manuscript is no sure indication of its age.
        (2) The Massoretic text may be based on older manuscripts or manuscripts that were better and more carefully copied.
    c. The general agreement among scholars is that 1QIs[a] is pre-Massoretic and dates from about 100 B.C. The spelling of the scroll is relatively late, that is, the *scriptio plena*. Sukenik explains this by saying that during the last century before the destruction of the Temple *scriptio plena* was being used to facilitate reading, both in new compositions and in ancient texts, although during the same period biblical manuscripts using the older orthography (that is, the *Hebrew University Isaiah*) were also in circulation. However, while the spelling of the scroll is relatively late, the grammatical forms indicated by that spelling are older than those preserved in the Massoretic text.

11. Significance of the *St. Mark's Isaiah* scroll.
    a. It is the only one of the scrolls that contains a whole book of the Bible.
    b. With the exception of some of the small fragments, it is the oldest of the manuscripts found in the cave.

c. On the whole the text agrees with the traditional manuscript. Such agreement gives reassuring testimony to the general accuracy of the traditional text, although it does not prove that the latter is the original text of Isaiah. It shows that any major changes that occurred in the transmission of the text had already been made before the writings of this scroll—in other words before the beginning of the Christian era.
d. Thus, the text was well on its way to standardization before this was done officially by the Massoretes.

B. *The Hebrew University manuscript of Isaiah* (1QIs^b)

1. Description
   a. It is not a complete copy of the Book of Isaiah.
   b. Its contents were not identified until some time after the discovery and purchase of the scrolls, because it was so tightly compressed that the attempt to unroll it was postponed until the other scrolls had been opened, and some skill for the delicate task had been developed.
   c. The scroll was found to consist of one large and several small pieces.
   d. The material had deteriorated to such a degree that the writing was in many places illegible except by means of infra-red photography.
   e. The large piece contains the last third of the book of Isaiah, from Chapter 38 to the end, with some gaps.
   f. The smaller pieces contain parts of Chapters 10, 13, 19-30, and 35-40.
   g. Apparently the scroll had already been in a fragmentary condition when it was deposited in the cave.

2. Relation of the scroll to the Massoretic text
   a. Unlike the St. Mark's scroll, the Hebrew University scroll agrees closely with the Massoretic text.
   b. 1QIs^b does not have the *scriptio plena* of 1QIs^a.
   c. 1QIs^b has variations on the Massoretic text, not all of which appear in the *St. Mark's Isaiah*, although on the whole it is much closer to the Massoretic text than 1QIs^a.
   d. The existence of two different texts read by the same sect shows the heavy responsibility and labor of those who later edited the Massoretic text.
   e. It may also be assumed that the sect possessed many manuscripts

of the Holy Scriptures which differed from each other in minor or major ways.

3. Dating of the scroll

   a. In the *Hebrew University Isaiah*, the final forms of all five Hebrew letters (*k*, *m*, *n*, *p*, and *ṣ*) are present. In the *St. Mark's Isaiah*, the two forms of *m* and *n* are used, but the "medial" form of the *m* often appears at the end of a word and the "final" form is sometimes found in the middle of a word. The other three letters in 1QIs[a] do not yet have special final forms, though the *k* and *s* are somewhat longer when written at the end of a word. In the *St. Mark's Isaiah*, a passage omitted by the first scribe and later inserted has a final *p*, which occurs nowhere else in the manuscript.

   b. The paleography then seems to indicate that 1QIs[b] is later than 1QIs[a], although its agreement with the Massoretic text does not indicate a definite date (as has already been discussed in relation to the dating of 1QIs[a]).

   c. It is believed that the *Hebrew University Isaiah* was made during the first century A.D.

C. Other fragments of manuscripts of Isaiah

1. More fragments for the Hebrew University manuscript have been found.

2. The Book of Isaiah seems to have been the most popular of the prophetic books in the Qumran community. In addition to the two scrolls from Cave One there are more-or-less extensive fragments of thirteen others from Cave Four.

3. Like the later and incomplete scroll from Cave One, the Cave Four fragments agree closely with the Massoretic text.

Topics for Study and Discussion

A. Describe the biblical materials found in the Dead Sea caves.

B. Describe the two important Isaiah manuscripts discovered and

   1. the probable dates of both;

   2. the similarities and differences between the two, and the importance of these similarities and differences

C. What is the significance of the discovery of both Isaiah scrolls among the manuscripts of the Dead Sea and the inferences that have been drawn from this discovery?

D. Discuss the variant readings recently adopted by the Committee for the Revised Standard Version of the Bible and some of the reasons advanced for adopting them.

XI

THE SCROLLS AND BIBLICAL STUDIES

This unit discusses the importance of the Qumran finds for Old Testament studies. Scrolls such as Daniel and Isaiah bring us closer to original copies of the Bible than any found so far and as such constitute our oldest copies of some of the books of the Old Testament. Aside from this, the biblical scrolls have yielded a great deal of data that is enabling scholars to reconstruct the textual history of the Old Testament. We now know that a variety of biblical texts was in circulation at the same time, at least up to A.D. 70. We also know that the Septuagint was made from a Hebrew text existing at that time and that therefore the differences between the Septuagint and the Massoretic text are not due to errors on the part of the Greek translators.

As a result of the discovery among the various recensions of the Old Testament of texts that corresponded to the Massoretic text standardized by the rabbis in the ninth century, we now know that the Massoretic text existed in the first century in much the same form as its later standardized version. Furthermore, the scrolls are important for biblical studies in that they help us

1. to substantiate and further understand passages in the standardized text,
2. to establish the historicity of innumerable passages and statements of the Bible, and
3. to show us that in its main substance and in its essential idea the Hebrew text was preserved with remarkably little change.

RECOMMENDED READING

Allegro, J. M., *The Dead Sea Scrolls*, pages 50-74
Burrows, M., *The Dead Sea Scrolls*, pages 102-116
Burrows, M., *More Light on the Dead Sea Scrolls*, pages 135-190
Cross, F. M., Jr., *The Ancient Library of Qumran and Modern Biblical Studies*, pages 120-145

Milik, J. T., *Ten Years of Discovery in the Wilderness of Judaea*, pages 21-35 and 129-139

Yadin, Y., *The Message of the Scrolls*, pages 73-89

THE SCROLLS AND BIBLICAL STUDIES

A. *General background*

1. About one third of the Qumran fragments are fragments of biblical manuscripts, and all the books of the Old Testament are represented except for the Book of Esther.
   a. The Book of Esther may have been rejected as part of the canon by the sect.
   b. Or it may be missing from the Qumran fragments purely by chance.
2. Nearly one hundred biblical scrolls were recovered from Cave Four; as a result there was material for sampling textual types in virtually every book of the Old Testament.
3. The material from the different caves and especially from Cave Four has produced different textual traditions for the same book.
   a. This attests to the fact that different traditions of the text were current in Palestine just before and after the turn of the Christian era.
   b. On the whole, three main traditions of biblical text were found— Samaritan, Septuagintal, and Massoretic.
   c. Examples of books found in more than one form are the following:
      (1) Jeremiah—one text corresponds to the LXX (Septuagint) text and one corresponds to the Massoretic text.
      (2) Isaiah—*St. Mark's Isaiah* is on the whole similar to the traditional text but differs from it at many points. The *Hebrew University Isaiah* agrees closely with the Massoretic text of later manuscripts.
      (3) Samuel—one version contains readings not found in either the LXX or the Massoretic text.
4. Similarities and agreements of some of the texts with the standardized Hebrew Bible attest to the existence of the Massoretic tradition before the final stabilization of this text in the eighth and ninth centuries.
   a. The *Hebrew University Isaiah* shows that a virtual standardization of the text had come about more or less spontaneously two or three centuries before the Massoretes made it official.

b. The Massoretic text existed at this period though not in fully standardized copies.
c. The Massoretic text in this period is for many books a single recension paralleled usually by one or more other recensions, usually of a type familiar to us from later documents, that is, the Samaritan or Septuagintal version of the text.
5. Certain books are more prominent in the Qumran library finds than others.
   a. The excavators found thirteen manuscripts of Deuteronomy, twelve manuscripts of Isaiah, and ten manuscripts of the Psalms.
   b. These figures are interesting in that these same books figure most frequently in New Testament quotations from the Old Testament.
6. The various recensions of the texts have basic similarities:
   a. These similarities show that the Old Testament text has been handed down over the centuries with great accuracy.
   b. The new finds do not require great changes in our accepted Bible.
   c. A remarkable degree of agreement between the scrolls and our present Hebrew Bible is evidenced.

B. *Examples of different textual traditions of the Bible found at Qumran*

1. Septuagintal tradition is shown in the historical books, Joshua, Samuel, and Kings.
   a. The text of these books found at Qumran is at wide variance with the traditional Massoretic text; it follows rather the Septuagint rendering.
   b. It becomes clear through these books that the Septuagint divergent text was not due to faulty translation from the traditional text, but to translation from a different Hebrew text.
   c. The Septuagint accurately reflects a Hebrew textual tradition at home in Egypt in the third to second centuries B.C.
   d. The Septuagint of the historical books can be used to study the pre-Christian texts of these books and the traditional Hebrew text.
2. Septuagintal tradition is shown in books of the Pentateuch.
   a. Among the thirty Pentateuchal manuscripts from Cave Four there were examples of the three textual traditions—Massoretic, Samaritan, and Septuagintal.
   b. Most of the texts reflect the proto-Massoretic tradition.
   c. Manuscripts of Deuteronomy and Exodus were found which reflect the Septuagintal tradition.

3. Paleo-Hebrew texts of Exodus and Numbers were found which reflect the Samaritan tradition.
4. The proto-Massoretic tradition and the Massoretic tradition are shown in the Isaiah manuscripts.
   a. Many of the differences between the *St. Mark's Isaiah* scroll and the Massoretic text can be explained by mistakes in copying.
      (1) Difficulties in copying arose because no system of vowels existed in Hebrew until the seventh century A.D.
      (2) Mistakes in the text can be explained by the three methods of reproducing the text—dictation, copying, and memory—which were used at the time.
   b. Agreements between this Isaiah and the traditional text give testimony to the general accuracy of the traditional text, although not proving that the latter is the original text of Isaiah.
   c. *St. Mark's Isaiah* shows that any major changes that occurred in the transmission of the text had already been made before the beginning of the Christian era.
      (1) It shows that a decisive history of the text of the Old Testament had already been completed by the time of Jesus, not only in the books of law but also in the books of the prophets.
      (2) Conspicuous differences in spelling and grammatical forms between this Isaiah and the Massoretic text make their substantial agreement in the words of the text all the more remarkable, considering how widely the earliest manuscripts of the New Testament vary, how radically the ancient Greek versions differ from the traditional Hebrew text, and what a long time intervened between the Dead Sea Scrolls and the oldest of the medieval manuscripts.
   d. This scroll shows us for the first time what Hebrew manuscripts of the Bible were like before they had been made to conform to a standardized text.
   e. This scroll helps to correct errors in standard text.
      (1) Burrows made a list of variant readings between this Isaiah and the traditional text.
      (2) Thirteen readings in which the manuscript departs from the traditional text were adopted in 1952 for the Revised Standard Version of the Bible by the Old Testament Revision Committee.
         (a) Example—"raisin cake" in 16 : 7 Isaiah. The *Habakkuk Commentary* scroll shows that the Hebrew word also

means able-bodied men, which makes more sense in context.
- (b) In eight of the thirteen changes the new reading of the text is supported to some degree by other ancient versions such as the Septuagint.
- f. The *Hebrew University Isaiah* agrees closely with the Massoretic text.
- g. Fragments of other manuscripts of Isaiah have been found in the caves. They agree closely with the Massoretic text and nowhere do they agree with the Septuagint when it differs from the Massoretic text.

C. *Canonization of the Bible in the light of Qumran manuscripts*

1. The finding of manuscripts of the Pentateuch and the prophets, especially the twelve, rules out speculations about late additions to prophetic works.
2. Ecclesiastes, sometimes dated in the second or first century B.C., appears in examples from Cave Four which dates ca. 175-150 B.C. and the text reveals development. The date of composition must now be pushed to the third century, B.C.
3. "The canonical Psalter of the second century B.C.," though fragmentary, indicates that the collection of canonical psalms was fixed by Maccabean times, bearing out current tendency to date latest canonical psalms in the Persian period.

D. *Light shed on oral, or possibly literary, sources lying behind the fixed edition of an Old Testament book*

1. Publication of fragments from Cave Four designated the "Prayer of Nabonidus."
2. This is closely related in language, style, and genre to Daniel 1-6.
3. It is possible that this new document preserves a more primitive form of the tale, which suggests a line of oral transmission.

E. *Significance of scrolls for biblical studies*

1. The scrolls bring us closer to original copies of the Bible.
    - a. The Book of Daniel is believed to have been written about 165 B.C. Qumran Daniel possibly was transcribed within one hundred years after the original. The Qumran Daniel is very close to the original biblical Daniel.
    - b. Book of Isaiah:

(1) Previously the oldest known biblical manuscript was the one called Codex Petropolitanus, dated A.D. 916.

(2) The Isaiah scroll takes us one thousand years closer to the original copy; it is the oldest manuscript of Isaiah in existence.

2. Scrolls yield data for the reconstruction of the textual history of the Old Testament.
   a. At least up to A.D. 70, various biblical texts were in circulation at the same time.
   b. The Septuagint translation was made from a Hebrew text current at the time.
   c. The Massoretic text existed at the time in much the same form as its later standardized version.
3. The scrolls are important because they substantiate and further our understanding of passages in the standardized text.
4. They help to establish the pre-Christian state of the Old Testament.
5. They help to establish the historicity of innumerable passages and statements of the Bible.
6. They show that in its main substance and its essential idea the Hebrew text was preserved with remarkably little change.
7. Scrolls indicate that there existed a tradition of biblical study which is outside the strict rabbinical tradition.

TOPICS FOR STUDY AND DISCUSSION

A. Discuss the importance of the discovery of the biblical manuscripts at Qumran.

B. Give examples of biblical books found in more than one textual tradition and discuss the importance of such finds.

C. Give an example of a book found in the Septuagintal tradition and discuss the light this sheds on the relationship of the Septuagint to the Massoretic text.

D. Write a short essay on the Septuagint.

XII

THE COMMENTARIES

The books of the Bible were the most important sources for study for the Qumran community, and like other teachers in Israel, the teachers of the sect believed that the words of the Scriptures could be applied to the events of their own time. The commentaries are important for several reasons:

1. They shed light on the internal problems of the sect and additional light on biblical texts.
2. There are allusions in these documents to the leader of the sect, known as the Teacher of Righteousness, and his enemy, the Wicked Priest, and the "man of lie" or "falsehood," and also the "House of Absalom."
3. In the *Nahum Commentary* the true names of historical personages are given for the first time, along with a clue to the identification of the Kittim.
4. The historical allusions are helpful in determining the date when the scrolls were first written and in telling us more about the sect, their history, and the history of the period in which they lived.

The *Habakkuk Commentary* is the most complete of the commentaries found, and it thus contains most of the allusions. In addition to the *Habakkuk Commentary*, fragments have been found of commentaries on Genesis 49, Pslams 37, 45, 57, 68, Isaiah (one in Cave Three and another in Cave Four), Hosea, Micah, Nahum, and Zephaniah, although the *Nahum Commentary* is the only one in which names of actual historical personages are mentioned.

Recommended Reading

Burrows, M., *The Dead Sea Scrolls*, pages 22-24, 91-94, 123-188, and 365-370 (Translation)

Burrows, M., *More Light on the Dead Sea Scrolls*, pages 166-167

Gaster, T. H., *Dead Sea Scriptures in English Translation*, pages 229-256 (includes a translation)
Van der Ploeg, J., *The Excavations at Qumran*, pages 55-56, 60-62 and 165-169
Vermes, G., *The Dead Sea Scrolls in English*, pages 214-246.
Yadin, Y., *The Message of the Scrolls*, pages 89-104

THE COMMENTARY ON THE BOOK OF HABAKKUK
A. *Discovery and description*

1. The Habakkuk scroll was found in Cave One in 1947.
2. It is one of the seven original scrolls of the first discovery. According to Theodore Gaster, the allusions in the *Habakkuk Commentary* "have been thought to constitute a connected biographical narrative which, once the characters are identified, might provide a definitive clue to the antiquity of the tale and thence possibly to that of the scrolls as a whole."
3. The scroll consists of two strips of leather sewn end to end with linen thread.
    a. Its beginning has been lost, but apparently only column one is missing.
    b. The bottoms of the columns have been eaten away.
    c. There are holes in some of the columns.
    d. The "hair side" on which the writing was done was carefully dressed and is smooth to the touch.
        (1) The smoothed surface was ruled into columns and lines and the margins between the columns were ruled.
        (2) The ruling was probably done with a sharp instrument, leaving a fine depression evident to touch and sight.
4. The scroll, when unrolled, is 5 feet long; originally it must have been 6 or 7 inches longer.
5. At present it is only 5 1/2 inches wide at the widest points; original width can be estimated at about 7 inches.
6. It is difficult to guess the exact number of lines in each page; scholars estimate an average of seventeen lines per page as the original number.
7. The first of the two strips contains seven columns of writing.
    a. The first column begins with words from the second verse of the first chapter of Habakkuk. Only a few words at the ends of the lines remain in this column; those at the bottom are from the fourth verse of the same chapter.

b. The second column has a considerable gap right down the middle and its first words are from the fifth verse of the first chapter of Habakkuk.
c. The other columns (of both strips) are relatively well preserved, especially in the upper parts where the edge is almost intact.
8. The second strip or sheet must have had margins set out for seven columns, but only six were used; the last column has only four lines of writing.
9. The writing of this scroll on the whole is good.
   a. The text is more clearly written and better preserved than that of the first Isaiah scroll; the scribe seems to have been more experienced.
      (1) The lines are straighter.
      (2) The letters are very clear.
      (3) There are relatively fewer mistakes.
      (4) The scribe leaves a small space between passages.
   b. The scribe uses ancient Hebrew script to write the Tetragrammaton —YHWH, the Hebrew for *Jehovah* or "The Lord."
   c. Corrections have been made to the text.
   d. The scroll is devoid of marginal marks seen in Isaiah, except for "X-like" signs at the end of some lines.

B. *Linguistic features*

1. The *Habakkuk Commentary* exhibits many of the same linguistic features of *St. Mark's Isaiah* scroll—peculiarities of spelling and grammar for which parallels have been found in Aramaic, in the Samaritan dialects, in the rabbinical dialects, and in the early medieval Hebrew poems.
2. The language is quite simple; it is drawn almost entirely from the Hebrew Bible.
3. The five Hebrew letters, which have final forms, are repeatedly used when occurring in the final position of the words in this scroll.

C. *Contents and analysis. The commentary is based on the Book of Habakkuk*

1. Habakkuk lived in the seventh century B.C. His prophecies, bearing his name, form one of the Twelve Minor Prophets in the Hebrew Bible.

2. In Chapter 1, Habakkuk spoke of the Chaldeans whose speedy arrival in Judea he foretold.
3. In Chapter 2, he foretold their punishment.
4. The *Habakkuk Commentary* quotes the text of all but the third chapter of the Book of Habakkuk.
   a. The third chapter of the book is a psalm which describes a theophany—a divine manifestation.
   b. Many scholars have long believed that the third chapter was not part of the original book, but its absence from the scroll proves neither the above nor the view that the third chapter was unknown to the sect.

D. *The method used by the author of the Habakkuk Commentary*

1. He quotes the text of Habakkuk, a verse, or a few words from a verse, at a time.
2. Immediately after the quotation the author adds his commentary or *pesher*.
3. The author sets out to explain how the commentaries come to be and how they should be applied to certain events of the day.
4. At times the same verse, or some part of the verse, is given two different commentaries or *pesharim*.
5. Each sentence or phrase is taken by itself, without inhibitions imposed by the context. Similarity of meaning or of sound may suggest an application, words may be combined or separated without regard to the plain intention of the author, and even the spelling is sometimes juggled to produce a new meaning.

E. *Application of the Book of Habakkuk is made by the author of the Habakkuk Commentary to the events known to himself*

1. The coming of the Chaldeans is applied to the coming of the Kittim, whom no one can escape.
2. The part which tells of the punishment of the Chaldeans leads the author to the discussion of the punishment which the Wicked Priest and his followers must undergo for their criminal behavior towards the Teacher of Righteousness.

F. *Dramatis personae*

1. The Kittim—the invaders.
2. The Teacher of Righteousness—the inspired and persecuted.

3. The Wicked Priest—rapacious, drunken, impious, perhaps diseased and certainly doomed.
4. The Man of Lie—probably a third character.
5. The Preacher of Lie—may be the same man or another person.
6. The House of Absalom—a group of people who for some unexplained reason should have helped the Teacher of Righteousness but instead kept silence.
7. God's Elect—the men of truth, the humble, the simple ones of Judah, those who have persisted in their faith in the Teacher of Righteousness.
8. The House of Guilt, the House of Judgment, and the last priests of Jerusalem.

G. *Summary of contents*

1. Kittim threatened to invade Jerusalem and all nations, which the writer considers a punishment fully deserved by the priests.
2. The Teacher of Righteousness, a priest believed to have a gift for interpreting prophecy, had difficulties with men who did not believe him and dealt treacherously with him in concert with a man called the Man of Lie.
3. A group called the House of Absalom and their party—perhaps the same group or perhaps another—instead of helping the Teacher of Righteousness when he suffered, remained silent.
4. The Wicked Priest—a man who ruled in Israel and who became proud, forsook God and the Law, amassed wealth by violent measures and wrought all manner of unclean abominations.
5. Either the Wicked Priest or the Teacher of Righteousness suffered some kind of horrible bodily affliction.
6. The Wicked Priest was punished by his enemies because of a wrong committed against the Teacher of Righteousness and his followers.
7. Something important happened on the Day of Atonement—different scholars have different theories. Possibly this is when the conflict between the Teacher of Righteousness and the Wicked Priest came to an open breach, and soon afterward the Teacher of Righteousness was arrested and brought to trial.
8. The Wicked Priest persecuted the Teacher of Righteousness. The purpose of this persecution was some kind of punishment.
9. One of the parties, probably the Wicked Priest, appeared on the Day of Atonement to some group, probably the followers of the Teacher

of Righteousness, with the intent of making them do something the commentator calls "stumbling". What happens then we are not told.

H. *Recognition of characters and historical events*

1. Difficulties were encountered in figuring out a time sequence.
   a. The plot is not clear; even the separate episodes are obscure.
   b. We cannot assume that the events occurred in the order in which we read of them.
   c. Each sentence or phrase brings to the author's mind events and persons in the history of his nation and his own religious community and he mentions them as they occur to him. Thus no chronological sequence can be inferred from the commentary.
   d. Whether the commentator thinks of the events as in the past, present, or future is still an open question.
   e. The allusions in the commentary are not specific. Perhaps persons and groups referred to are deliberately disguised to avoid censorship and persecution. For his contemporary readers who knew the historical background and could recognize the allusions obscure to us, the author's meaning was no doubt unmistakable.
2. Since none of the references to the *dramatis personae* are specific, many theories as to the identities of the different people have been advanced.
   a. It is felt that the Kittim are the Romans. This is the general view. Few think the reference is to the Seleucids.
   b. Many theories exist, but there is no general agreement as to who the other persons are. Many scholars feel that the Wicked Priest may have been the Hasmonean King, Alexander Jannaeus, who reigned from 104-78 B.C.

I. *Significance of the Habakkuk Commentary*

1. It gives us the text of the book of Habakkuk, which is one thousand years older than any Hebrew text so far known. This is of importance to biblical criticism.
2. A great deal will be learned once the identities of the people are established. Even so, the text enables us to learn about the problems of the members of the sect who wrote the scroll, and about the Teacher of Righteousness.
3. We learn that the Teacher of Righteousness was clearly the leader and perhaps the founder of the community. He was evidently believed

by his followers to be endowed with the gift of interpreting prophecies; in fact, he could explain what was obscure even to the prophets themselves.

J. *Dating of the scroll*

1. Sukenik dates the scroll shortly before the destruction of the Temple (about A.D. 60-70); Albright puts it a little earlier, near the beginning of the Christian era.
2. This scroll, along with the *Genesis Apocryphon*, exhibits some of the latest forms of writing found in the scrolls.

THE NAHUM COMMENTARY

A. *Description*

1. The *Nahum Commentary* was published in 1956.
2. This commentary is of the same type as the *Habakkuk Commentary*: the prophet's words are seen and explained in the perspective of the writer's day.
3. Like the other commentaries, it speaks of a conflict; but unlike the others, it mentions names: Demetrius and Antiochus, along with the "rulers of the Kittim" and the "kings of Greece."
    a. Many scholars now feel that Antiochus is Antiochus Epiphanes, and the Kittim are the Romans. Demetrius is probably Demetrius III, who about 88 B.C. came into conflict with Alexander Jannaeus, who reigned from 104-78 B.C.
    b. Many scholars, such as Allegro and Gaster, feel that the Wicked Priest alluded to in all the commentaries is Alexander Jannaeus.

B. *Contents and explanations of contents*

1. The commentary speaks of a "(Deme)trius, king of Greece who tried to enter Jerusalem by the counsel of the "seekers after smooth things."
    a. Syria had three kings called Demetrius: Demetrius I (162-150 B.C.); II (145-126 B.C.); III (some time between 95 and 83 B.C.).
    b. Demetrius III was one of five brothers who disputed each other's claims to the kingdom of their dead father Antiochus VIII, and waged war to seize as much as possible of their paternal heritage. Demetrius III (or Demetrius Eucaerus) saw a chance of making himself master of Damascus and some of the surrounding territory, but while fighting his brother, Philip, in the north of the

country in 88 or 87 B.C., he was taken prisoner by his brother and died in captivity.
  c. This is the Demetrius who was called in by the Pharisees in their struggle against Alexander Jannaeus. He invaded Palestine in the hope of extending his territory, but went no farther than Sechem. He retired after winning a battle, when six thousand Jews who had been on his side went over to Alexander.
  d. We know that Demetrius I sent several generals to Judea to attack Judas Maccabeus, at a time when Jerusalem was still in the power of the king. It cannot therefore be said easily of him that "he tried to enter Jerusalem" while it may well be supposed that Demetrius III had this object in view because it was the capital of his adversary, Alexander. Demetrius II seems to be out of the question as a candidate for the Demetrius of the commentary.
  e. Hence, a number of scholars think it probable that the author of the *Nahum Commentary* meant the third king of that name when he spoke of Demetrius. If so, he cannot have written before 88 B.C..
2. An incomplete line of the text contains the words: "the kings of Greece (Syria) till the rise of the rulers of the Kittim."
  a. With the Greeks thus contrasted with the Kittim, many scholars feel that the Kittim can be identified with the Romans, as in Daniel 11 : 30, and as many hold, in the *Habakkuk Commentary*.
  b. If so, the text must refer to the coming of the Romans to the Near East, especially Syria. This took place in many stages and the Romans only really interested themselves in Syria when Pompey led his armies in triumph through the Near East and took Jerusalem in 63 B.C.
3. The commentary also speaks of a "Raging Lion" (literally, "The Lion of Wrath"), a personage known to the author and regarded by him as the "ravening lion" of Nahum 2 : 13. Many scholars feel that the ravening lion refers to the same person as the Wicked Priest, and that if the two are the same then the Wicked Priest must be Alexander Jannaeus. Other scholars feel that this cannot be proved and that the question of identification still remains open.
  a. The ravening lion with his lords and counselors did much evil.
  b. In the *Nahum Commentary*, based on Nahum 2 : 11-12, reference is made to the crucifixion of a number of Jews by the king, an event mentioned by Josephus, Antiquities XIII, 14 : 1-2, as having occurred during the reign of Alexander Jannaeus about 88 B.C.
  c. Antiochus Epiphanes had put Jews to death by crucifixion, but

the first Jewish ruler who is known to have done so is Alexander Jannaeus (as we have seen above), who was the adversary of Demetrius.
- d. The question arises whether Alexander is not the Raging Lion.
- e. We may go a step further and ask whether the Raging Lion is not the same as the Wicked Priest, and/or the Man of Lies of the *Habakkuk Commentary*. The latter occurs, at any rate, in the different commentaries (Habakkuk, Micah, Psalms 37—that is, in three out of four commentaries of any size yet published), which suggests that he was *the* great enemy of Qumran. Hence the identification of the Wicked Priest (the opponent of the Teacher) with Alexander Jannaeus, has much to be said for it, though it is not yet fully proven.
- f. In fact, even before the recovery of the *Nahum Commentary*, many scholars noted how well the tyrant Alexander Jannaeus fitted the characteristics of the sect's persecutor.

PSALMS COMMENTARY

A. It was discovered in Cave Four.
B. Those parts of it published to date, are written on two pieces of skin measuring 10 by 20 centimeters and 5 by 9 centimeters, respectively.
C. A third fragment of the same commentary was only recently published.
D. The fragments contain a commentary on Psalm 37, similar in style to the Habakkuk Commentary and in all probability written about the same time.
   1. Its subject is influenced by the nature of Psalm 37, which deals with the victory of the just over the wicked and the meek over the evil-doers.
   2. This subject is close to the beliefs of the sect, and could easily be applied to the persecution of the Teacher of Righteousness by the Wicked Priest.
E. The importance of the *Psalms Commentary* lies in its biographical data about the Teacher of Righteousness.
   1. It confirms that he was a priest.
   2. It affirms that he will be under attack.
F. The *Psalms Commentary* refers to the leaders of Jerusalem in terms similar to those used in the *Habakkuk Commentary*: "The Princes of wickedness who have cheated His holy people."

G. Through this commentary we may learn the sect's version of Psalm 37.

H. There are several interesting differences between the Massoretic text of the Psalm and the text of the *Psalms Commentary*.

OTHER COMMENTARIES

A. All that is left of the other commentaries—those on Isaiah, Micah, Zephaniah, Hosea, and the Psalms—consists of small pieces only.

B. The commentaries on Micah and Psalm 37 mention the Teacher and his opponent.

C. Column VIII, fragment 16, lines 7-16, of the *Manual of Discipline* contains an extract from the *Commentary on Isaiah*. In this extract there is an indication of a date, but it is difficult to interpret it.

D. There is a commentary on Ezekiel in Column XV, lines 1-3, of the *War Scroll*, which seems to be an extract from a popular writing composed after A.D. 70 and before A.D. 132.

TOPICS FOR STUDY AND DISCUSSION

A. Discuss briefly the discovery of the Habakkuk scroll and its general contents. Discuss the methods used by the author in writing the commentary.

B. Describe the events narrated in the Habakkuk scroll and the *dramatis personae* involved in these events.

C. Discuss:
   1. What is the *Habakkuk Commentary* based on and how does the author relate the events in the original story to himself and to his times?
   2. What is the significance of the *Habakkuk Commentary*?

D. Discuss the importance of the *Nahum Commentary* and the light it has shed on the identification of the following:
   1. Demetrius
   2. the Kittim
   3. the Raging Lion

E. List some of the commentaries found other than those on Habakkuk and Nahum, and describe briefly the contents and importance of the *Psalms Commentary*.

GENERAL REVIEW

Required Reading

This is a review unit; you should therefore go over Units 1-12 and read those assignments that you think are necessary. You are also advised to read the written answers to the assignments done for Units 1-12. As a general review, read the following: Edmund Wilson, *The Scrolls from the Dead Sea*, pages 1-53 and 113-121, or any of the general works listed in the Bibliography. The chapter on the Essene Order should serve as a good introduction for the remainder of this course.

Topic for Study and Discussion

Professor W. F. Albright described the discovery of the Dead Sea Scrolls as "the greatest manuscript discovery of modern times." Discuss this statement in detail with reference to contents, general significance, and importance to biblical studies.

XIII

THE THANKSGIVING HYMNS

The scroll of the *Thanksgiving Hymns* is one of the most important scrolls because its hymns advance the study of the religious ideas and doctrines of the sect which preserved them. It is an invaluable document for research on the comparative doctrines of this sect and the background of Christianity. To mention only a few, this scroll contains the doctrines of dualism, predestination, salvation through election and immortality. You are required to read *at least* two books, but you will do well to read all you can on this scroll. This collection of hymns seems to be the product of a single author whose experience and feelings they vividly reflect.

Read the translation of these hymns in one of the following books:
Burrows, M., *The Dead Sea Scrolls*, pages 400-415
Gaster, T. H., *Dead Sea Scriptures in English Translation*, pages 123-202
Mansoor, M., *The Thanksgiving Hymns*
Vermes, G., *The Dead Sea Scrolls in English*, pages 149-201.

Make notes on the religious ideas and doctrines expressed in the hymns and compare these with corresponding doctrines and ideas in Judaism and Christianity. This should serve as a good preparation for Unit 19, "Qumran Writings and Christianity."

REQUIRED READING

Allegro, J., *The Dead Sea Scrolls*, pages 124-133
Burrows, M., *The Dead Sea Scrolls*, pages 400-415 (Translation of text)
Burrows, M., *More Light on the Dead Sea Scrolls*, pages 292-296, 324-336, 342-352, and 379-382
Gaster, T. H., *Dead Sea Scriptures in English Translation*, pages 123-202 (Translation of text)
Mansoor, M., *The Thanksgiving Hymns* (Read the entire introduction to the book.)
Sukenik, E. L., *The Dead Sea Scrolls of the Hebrew University* (Read the introduction to the *Thanksgiving Hymns* in the English edition.)

Van der Ploeg, J., *The Excavations at Qumran*, pages 175-178
Vermes, J., *Discovery in the Judean Desert*, pages 187-196
Yadin, Y., *The Message of the Scrolls*, pages 104-112

THE SCROLL OF THE THANKSGIVING HYMNS

A. *The discovery*

1. The scroll of the *Thanksgiving Hymns* was found in Cave One in 1947.
2. Small fragments of this scroll were also found in 1949.
3. In the summer of 1952, five additional fragments of this scroll, including one on papyrus, were among the finds in Cave Four.
   a. At some points these fragments complete the numerous gaps in the hymns.
   b. Four or five fragments from Cave Four of manuscripts containing psalms similar to, but not found in, the *Thanksgiving Hymns*, were also discovered, but whether they belonged to the same collection is an open question.

B. *Description*

1. This scroll was found in two parts—"two shapeless bundles."
   a. First part
      (1) It contained three separate folded (not rolled) sheets.
      (2) Each sheet had four columns of text.
      (3) The sheets are about 13 inches high, containing as many as forty lines to a column.
      (4) These columns are the same width, and the writing is the same size as that in the complete scroll of Isaiah.
   b. Second part
      (1) This part, when found, was a crumpled mass of some seventy fragments, difficult to unroll.
      (2) The greater part of the parchment is dark to extremely dark brown. Some pieces have become black due to the ravages of time.
      (3) Thanks to infrared photography, scholars were able to read some previously illegible sections.
2. Description of the text as a whole
   a. It is poorly preserved, the numerous lacunae that interrupt the

context not only in the upper and lower edges but also in the middle of the columns.
   b. In some columns only the right or left half of the column is preserved.
3. So far, eighteen plates, each with twenty to forty preserved lines, have been published.
4. In addition, six plates containing sixty-six fragments of hymns have been published. Most of these fragments are very badly preserved. In only a few instances do these fragments help in completing the gaps in the better-preserved texts.
5. There were at least two scribes:
   a. The columns from the first bundle are written by a careful scribe whose handwriting is similar to that of the *Manual of Discipline* and the *Habakkuk Commentary*.
   b. The second scribe takes over from line 22 of plate XI in the middle of a hymn. The writing of this scribe is careless and contains several errors.
6. Altogether there are some thirty to thirty-two hymns in columns i-xviii, disregarding the fragments.
7. The Hebrew title *Hodayot* or *Thanksgiving Hymns*, generally accepted by all writers, was given to this collection by Professor E. L. Sukenik of the Hebrew University for two reasons:
   a. Many of the hymns begin with the stereotyped formula, "I praise Thee, O Lord, because..."
   b. The opening is followed by a statement of some favor or favors for which the author is grateful.

C. *Style of the hymns*

1. It is similar to the poetical style of biblical Hebrew, especially that of the Book of Psalms.
2. Several expressions in the hymns are derived from biblical Hebrew idioms. In places the text sounds like a mosaic of biblical phrases, especially from the later books of the Bible.
3. Biblical parallelism occurs but not to any great extent.
4. There is no regular meter in the hymns, rather a great variety of metrical structures.

D. *Author(s) of the hymns*

1. The question of authorship is far from being settled.

2. In numerous instances the hymns seem to be a product of a single author whose own personal experiences and feelings they reflect.
3. A suggestion has been made that the "I" in the hymns is the author himself, possibly the Teacher of Righteousness.
   a. It is difficult to equate the Teacher of Righteousness with the author, as the former is never mentioned in these hymns.
   b. There are, however, passages in the first person singular which seem obviously autobiographical.

E. *Contents and date*

1. The author describes his persecution and that of his people by the enemy of the sect.
2. The author thanks and praises God for deliverance from the enemy and other evils that beset him and his people.
3. The date of the *Thanksgiving Hymns* is believed to be the first century B.C.

F. *Frequent recurrences of expressions and ideas throughout this scroll constitute an important source for the comprehensive theological doctrines of the sect. Main ideas and doctrines expressed in the hymns are*:

1. The world is created by God; His rule is absolute. God has also created man.
2. God's justice and sovereignty are absolute and unquestionable by right of His being the Creator.
3. God is the "God of knowledge." He has foreseen all the deeds of man and has used this prescience to lay down His unalterable plan for the world. God's foreknowledge and providence encompass everything that happens in the world.
4. God has predestined every man from birth for evil or for good, for destruction or for salvation. He has determined the fate of His creatures before the creation.
5. The belief in divine predestination and foreknowledge is linked with that of dualism, the division of mankind into the two lots of the wicked and the righteous.
6. Man as a mortal creature is frail, sunk in sin, and utterly dependent upon God. He can be raised only by the sovereign, unconditional grace of God.

7. Salvation of man is attained not through man's act of righteousness but through faith and divine grace. It consists not only of deliverance through calamity, but also deliverance from sin itself.
8. Salvation means not only forgiveness and cleansing from sin but also participation in a divine fellowship.
9. The wicked are created so that God's power can be displayed in their downfall and destruction.
10. The divine spirit is infused into the elect by the grace of God. By this spirit the elect are guided.
11. The gift of knowledge means, for the members of the sect, a fact of salvation which no one outside the group can share; only those whom God has elected for His covenant are capable of such divine knowledge.
12. The author and his people believe that they are living in a transitional period that is dominated by the battle between good and evil in the "end of days." Their future lies in fellowship with the angels and the heavenly spirits of knowledge and truth.
13. Angelology
    a. The Almighty is surrounded by His angels and members of the sect look forward to praising Him ultimately in their company.
    b. There are two classes of angels—the good and the evil:
        (1) Good angels are called "sons of heaven", "heroes of heaven", "host of heaven," "spirit of knowledge."
        (2) Bad angels are called "prince of darkness," "angel of hostility", "Belial."
    c. The evil angels have in their hands the dominion of the sons of iniquity.
14. One of the recurrent themes in the hymns is that which refers to the presence of the righteous before the Divine Majesty and the association with the angels.
15. There are several expressions in the hymns which probably allude to resurrection, but some scholars feel that the sect laid no particular emphasis upon it.
16. Messianism
    a. No *clear* reference to the Messiah occurs in these hymns.
    b. The possibility of a Messianic interpretation has been favored by some scholars who regard column iii, lines 1-18, as a Messianic hymn.

(1) This hymn contains a description of a woman "who brings forth a male child, a wondrous counselor."
(2) The interpretation of this hymn remains obscure and cannot be regarded as a definite reference to the Messiah.

TOPICS FOR STUDY AND DISCUSSION

A. Give (1) an account of the discovery of the *Thanksgiving Hymns* and (2) a description of the scrolls themselves.
B. Compare the style of the hymns with that of the biblical Psalms. Write a note on the author(s) of the hymns.
C. List the main religious ideas and doctrines expressed in the *Thanksgiving Hymns*.
D. Discuss the following doctrines:
   1. Dualism
   2. Predestination
   3. Sin
   4. Salvation

XIV

DOCTRINES OF THE QUMRAN SECT

This unit discusses the doctrines of the sect as reflected in the Qumran manuscripts.

REQUIRED READING

Allegro, J. M., *The Dead Sea Scrolls*, pages 124-133
Burrows, M., *The Dead Sea Scrolls*, pages 227-245
Burrows, M., *More Light on the Dead Sea Scrolls*, pages 277-342
Mansoor, M., *The Thanksgiving Hymns*, pages 52-93
Milik, J. T., *Ten Years of Discovery in the Wilderness of Judaea*, pages 99-128.
Van der Ploeg, J., *The Excavations at Qumran*, pages 90-130
Vermes, G., *The Dead Sea Scrolls in English*, pages 34-52
Yadin, Y., *The Message of the Scrolls*, pages 160-189

DOCTRINES OF THE SECT

A. *The sect believed that only through the observance and study of the laws could its members expect union with God*

1. It is evident from the number of biblical commentaries and books found at Qumran that interpretation of scripture played an important part in the life of the sect.
2. The Manual of Discipline required that each group give over one third of the nights of the year to the study of the laws.
3. Other documents support the theory that a return to the law of Moses was one of the objectives of the Qumran community. The *Damascus Document* declares that the duty of the member of the community is "to walk uprightly in all His ways."

B. *Only people thought by the community to be worthy of the Law and to be worthy of eventual fellowship with God were the members of the community*

1. Membership in the community thus meant election to the group of the saved and the token of salvation. This is clearly indicated in the *Manual of Discipline*.
2. Each member of the community was set aside by God as one of the "children of Grace" and each found the fruits of grace in wisdom, justice, and sanctity.

C. The community was to be led to salvation by a series of spiritual guides sent by God

1. Moses was the most important. His name was so holy that the *Damascus Document* forbids its use in the taking of oaths.
2. The second guide was Zadok, the anointed one, who presumably founded the sect.
3. The Teacher of Righteousness was the third guide; only through faith in him and fidelity to his doctrine could a member be saved.

D. The community believed in divine grace and predestination

1. There was a clear division between God's elect through His grace and those He had not elected.
    a. The author of the *Thanksgiving Hymns* felt that he was among the elect and expressed that feeling in the psalms.
    b. The sect felt that man's works have no justification; only the divine grace of God will save man.
    c. The sect felt that the Teacher of Righteousness was delivered by God's grace.
    d. The highest aspiration of all the members of the sect was to stand before God with the other "elect of mankind."
2. Fellowship with God and salvation through divine grace is the result of absolute predestination.
    a. The members of the sect felt that all men are sinful and bad. If God granted His grace to man, then the sins of man were forgiven.
    b. The man who had received God's grace was able to walk in the way of God's command, practice the commandments, and adhere to the law of Moses—these things cannot be achieved through human endeavor, but come only as a result of divine grace.
    c. A man possessing this grace could withstand any affliction through his reliance on God.
    d. Contrary to the usual view in the Bible and in the Talmud, the wicked of the Qumran documents (those who had not received divine grace) were not even allowed to repent.

e. A person who is elected to divine grace joins the company of angels praising God and accomplishes this through his membership in the sect.
3. The two spirits of light and darkness exemplify the dualistic tendency which permeated the Qumran doctrine and is evident in most of the literature recovered to date.
   a. Intimate fellowship with God was held to take place only through the agency of the spirits of light and truth.
   b. Man's membership in either the group of the elect or the non-elect determined his predestined end. Each man acted righteously or not, according to whether he was of the spirit of light or the spirit of darkness.
   c. God created both these spirits with equal measure and caused man to know them so that they might know both good and evil.
   d. The angels, as well, are divided into the two camps of light and darkness.
      (1) In the *War Scroll* we are told that the angels will carry on the war in heaven while the Sons of Light combat the Sons of Darkness on earth. During the last of the seven battles described in the *War Scroll* the angels will come and help the Sons of Light defeat the Sons of Darkness for the last time.
      (2) The angels of light are identified with the archangel Michael, the prince of light, and the angels of darkness are identified with Belial.
   e. Both spirits—the spirit of light and the spirit of darkness—constantly contend for the heart of man. The Sons of Light should hate the Sons of Darkness and vice versa.
   f. Men elected to the spirit of light and truth had to submit to trials and temptations from Belial and the Sons of Darkness. The just are tempted but must not waver during this time of trial.
4. The sect believed in signs of grace:
   a. Knowledge and understanding are signs and gifts of divine grace which will lead man to God.
   b. Outward signs of inward grace are recognizable in the man who is to inherit the spirit of light.
      (1) The *Manual of Discipline* records that each candidate for admission to the community was carefully watched during the two years he served as a novice in order to discern the signs of grace. If none were found in him he was denied membership in the sect.

(2) The signs of the man who was not among the elect are clearly listed in the *Manual of Discipline*.
5. Creation—the sect maintained that:
   a. The mysteries of God are past the comprehension of mortal man.
   b. God rules the world by virtue of being its creator, and creation of the world occurred as an act of God's will.
   c. The creation of the world preceded the existence of the creatures created by God. A common expression in the Qumran writings is "before Thou created them, Thou knew their deeds."
   d. In the Book of Psalms the divine rule of the world is demonstrated in nature—the harmony of the universe, the cycles of the sun and moon, the alternations of night and day, the presence of the stars, and the occurrence of the winds.
6. Immortality—the sect believed the following:
   a. Belief in immortality is evidenced by such passages as "wisdom of life, knowledge of eternity, eternal life, eternal bliss, and eternal destiny."
   b. The idea of the eternal nature of the community was connected to the belief that the individual members are immortal.
   c. This belief presupposes faith in the immortality of the soul but not in the immortality of the whole man.
7. Members of the sect were unconcerned with the resurrection of the body because they expected the universal judgment to occur during their own time. No resurrection was foreseen, but instead an assumption of the body, sanctified and purified through the ritual of the sect, was expected.

TOPICS FOR STUDY AND DISCUSSION

A. Outline the doctrines of the Qumran Sect.
B. Discuss dualism and predestination as taught by the sect.

XV

JEWISH SECTS: PART 1 - ASSIDEANS, PHARISEES, SADDUCEES, AND ZEALOTS

To understand the sect of the Dead Sea Scrolls, its tenets and doctrines, it is important to study the pre-Christian Jewish sects and contemporary Judaism.

A series of different sects, indicating considerable controversies and divergencies, emerged in Judaism during the period of the Second Temple (516 B.C.-A.D. 70) and especially during the Second Commonwealth in Palestine, which may be considered to have lasted from the successful Maccabean revolt for independence in the second century B.C., through the Roman period to the fall of Jerusalem and the destruction of the Temple in A.D. 70.

The first dissenting sect was that of the Samaritans, who maintained that Judaism was to be based on the Pentateuch alone. However, we are not discussing this Sect in this work. Later the religious controversy evolved around two main issues: One (Sadducees) held that the Scriptures without further rabbinical interpretation constituted Judaism; the other (Pharisees, who were destined to become the preservers and transmitters of Jewish religion) insisted that the traditional Oral Law, as interpreted by the rabbis, was a necessary supplement to the Mosaic Written Law. A third sect, the Essenes, constituted an ascetic group of dissident Jews who lived communally, repudiated Temple worship and animal sacrifices, and emphasized Messianic expectation. The Essenes have been identified by many scholars as the sect of the Dead Sea Scrolls.

These sects represented philosophies ranging from conservatism to extremism, from asceticism to activism, and from rigid orthodoxy to religious liberalism.

The main differences between these sects in Judaism of that period reflected not only religious issues but also social, political, and economic issues. It is therefore important to discuss all the sects of that period in relation to this course.

RECOMMENDED READING

Although the information on Jewish sects given in this unit and the following is basic and adequate for the purpose of this course, you are nevertheless strongly advised to read at least one of the following:

    Baron, S. W., *A Social and Religious History of the Jews*, Volumes I and II

    Herford, R. Travers, *Judaism in the New Testament Period*

    Klausner, J., *Jesus of Nazareth: His Life, Times, and Teaching*

    Lauterbach, J. Z., *Rabbinic Essays*, an excellent work on the teachings of the Pharisees

    Lightley, J. W., *Jewish Sects and Parties in the Time of Jesus*

    Mansoor, M., "Jewish Sects", 1963 edition of the *Encyclopedia Britannica*

    Zeitlin, S., *The History of the Second Jewish Commonwealth*

For the relation between the sect of the Dead Sea Scrolls and the Jewish sects, you should read one of the following:

    Cross, F. M., Jr., *The Ancient Library of Qumran*

    Dupont-Sommer, A., *The Jewish Sect of Qumran and the Essenes*

    Van der Ploeg, J., *The Excavations at Qumran*

You can also read about these sects in any of the standard or biblical encyclopedias. The reading material for this unit is the same for the next unit (16).

THE VARIOUS SECTS

A. *Hassideans*

Assideans or Hassideans (Greek form of Hebrew *Hasidim*, "the pious ones") were a Jewish religious group or sect whose date of origin is unknown. It was probably organized during the fourth or third century B.C. to revive and promote the observance of Jewish rites, to study the Law, and to uproot paganism from the land. The group is first mentioned by this name during the persecutions of Antiochus IV (Epiphanes), king of Syria (175-164 B.C.), in the second century B.C. when its members joined the Maccabean opposition led by Mattathias in his revolt against the Syrians. They formed the nucleus of the Maccabean revolt and refused to compromise in any way with the Hellenizing policy of the Syrians. They suffered torture and martyrdom rather than desecrate the Sabbath and other Jewish observances. There are explicit references to the Assideans in the Books of Maccabees and in the Talmud. In I Maccabees 2 : 42, it is recorded that the Assideans were "mighty men in Israel . . . such as were devoted to the Law."

The Talmud refers to the strict observance of the commandments by the "Hasidim," to their ardent prayers which they would not renounce even at the risk of their lives, and to their rigid observance of the Sabbath. Because of their meticulous legal observance, they have also been linked with the Essenes. However, the consensus of scholars is that the Assideans were the spiritual forerunners of the Pharisees.

B. *Pharisees*

1. Origin

   a. The Pharisees were a Jewish religious and political party during the Second Temple period which emerged as a distinct group shortly after the Maccabean revolt, about 165-160 B.C., probably springing from the Hasidim, or Assideans. (See above). Traditionally the Pharisees were the successors of Ezra and the early scribes ("Men of the Great Synagogue"). They cherished Ezra, next after Moses, as the founder of Judaism.

   Though the Pharisees exercised great political power, they were not primarily a political party. They represented the orthodox party within Judaism. To them, Judaism was contained not only in the Pentateuch (which alone the Sadducees recognized), but also in the traditional Oral Law, by which they tried to adapt old codes to new conditions. In contrast to the Sadducees, the Pharisees believed in the resurrection of the dead, life after death, reward and retribution on the Day of Judgment, the advent of the Messiah, and the existence of angels. The Pharisaic doctrine admitted divine knowledge and predestination but maintained man's free choice and therefore responsibility for his deeds.

   b. The meaning of the word *Pharisee* is uncertain. It is generally believed that the name derives from a Hebrew stem, *parash*, "to be separated"; hence *Pharisee* would mean "the separated one," or "the separatist." According to some scholars, *Pharisees* would mean "those who are set apart," that is, avoiding contact with others for reasons of ritual purity, or those who "separated themselves" from the heathen and from heathenizing tendencies and forces within their own nation, such as the Sadducees.

   c. The Pharisees tried to keep all that was Jewish set apart and thus "undefiled." Basing everything upon the Torah, the Pharisees insisted upon strictest observance of the ordinances of Judaism in all aspects of life. Because of the Pharisees' insistence on scrupulous observance of the Torah, their views led to a separatist attitude toward all of life. Although at first the Pharisees were relatively small in number, they represented the religious beliefs, practices, and social outlook of the majority of Jewish people of their day. In Josephus and in the New Testament they appear as the spokesmen of the majority of the population. Their activities were directed to the masses whom they sought to imbue with a spirit of holiness by spreading traditional religious teaching. As years went on, it became more and more apparent that the hearts of the masses were with the Pharisees and by the first century A.D. they sat in "Moses' seat" (Matthew 23 : 2). The Pharisees, however, were nonpolitical, their religious values towered so high above all other concerns that they were ready to submit to foreign domination, so long as it did not interfere with their inner way of life, rather than to an impious government of their own. On one occasion, three successive Pharisaic delegations appeared at great personal peril before Mark Antony, pleading for the removal of Herod (73-4 B.C.). Again, during the great war with the Romans, two Pharisaic leaders, Johanan ben Zakkai and Josephus, made peace with Vespasian (A.D. 69-79).

2. Historical background
   a. For two centuries following the exile, the high priesthood earned the right to political and religious leadership of the Jewish people. The Temple cult and the affairs of the country were controlled by the Sadducees, the representatives of the priestly aristocracy, and by the Hasmonean rulers who were supported by the Sadducees. The Pharisaic leaders who usually rose from the ranks of the masses raged a long and bitter struggle against the Sadducees in an effort to democratize the Jewish religion and remove it from the rigid control of the Temple priests. As L. Finkelstein has pointed out, many of the ceremonies introduced by the Pharisees in the home were originally part of, and limited to, the Temple cult. Thus, learned men of Israel of nonpriestly descent began to play an important role in the conduct of the religious and, to a lesser extent, secular affairs of the people. While the priesthood exhausted itself in the ritual of the Temple, the Pharisees found

their main function in teaching and preaching the Law of God. In this sense, Pharisaism cleared the ground for Christianity.
  b. By the beginning of the second century B.C. we find that the Sanhedrin (the supreme Jewish council and tribunal of the Second Temple period) was composed of both priests and lay leaders. Since one of the chief problems of the Sanhedrin was to find in the ancient Torah of Moses the answers to and decisions about new questions that would meet the circumstances of the day, a conflict developed between priests and laymen over opposing views on this problem. The differences between Sadducees and Pharisees over the interpretation of the Torah also became apparent. The Pharisees endeavored to extend their influence over the Temple to undermine the authority of the Sadducees. The antagonism between the two parties extended to many spheres; generally the Pharisees admitted the principle of evolution in their legal decisions, while the Sadducees were incapable of adapting to the changing environment and hence clung to the letter of the written text. These differences, which had a political as well as religious aspect, became fundamental and ultimately brought about two distinct and opposing parties: the Pharisees and the Sadducees.
3. Theological doctrines
  a. Judaism

  From the prophets the Pharisees learned to think of God as a spiritual being—omnipotent and just, all-wise and all-knowing, all-merciful, and like a father loving *all* His creatures. He was not to be pictured in any image and could not be likened to any other being. He was not limited to any place but was omnipresent. For the Pharisees, God was omnipotent, nothing being impossible for Him, not even making man choose good or evil. But man must have freedom of will if he is to be a moral being, which God wants him to be. So God gave him the power to choose between good and evil. He created in him two impulses, a good one and a bad one, advised him to do good and gave him the Torah as a guide to help him. The Torah, as the Pharisees understood it, also taught this God-conception. None of the expressions in the Torah which speak of Him in anthropomorphic terms was to be taken literally. They conceived of God as the One whom no human being could fully comprehend, for He is transcendent, and therefore they avoided using even any of the other biblical names of God except in prayer and in reading of the Scriptures. They apparently felt that no name could designate His essence or describe the totality of His being. They spoke of Him in such terms as "the Creator of the World," "the Merciful One," "the Divine Presence" (*Shekhina*), and "the Spirit of Holiness." The latter two designations were never taken by Pharisees or rabbis as separate entities. They were merely used, like so many other designations, to describe some attributes of God which no man can fully comprehend.

b. Torah

The Pharisees thought that the Torah which God gave to Moses was twofold, consisting of the Written Law (the Torah) and the Oral Law. The first express reference to the "Two Laws" is ascribed in the Talmud to Hillel. For the Pharisees, the Torah was divine revelation to man, contained in the five books of Moses as supplemented and explained by the teachings of the prophets and by other, unwritten, traditions of the fathers. Its purpose was to ennoble man by guiding him in the right way of life. Since the Pharisees did not follow the letter of the Law blindly when it conflicted with reason or conscience, they found no great difficulty in harmonizing the teachings of the Torah with their advanced ideas or in finding their ideas suggested or implied therein. The Pharisees insisted on the binding nature of Oral Law which, in their opinion, had been revealed to Moses simultaneously with the written Torah. In that Law were reflected traditions and practices which had developed in the preceding centuries. To support such scriptural links, the Pharisees developed a ramified system of hermeneutics. Their view of the Law was that its teaching and commandments had to be interpreted in conformity with the standard of the teachers of each generation and made to harmonize with the advanced ideas of the era. Accordingly, when in the course of time they had outgrown a certain law, they unconsciously gave it a new and more acceptable meaning. For the Pharisees believed that men must use God-given reason in interpreting the Torah. So the teachings of the Torah were to be interpreted to harmonize with the truth resulting from man's God-given reason. The Law could never mean anything else than what the teachers understood it to mean. Hence the Pharisees interpreted the Law according to its spirit and ignored its letter when reason and human conscience were against it.

The Mosaic law, for instance, of "an eye for an eye" was interpreted by the Pharisees as monetary compensation and not retaliation. It was due to this progressive tendency of the Pharisees that their interpretation of the Torah continued to develop and remained an ever-living force in Judaism.

c. Divine worship

The Pharisees believed that from the rising of the sun until its setting, the Lord's name must be praised (Psalm 113 : 2) and that there was no place where God could not be found and reached in prayer. Hence they concluded that God can and should be worshipped even away from the Temple and outside of Jerusalem. They felt that worship consisted not of bloody sacrifices but of prayer and study of God's law. Hence they fostered the synagogue as a unique institution of religious worship—outside of, and separate from, the Temple. The synagogue may be considered a Pharisaic institution. Not that the Pharisees first founded it, but they developed it, raised it to high prominence, and gave it central place in the religious life of the people.

d. Divine providence and free will

The Sadducees believed that God does not concern Himself with human affairs. The individual is left to his own resources. To the people as a group He gives His protection if they fulfill His commands, just as He punishes them for violating laws stipulated in His covenant. The Pharisees believed that God takes cognizance of all our doings. The Pharisees, Josephus tells us, "ascribe all to Providence and to God and yet allow that to do what is right or contrary is principally in the power of man; although fate does cooperate in every action." With the belief in divine providence and prescience the Pharisees combined the belief in the freedom of the will. This is also confirmed by Talmudic reports of the followers of the Pharisees, who declare "Everything is in the hands of God but the fear of God," and although "everything is foreseen, yet freedom of choice is given." This represents the long-accepted doctrine of the Pharisees. As the Talmud puts it, "If a man chooses to do good, the heavenly powers help him. If he chooses to do evil, they leave the way open to him." Thus, the Pharisees concluded that indeed God can, but does not desire to, determine man's choice of conduct. He wants man to choose for himself.

e. Divine retribution

The belief in man's responsibility for his conduct leads to the belief in divine retribution. We have no record of speculation on the part of the early Pharisees as to the vexing question of why the righteous suffer and the wicked prosper. At any rate, they solved the problem by postulating a belief in a life after death. According to Josephus, the Pharisees believed that souls have an immortal vigor and "that under the earth there will be reward and punishment according as they have lived virtuously or viciously in this life." The Pharisees were not philosophers and probably did not stop to realize the philosophical difficulties of their naive solutions. They were practical teachers of religion and for the purpose of teaching religion and right conduct this was a practical, if unsophisticated, answer.

f. Immortality and resurrection

According to the Talmud and the New Testament, the Pharisees believed in the resurrection of the dead. Man's career is not ended with death. This belief in another world thus makes possible the belief in divine justice and divine retribution in the face of apparent injustices on earth. Here again was a practical solution to a nagging problem which threatened to tempt man from virtue and caused him to abandon the pursuit of righteousness. Immortality and resurrection are generally attributed to Greek or Persian origins, yet to the Pharisees it was a genuine Jewish belief based on passages in the Torah.

g. Humanity

The Pharisees were also concerned with the salvation of their people and of humanity and with the future of this world when all mankind will join Israel in accepting the Torah and believing in one God. For the Pharisees believed in one humanity as they believed in one God. According to the Pharisees, all men are born equal. Israel's position among the other nations is that of an older brother, since it was the first to recognize God as the Father. And it is Israel's duty and function to help other peoples to do so. According to the Pharisees it was for this purpose that God gave the Torah to Israel in the wilderness and not in Palestine. Probably with this in mind, the Pharisees engaged in an active propaganda for Judaism. In the words of the New Testament, they did "compass sea and land to make one proselyte" (Matthew 23 : 15).

h. New Testament references to the Pharisees
While the Pharisees as a whole set for themselves a high degree of ethical standard, not all Pharisees lived up to it. The Talmud itself lists seven hypocritical types of Pharisees. The New Testament's derogatory references to the Pharisees (Matthew 23 : 5, 23ff; Luke 18: 1ff; *et al.*) as "hypocrites" and "offspring of vipers" were probably directed at this minority of insincere hypocritical members who were condemned by leaders of the Pharisees themselves. The Pharisaic leaders were well aware of the presence of insincere followers. They called them, in the Talmud, "sore spots" or "plagues of the Pharisaic party" (Sotah III : 4 and 22b). And while they deplored these backsliders, they had no means of getting rid of them. It is mistakenly held by some writers that New Testament references are aimed at the entire Pharisaic group itself. Many of the Pharisaic doctrines have a great deal in common with those of Christianity. Saul of Tarsus (Paul) boasted of being a Pharisee and the son of a Pharisee, brought up "according to the perfect manner of the law of the fathers" (Acts 22). He was a pupil at Jerusalem of Gamaliel (Acts 22 : 3), a "doctor of the law" (Acts 5 : 34), probably grandson of the great Pharisee Hillel. Paul was proud of this teacher-pupil relationship of his youth (Acts 23 : 6, 26 : 3-7).

4. Evaluation
The active period of Pharisaism, which was the most influential in the development of orthodox Judaism, extended well into the second and third centuries A.D. Though criticized by Jesus for their pedantic stress on the legalistic aspects of religion, the Pharisees are to be given credit for preserving and transmitting Judaism. The deepest and most stable elements among the forces which built Judaism and the Jewish people were contained in Pharisaism. Unlike the Zealots, they rejected the appeal to force and violence, believing that the God of the nation was in control of history and that Israel and the nations would be redeemed in God's good time and that every true Jew should live in accordance with the Torah. It is not surprising, therefore, that the Pharisees devoted a great deal of their effort to education. After the destruction of the Temple and the fall of Jerusalem in A.D. 70, it was the synagogue and the schools of the Pharisees that continued to function and promote Judaism.

C. *Sadducees*

1. The Sadducees (Hebrew *tzedukim*) were members of a Jewish reli-

gious sect of the latter half of the Second Temple period, formed about 200 B.C. as the party of high priests and aristocratic families. The party was opposed to the Pharisees down to the time of the destruction of Jerusalem in A.D. 70. They questioned the validity of oral tradition which was firmly upheld by the Pharisees. Both in Josephus' writings and in the New Testament, Sadduceeism is represented as associated with certain definite religious positions. The Sadducees stood for the conservative trend in matters of religion. While paying great attention to the letter of the Law, they rejected the Pharisaic supernatural beliefs, claiming that they had no basis in Mosaic Law. They denied the doctrine of the resurrection of the body (Mark 12 : 18, Matthew 22 : 23, Luke 20 : 27, and Acts 23 : 8). According to Josephus the Sadducees denied the immortality of the soul. They also rejected the Pharaisaic doctrine regarding the existence of angels and ministering spirits (Acts 23 : 8). Many Christian doctrines have more in common with those of the Pharisees than with those of the Sadducees. We can therefore see why the Apostolic Church, in her first years, had most to fear from the Sadducees (Acts 4 and 5).

2. The most probable explanation of the uncertain name "Sadducees" is that it is derived from Zadok, the high priest in the days of David (II Samuel 8 : 17, 15 : 24) and Solomon (I Kings 1 : 34ff and I Chronicles 12 : 28). Ezekiel (40 : 46, 43 : 19, and 44 : 10-15) selected this family as worthy of being entrusted with the control of the Temple; in fact, descendants of this family formed the Temple hierarchy down to the second century B.C. However, not all priests were Sadducees. Hence the name "Sadducee" may best be taken to mean anyone who is a sympathizer with the Zadokites, the priestly descendants of Zadok.

3. The Saducean party was composed largely of the wealthier elements of the population—influential priests, wealthy merchants, and worldly aristocracy. They dominated the Temple and its rites and many of them were members of the Sanhedrin (the supreme Jewish council and tribunal of the Second Temple period). Thus this party was influential in political and economic life.

4. The main difference between the Pharisees and Sadducees, concerned their *attitude* toward the Torah. The supremacy of the Torah was acknowledged by both parties. However, the Pharisees assigned to the Oral Law a place of authority side by side with the written Torah, and determined its interpretation accordingly, whereas the Saddu-

cees refused to accept any precept as binding unless it was based directly on the Torah. The theological struggle between the two parties, as J. Z. Lauterback puts it (*Rabbinic Essays*, pages 23-162), was actually a struggle between two concepts of God. The Sadducees sought to bring God down to man. Their God was anthropomorphic and the worship offered him was like the homage paid to a human king or ruler. The Pharisees, on the other hand, sought to raise man to divine heights and bring him nearer to a spiritual and transcendent God. From Josephus and the Talmud we learn that one of the main differences between the Pharisees and the Sadducees was the peculiar attitude of each towards those laws not contained in the Pentateuch but merely based on tradition. The Pharisees considered such laws to be absolute authority and equal to the Written Law, while the Sadducees denied them such an authoritative and compulsory character. Because of their strict adherence to the letter of the Law, the Sadducees acted severely in cases involving the death penalty. The Mosaic principle of *Lex Talionis* (Exodus 21 : 24), for instance, was interpreted literally rather than construed as monetary compensation—the view adopted by the Pharisees. The Sadducees were opposed to changes and innovations and refused to accept the oral traditions with which the Pharisees supplemented the Written Law. It was never a question of whether certain laws were derived from tradition, but whether those laws that were admittedly derived from tradition were obligatory.

5. Apart from the aforementioned major differences between the Pharisees and the Sadducees as to the oral tradition and the supernatural beliefs, there were numerous legal-ritualistic details upon which these two parties differed, especially upon those connected with the Temple. On the whole, it can be said that while the Pharisees claimed the authority of piety and learning, the Sadducees claimed that of blood and position. The rivalry between the Pharisees and Sadducees was, in a sense, the renewal of a conflict between the prophets and the priests of pre-exilic times. Following the restoration of the Temple and its sacrificial cult, the priests were also restored to their former position as religious leaders. But the rise of laymen and "scribes" who possessed a knowledge of the Law aroused doubts as to the undisputed authority of the priests. Greek rule probably helped to weaken priestly authority, for among the Greeks themselves priests were the servants, not the leaders, of the community. Thus the learned men of Israel of nonpriestly descent

began to play a role in the conduct of both the religious and secular affairs of the people, and in the beginning of the second century B.C. the Sanhedrin was composed of both priests and lay leaders.

6. We must remember that the Sadducees were the conservative priestly group, holding to the older doctrines and cherishing the highest regard for the sacrificial cult of the Temple. They retained primitive notions both about God and the purpose of service offered to Him in the Temple. They were strongly opposed to any reform in the sacrificial functions of the Temple.

7. The Sadducees' attitude toward prayer and sacrifice differed greatly from that of the Pharisees. Perhaps the most effective means by which the Pharisees impressed upon the minds of the people the lesson that sacrifices were not the most acceptable form of worship was the institution of a synagogue in the very precinct of the Temple. It put synagogue worship on a par with the sacrificial cult. This fact makes likely the assumption that the institution was forced on the priests by the Pharisees. Josephus and the Talmud say little about the Saducean position on prayer but the Sadducees would naturally not favor a religious service consisting of prayer and study alone, as this would tend to lessen the importance of the sacrificial cult and thereby weaken their own position as priests.

8. The Sadducees seemed not to believe in fate. On the problem of human conduct and activities, the Sadducees seemed to believe that God is not concerned with men's affairs. As Josephus puts it: "And for the Sadducees they take away fate and say there is no such thing, and that the events of human affairs are not at its disposal, but they suppose that all our actions are in our own power, so that we ourselves are the causes of what is good and receive what is evil from our own folly." (*Ant.* XIII, v. 9). In other words, they do not believe in Divine Providence. Unfortunately we possess no statement from the Saducean side of their beliefs and principles. There are controversial references in rabbinical literature to the Sadducees on the interpretation of the Law. The Sadducees have been represented as lax and worldly-minded aristocrats, primarily interested in maintaining their own privileged position, and favoring Greco-Roman culture.

9. In the New Testament, John the Baptist jointly condemned the Pharisees and the Sadducees, calling them a "generation of vipers" and challenging them both to "bring forth fruits meet for repentance" (Matthew 3 : 7ff). In his denunciation of their doctrines,

Jesus, too, grouped Sadducees and Pharisees together (Matthew 16 : 6ff), and both parties were said to have posed questions designed to perplex Jesus (Matthew 15 : 1). According to Acts (4 : 1, 5 : 17, and 23 : 6-8), Peter and John were imprisoned by them.

10. Conclusion

    Historically the Sadducees came under the influence of Hellenism and later were in good standing with the Roman rulers, though unpopular with the common people from whom they kept aloof. The Sadducean hierarchy had its stronghold in the Temple, and it was only during the last two decades of the Temple's existence that the Pharisees finally gained control. Since the whole power and *raison d'être* of the Sadducees were bound up with the Temple cult, the group ceased to exist after the destruction of the Temple in A.D. 70. By the end of the first half of the second century, the Pharisaic teachers and leaders of Judaism were practically alone in the field.

D. Zealots (*Hebrew* Quanna-eem, *Greek* Zelotes, *English* Cananaean)

1. The Zealots belonged to a sect whose members relentlessly opposed the attempt to bring Judea under the dominion of idolatrous Rome. They regarded themselves as zealous defenders of the Law and the national life of the Jewish people. The Zealots were first influential in Galilee and later in Jerusalem, especially from the time of Herod (37 B.C. to A.D. 4) until the fall of that city in A.D. 70. They were members of one of the parties that loosely formed what Josephus called "the fourth philosophy" and by this definition were distinguished from the Pharisees, Sadducees, and Essenes. The main characteristic of the "fourth philosophy" was strong opposition to foreign rule. Josephus mentions two incidents involving activities of Zealots during the rule of Herod. The first concerns ten citizens of Jerusalem with concealed daggers who entered a Roman theater. Herod was informed of the plot, and the conspirators suffered torture and death. The people were indignant and in their wrath tore to pieces the spy who had relayed the plot. The second incident occurred when Herod placed a large golden eagle over the gate of the Temple. Two rabbis exhorted their disciples to sacrifice their lives rather than allow this violation. Forty young men and the two leaders pulled down the eagle but were put to death by fire.

2. Under the leadership of Hezekiah (a Zealot martyr who was beheaded by Herod without trial) and his sons, the Zealots became an aggressive and relentless political party which would accept no compromise and make no peace with Rome. Josephus says it was

the introduction of Roman institutions, antagonistic to the spirit of Judaism (such as the gymnasium, the arena, and idolatrous trophies) which provoked the indignation of the people. The Zealots were particularly active in A.D. 6 at the time of the revolt of Judas of Gamala, in Galilee, who led the opposition against the taking of the census, that is, the assessment of property for taxation by Quirinius, governor of Syria, on the grounds that compliance with the Roman demand would constitute an act of enslavement. Some scholars, therefore, believe that the Zealot party was formed during this revolt, but there is little evidence to support this view. As stated by Josephus, the Zealots boastfully called themselves *Quanna'eem* ("zealots") on account of their religious zeal. He refers to the Zealots as members of a party that started a reign of terror in A.D. 66 against Rome. The Zealots are mentioned but not described in the Gospel (Luke 4 : 15). The term "Zealots" is applied as a designation of Simon, a disciple of Jesus, in Luke 6 : 15 and Acts 1 : 13. The same disciple is called "The Cananaean" (from a Hebrew and Aramaic stem *kanna*', "to be zealous") in Matthew 10 : 4 and Mark 3 : 18.

3. The Zealots considered it an act of disloyalty to God to acknowledge Roman domination over Judea. The right of the Quanna'eem to assassinate any Roman who dared enter the consecrated parts of the Temple was officially recognized in a statute inscribed upon the Temple wall and discovered by the French archaeologist Clermont-Ganneau in 1871. In contrast to the Pharisees, Zealots refused to pay taxes and harassed the Roman administration with every means at their disposal. It was during the period immediately preceding the great rebellion against Rome in A.D. 66 that the Zealots won followers from all social classes. The Roman successes in Galilee in A.D. 6 weakened the Jewish government in Jerusalem and strengthened the position of the Zealots who fled to Jerusalem and played an important role in the defense of the city. They terrorized their political opponents who accepted foreign rule, deposed the high priest, and elected a successor by lot. In one instance, in order to force the wealthy and more practically inclined citizens to act against the Romans, the Zealots set fire to the storehouses containing the corn needed for sustenance during the siege. However, the population rose against them and drove the Zealots under Eleazar ben Simeon into the inner court of the Temple. With the support of the Idumeans, the Zealots regained control of Jerusalem under the leadership of

John of Gischala and resumed their acts of horror. It is from this sect that the Sicarii, the ultra-extreme sect, was engendered. One of the chief leaders of the revolt in A.D. 66, Menahem, son of Judah the Galilean, appeared to have claimed Messianic status. Surrounded with royal pomp, he went up to the Temple to be crowned but was slain by rivals of his own party. His comrades fled the city to Masada on the shores of the Dead Sea. When the final siege of Jerusalem by the Romans began, the Zealots advocated and used extreme measures which brought about the final destruction of the city in A.D. 70.

4. Some authorities maintain that the Zealots can be traced to the Hassidim (*Assideans*), a religious sect of the Maccabean period (see above). Some find a positive relationship between the Maccabees and the Zealots, while Josephus asserts that the Zealots were a new party, having no connection with the Maccabees. The Zealots were not as Josephus pictured them, purely selfish and secularly motivated; but rather, like the early Maccabees, they were deeply patriotic and motivated by a dynamic theology of zeal for the Torah. Traditional Jewish history, however, has declared itself in favor of the Pharisees, who regarded the house of study more important to the Jews than the State and Temple. Some modern historians nonetheless believe that the Zealots also deserve their due recognition for a sublime type of steadfastness. Unsuccessful attempts have been made to identify the sect of the Dead Sea Scrolls with the Zealots.

E. *Sicarii*

"Sicarii," also known as "Assassins," is a term applied to the extreme members of Jewish Zealots who fanatically opposed Roman rule in the two decades immediately preceding the destruction of Jerusalem in A.D. 70. Members of this group concealed small daggers or *sicae* under their cloaks; hence their Greek name *sikarioi*, "daggermen," "assassins." At public places and popular assemblies they stabbed their opponents who were friendly to the Romans or any person found committing a sacrilegious act. According to Acts 21 : 38, bands of assassins (*AV* "murderers") pillaged villages and terrorized Judea in A.D. 50-70. At the beginning of the revolt against the Romans, the Sicarii, with the help of other Zealots, gained secret access to Jerusalem, where they committed ruthless acts. After the destruction of the Temple some of their leaders, including Menahem ben Ya'ir, Eleazar ben Ya'ir, and Bar-Giora, who were among the most important figures of this war, fled to Masada fortress and eventually committed suicide before the fortress was taken by the Romans in A.D. 73. Others who fled to the forests of Jardes after the destruction of Jerusalem were annihilated by the Romans.

Topics for Study and Discussion

A. Write a general outline of the sects studies in this unit.
B. "The Pharisees were the preservers and transmitters of Judaism." Discuss this statement.
C. What are the main differences between the Pharisees and the Sadducees?
D. Write a paragraph on each of the following:
   1. Assideans
   2. Sicarii
   3. The origin of the name "Pharisee"
E. Discuss the theological doctrines of Pharisaism.

XVI

JEWISH SECTS : PART II-ESSENES AND THERAPEUTAE

Recommended Reading

Your reading assignment for this unit is the same as that in Unit 15 for the Pharisees and Sadducees.

Description of the Sects

A. *Essenes*

1. Background

The Essenes were members of a religious communalistic Jewish sect or brotherhood in Palestine in the latter half of the Second Temple period (ca. second century B.C. to A.D. 70). It is generally believed that the Essenes made their first appearance during or toward the end of the Maccabean revolt, in the second century B.C., when the priesthood under Sadduceeism was in its lowest repute, especially because of its close association with Hellenism. Its members clustered in monastic communities from which women were, with few exceptions, excluded. They lived austerely and held everything they owned in common. In their religious outlook, the Essenes were closer to the Pharisees than to the Sadducees, but they had their own specific beliefs and observances. Wherever possible, the Essenes, who lived in several cities and communities, withdrew from the defilements of everyday life into their own "purified" monastic centers, where emphasis was laid on meticulous ceremonial purity such as communal baptism and communal meals rather than religious or philosophic speculation. The Essenes supported themselves by manual labor, generally in agricultural but never military pursuits. The proceeds of their labor replenished the common fund. They kept no slaves and abhorred slavery. To study the Torah in its minutest details the Essenes devoted their whole lives to this task. Accordingly, they opposed ownership of private property and adhered to celibacy. On the Sabbath they listened to reading of the Scriptures with allegorical interpretation of the text. In the course of time the communities developed into more closely linked units. Finally, however, in order to give undivided attention to the Torah they divided into separate groups in several locales. By the end of the first century B.C. their main group was located on the northwestern shore of the Dead Sea region, organized as a real monastic order. The Essenes, according to Philo, were never numerous. There were four thousand in his day. They replenished their numbers by adopting proselytes after a probationary period. Although as a body they preferred the country to the city, we find some individuals taking part in political life. Essenes are known even to have participated in the wars against the Romans. One of Josephus' accounts tells us that Herod the Great respected and tolerated the Essenes and did not compel them to take an oath of loyalty to him. However, during the war against the Romans they were badly thwarted, tortured, and put to trial in every way "in order that they might blaspheme the Lawgiver or eat one of the forbidden things," but they held to their faith and gladly went to death rather than forsake their beliefs. The discovery of the Dead Sea Scrolls has cast a new and interesting light on the nature and beliefs of the Essenes or some sect closely associated with them.

2. Meaning and origin of the name
   a. The etymology of the name *Essene* has elicited a wide diversity of opinion. Perhaps it is because of the difficulty of accounting for the word *Essene* that many works have been devoted to the subject. No categorical epithet for the Essenes occurs in Hebrew. None of the theories on the exact meaning and origin of the Essenes either prior to or following the discovery of the Dead sea Scrolls has been generally accepted. In spite of numerous efforts, the etymology of *Essenes* remains as uncertain as it ever was. Greek writers refer to the Essenes by names of which the most common are *Essenoi* and *Essaioi*. The derivations are disputed. The English Essene comes, through the Latin, from the Greek. This form is unknown to Philo who invariably uses the alternative. Josephus uses both names, the former more frequently. Both Philo and Josephus assert that the title *Essenes* originates from the particular holiness characterizing the followers. He selects a Greek term with a slight and remote phonetic resemblance to *Essaioi*, "the holy ones," which was intended much more to associate the name with

the concept of holiness in the mind of his Greek readers than to offer a strict grammatical or etymological explanation.
  b. Although both Philo and Josephus connect *Essenes* with holiness, both remain content with a rather vague association. Neither of them declares simply that *Essenes* signifies "holy ones." It has generally been accepted as practically certain that *Essenes* is modeled on some Hebrew or Aramaic original, and hypotheses intending to prove its non-Semitic derivation may therefore be discounted from the start.
  c. A view on the etymology of *Essenes* advanced by Geza Vermes identifies the Qumran sect as Essenes ("the healers") and regards the latter as a popular, not official, designation of the sect. The word is linked with Aramaic as "to heal." This is supported by Philo in whose mind all service of God aims at holiness and spiritual freedom, and that this aim can be achieved only through the healing of the sickness caused by the sinful passions of human nature.
  d. One clear conclusion emerges from the above, namely that none of the theories is weighty enough for exclusive adoption.
3. Essenes and Pharisees
  a. Historically the Essenes have a great deal in common with the Pharisees; both stressed the need for personal piety and separation from the impurities of daily life. Yet, Essenes and Pharisees differed in many details of doctrine and practice. Josephus, for instance, tells us that while the Essenes believed in immortality, they rejected the doctrine of bodily resurrection.
  b. The Pharisees took an active part in the Jewish life of the masses; in fact, they continued to participate in Temple worship even though that worship was controlled by the Sadducees. The Essenes, on the other hand, formed a separate sect. The reason seems evident; they deemed themselves the only true Israel, they regarded the religious observances in the cities and the Temples as corrupt; they refused, therefore, to participate and went to the wilderness of Judea to seek God there.
  c. K. Kohler, Jewish scholar, terms the Essenes "a branch of the Pharisees who conformed to the most rigid rules of levitical purity while aspiring to the highest degree of holiness." Kohler's main thesis is that the Essenes were essentially Jewish in origin and belonged to the Pharisees. Thus they did not on the whole

constitute a distinct, well-defined body to be segregated from the general mass of Jews; the Essenes did not at any time secede from official Judaism.

4. Rites and doctrines
   a. It is probable the Essenes first lived as small communities or brotherhoods of men intent on strict observance of the Torah; this led naturally to a strong emphasis on ritual precision. The Sabbath was observed with particular strictness. The levitical laws of holiness were rigidly observed. The Essenes met at dawn for traditional prayers, worked until 11 a.m., then gathered and, clad in white linen garments, bathed in cold water. They had their midday meal together, with a grace recited by a priest before and after the meal. After working until the evening, they again ate together. We are told that the silence prevailing at the meal was amazing. The Essenes lived a simple life, devoting much of their time to prayer and study yet requiring each member to perform some manual labor. Their principal occupations were handicrafts and farming.
   b. The younger ministered to the elder and this natural respect replaced artificial rank. Seniority and learning were the basis of position in the Essene society. In all their activities the leaders directed the procedure and named the persons to officiate; only in deeds of mercy and charity could individuals use initiative, as in acts of benevolence towards the aged or the sick.
   c. Josephus describes the strict discipline of the Essenes. An individual member of the community was obliged to live in constant submission to his overseer: "They do nothing but according to the injunctions of their curators; only these two things are done among them at everyone's own free will, which are to assist those that want it and to show mercy; for they are permitted of their own accord to afford succor to such as deserve it, when they stand in need of it, and to bestow food on those that are in distress, but they cannot give anything to their kindred without the curator's consent." (*Wars*, II, viii, 6)
   d. In principle, the Essenes objected to oaths, but an oath once taken could not be rescinded. Herein lay the chief disciplinary power of their officers, for since they observed strict purity in their food and refrained from eating anything prepared by outsiders, persons excommunicated could soon be starved into obedience. However,

expulsion seems to have been almost unknown and disobedience rare.

e. The Essenes declined to take part in Temple rites involving animal sacrifice and brought to the altar offerings of flour and oil only. They zealously studied the books of their ancestors and had some knowledge of medicine. Despising luxury and pleasure, the Essenes would not anoint their bodies with oil—a practice which they probably regarded as sybaritic. Blasphemy against God was punishable by death. A candidate for the society had to wait a year before he was given the emblems—a hatchet, belt, and white garment. Then he was allowed to follow their routine and receive "more purifying washings for holiness" but he was not yet permitted to take part in their common meals. If he proved himself worthy for two more years he was then admitted to the society, but not until he had taken fearful oaths to observe the rules. Among these were many ethical injunctions, a pledge of loyalty to the society, and a promise to "keep the books of the sect and the names of the angels."

f. Josephus, who states that he himself underwent this probationary period but then resigned, can therefore be trusted in his accounts of the external life and tenets of the Essenes, but cannot be regarded as having possessed an inner knowledge of their secrets, as the Essenes revealed them only to persons who joined their order. The oath exacted from the initiate, before he was allowed to share the common meal, is given by Josephus: "To be pious to God, to practice justice towards men; never to injure anyone, either of his own accord or under compulsion, always to hate the wicked and side with the just; ever to show faithfulness to all mankind and to be true to those in authority, for all power comes from God; never when in office to force his personal views or authority or to assume a special dress or luxury; to love truth and hate falsehood; to keep his hands pure of theft and his soul from unrighteous gain; not to have any secret from his brethren and never to betray one of theirs, even at the cost of his life; to pass on the traditions he himself had received; never to be a brigand; to safeguard the sacred books and to preserve, with care, the names of the angels that had been taught him."

g. According to Josephus, the Essenes attributed all things to fate. Some of them purported to foretell the future by close study of books, various holy matters, and utterances of prophets. They believed in the immortality of the soul but not of the body from which, in their view, the soul will be gladly delivered. Josephus stresses the beliefs of the Essenes and states that their doctrines were borrowed by the Pythagoreans and Stoics. He observes that the Essenes are the oldest of ascetics and it was from Egypt that their doctrines spread abroad. Certain scholars believe the Essenes were under foreign influence. They point to the fact that the Essenes worshipped facing the sun and not facing the Temple. Essenic belief in immortality is attributed to Greek or Iranian influences. The nature of these beliefs, however, was thoroughly Jewish and we find it among the Pharisees and the Qumran sect.

h. The Essenes and the New Testament. There is no reference to the Essenes in the New Testament, although other sects (Pharisees, Sadducees, and Zealots) are mentioned there. It is probable that John the Baptist was influenced by Essenism. He lived, preached, and baptized in the Jordan River only a few miles from a community of Essenes. Some New Testament scholars also believe that the Apostolic Church may have been influenced. This influence, however, has been invested with the specific spirit and character of Christianity.

i. To the student of New Testament times and religious history, the very existence of a pre-Christian monastic community of brotherhood within Judaism is of great interest. While the existence of Ascetics or Gymnosophists was mentioned in the accounts of the Greeks who followed Alexander to India, Essenism was the first form of organized monasticism in the ancient Mediterranean world.

5. Varieties of Essenism

   a. A study of the Essenes is complicated by the term *Essene* itself which was used to describe individuals and brotherhoods differing widely in significant tenets. Josephus, for instance, speaks of an Essenic order whose members did not practice celibacy. They approved of restricted conjugal intercourse until children had been born. On the other hand, Pliny asserts the Essenes avoided women and abstained from marriage altogether. Another body of pre-Christian Jews who lived a monastic life were the Therapeutae, described below. The Qumran (Dead Sea Scrolls) sect has also been identified as an Essene or Essene-like sect (see below).

   b. The Essenes did not apparently break away from official Judaism as a separate sect; little can be said of the Essenes that does not fall within the Pharisaic category. In fact, there were numerous instances among the Pharisees of persons who, singly or collectively, lived the Essene life. These men were no recluses, rather they were leaders who carried religion into life. Menahem, an Essene, foretold the rise of Herod to power. John, the Essene, was a general in the Roman War. Some scholars regard the Essenes as a subdivision of the Pharisees. Probably both Essenes and Pharisees sprang from the pre-Maccabean Hassideans. It is only by carefully gathering instances of individual holiness of a type unusual in Judaism that the Essenes can be isolated. These scholars maintain there is no argument for the assertion that Essene tenets lie far off the established track of Judaism. Abstinence is possibly the only exception, yet this, too, is not unknown in the Talmud. Private fasts and asceticism are also mentioned in rabbinical literature. That they are deprecated is another matter.

   c. Common to the above-mentioned varieties of Essenes is the cir-- cumstance that each lived a monastic life and formed a homogeneous body, ruled by officers acting in accordance with traditional laws and possessing initiatory oaths and ceremonies incumbent on the neophyte. Greek sources make it clear that they are speaking of sects. On the other hand, rabbinical writings speak of individuals or informal groups, lacking the cohesion and permanence which the Greek sources imply. Probably both are correct, for allowance must be made for the fact that the Greek accounts are connected descriptions, possibly even colored by the desire to heighten parallels to other bodies, while rabbinical sources contain only incidental references with the comprehensive designation *Essene* never mentioned.

6. The Essenes and the Dead Sea Scrolls

   a. Shortly after the discovery of the Dead Sea Scrolls, scholars began to note similarities and differences between the Essenes as described by Josephus, Philo, and Pliny and the community described in the scrolls. Scholars have already noted that both the Qumran sect and Essenes were groups which had separated themselves from the "normative" Judaism of their day, including Temple services. Each had rules of discipline. A superintendent or overseer was responsible for the life of members. Possessions were held in common. A newcomer had to undergo a period of probation, and

the uninitiated were excluded from the community meal. Ritual washing was practiced.
  b. On the other hand, there are differences between descriptions of the Essenes as given in Josephus, Philo, and Pliny and descriptions of the practices of Qumran. Although they repudiated animal sacrifice, the Essenes sent gifts of incense to the Temple. The attitude at Qumran was one of complete separation from the Jerusalem priesthood. Descriptions of the Essenes do not indicate the prominence of priests in their movement as do Qumran writings for their own community. Moreover, there is no reference to an Essene leader who compares with the Teacher of Righteousness of the Qumran sect.
  c. The majority of scholars classify the Qumran community as Essene, or an Essene-like sect. Others have, with not much success, point out parallels with Pharisees, Sadducees, Zealots, Ebionites, and other groups. (This problem is discussed in detail in Unit 18).

B. *Therapeutae*

1. Background
  a. The *Therapeutae* (Greek for "healers" or "attendants") were members of an ancient sect of Jewish ascetics, closely resembling the Essenes, believed to have settled on the shores of Lake Mareotis in the vicinity of Alexandria, Egypt, during the first century of the Christian era. Their way of life resembled that of the Essenes but was carried to a further degree of contemplation. The only original account of this community is given in *De Vita Contemplativa* ("Concerning the Contemplative Life"), an essay attributed to the Jewish philosopher Philo of Alexandria (20 B.C. to A.D. 40). Their origin and fate are alike unknown.
  b. The sect was characterized as being unusually severe in discipline and mode of life. Unlike the Essenes, the group was composed of both men and women.
  c. According to Philo, members of this sect devoted their time to contemplation. The Therapeutae prayed twice every day, at dawn and at eventide. The interval between early morning and evening was spent entirely on spiritual exercise. They read the Holy Scriptures and sought wisdom from their ancestral philosophy by taking it as an allegory, since they thought that the words of the literal text were symbols of something whose hidden nature is revealed by studying the underlying meaning. Upon joining this sect a man no longer belonged to the world and voluntarily assigned his property

to his heirs. So far as is known, prayer and study were the sole occupations of the Therapeutae.

2. Daily life of the sect
   a. Members of this community lived in separate and scattered houses. These were near enough to afford mutual protection in times of danger and emergency, yet not too close to deprive members of the solitude they so cherished for the purpose of meditation. Each house contained a chamber or sanctuary, consecrated to study and prayer. (Compare Matthew 6 : 6, "But when you pray, enter into your closet, and having shut your door, pray to your Father who is in secret, and your Father who sees in secret shall reward you.") Within the walls of this sanctuary, members were initiated into the mysteries of their sanctified life. Attendance to bodily needs, such as food, was entirely relegated to the hours of darkness. No drink or food or any other things for the needs of the body were permitted to be taken into the sanctuary, nothing but the books of the Law, the Prophets, the Psalms, or anything which fostered and perfected knowledge and piety. In addition to the Old Testament, the Therapeutae had books, composed by the founders of their sect, on the allegorical methods of interpreting Scripture. Philo's account refers to the composition of "new psalms" to God in various meters and melodies.
   b. For six days a week the Therapeutae lived apart and sought wisdom in solitude, in their respective sanctuaries, never passing through the outside door of the house. Some recluses ate every other day, while others succeeded in eating on one single weekday only. On the Sabbath men and women met in the common sanctuary, a double enclosure with one portion for men, the other for women; for women, too, were regularly part of the audience and attended with the same ardor as the men. The wall separating the sexes rose up from the ground to three or four cubits, while the space above it, up to the roof, was left open. Thus the modesty becoming the female sex was preserved, while the women, sitting within earshot, could easily follow what was said, since there was nothing to obstruct the voice of the speaker. All listened to a discourse by the eldest and most skilled in their doctrines. After attending to their souls they indulged their bodies. However, their indulgence even then did not exceed coarse bread, flavored with salt and sometimes hyssop, and a drink of spring water.
   c. A special common assembly was also held every fiftieth day or

after seven sets of seven days had passed. The sect, according to Philo, revered the simple number seven and its square, but the most sacred of numbers was fifty. Thus on the eve of the fiftieth day they observed the *Pannuches*, "all-night festival." They assembled together, white-robed and cheerful-faced, yet with the utmost seriousness. First they took their stand in a line, eyes and hands stretched toward heaven. Standing in this way, they prayed to God that their feasting would be accepted. After the prayers, members took seats according to the order of their admission. The banquet was also shared by women. The order of reclining at the assembly was so arranged that the men sat by themselves on the right and the women on the left. They had no slaves to wait upon them because they felt that the ownership of servants was entirely against nature, for nature ordained that all men be free. Attendants at the banquet, however, were young members of the community carefully selected for their special merit. In this assembly or banquet of the fiftieth day no wine was served, only clear spring water. The table, too, was kept pure from the flesh of animals; the food again consisted of bread flavored with salt or hyssop, "as a relish for the daintier appetite." The members abstained from wine and meat because the former acts like a drug producing folly while the latter stirs up that most insatiable of animal passions.

d. After taking their seats and becoming silent, all listened devoutly to the president, who discussed some philosophical question arising in the Holy Scripture or solved one propounded by one of the members. The president lingered over his instruction and spun it out with repetitions, "thus permanently imprinting the thoughts in the souls of his audience." He made no attempt to win a reputation for clever oratory, but rather to gain a closer insight into some particular problem and, having gained it," not to withhold it selfishly from those who, if not so clear-sighted as he, have at least a similar desire to learn." The discourse was followed by the singing of a hymn, composed as an address to God, first by the president himself. After him, all the others took their turn, while the rest listened in complete silence, except when they had to chant the closing lines or refrains, when all lifted up their voices, men and women alike. Then came the meal of the simple type already described. After the supper they held the *per vigilium*, "the sacred vigil," celebrated with antiphonal and joint singing of hymns of thanksgiving and with choral dancing in imitation of Moses and Miriam at the Red Sea (Exodus 15). Philo, who describes this sect in loving detail, remarks that the choir of the Therapeutae in matching "note in response to note and voice to voice, the treble of the women blending with the bass of the men, created a harmonious concert, musical in the truest sense." Thus they continued till dawn. At sunrise they stood with face and body turned to the east and hands stretched up to heaven and prayed for bright days and knowledge of the truth and that the light of truth might illuminate their minds for keen-sighted thinking. After the prayers they departed, each back to his sanctuary, for contemplation and study. Because of their piety, Philo characterized the Therapeutae as "the citizens of the heaven and of the universe."

e. Although the Therapeutae, like the Essenes, left no permanent traces on Jewish life, their semimonastic communities were probably the prototype of a large development in the Christian Church. N. Bentwich (*Hellenism*, page 173) observes in this connection that the emphasis on individual salvation and the breaking away from the national life and the national law cut off these sects from the Jewish people and, as soon as they had made themselves distinct, led to their absorption into the antinational Christian body.

3. Differences of opinion concerning the identity of this sect
   a. Some early authorities believed that the Therapeutae were a Christian order because of the similarity of their asceticism with that of Christian monasticism. However, the concensus of modern scholars is that they were a radical offspring of pre-Christian Judaism, probably Essenism.
   b. To the modern reader, the importance of the Therapeutae, as of the Essenes, lies in the evidence they afford of the existence of the monastic system before the Christian era. The discovery of the Dead Sea Scrolls in the wilderness of Judea has certainly confirmed this view. Although no clue is given as to their origin, the description in Philo's *De Vita Contemplativa* does not account for the origin of the name *Therapeutae*, and this tends to show that the sect had already been well established before Philo's time. Eusebius (A.D. 260-339) was so struck by the similarities between the Therapeutae and the Christian monks of his own days as to claim that they were Christians converted by the preaching of St. Mark It is, however, now generally acknowledged that the Therapeutae were a variety of Essenes, distinguished by a love of contemplative

devotion. They shared with the Essenes the dualistic view of body and soul and the affection for the secret doctrine which underlies the literal word of the Scriptures.

Topics for Study and Discussion

A. Give a general description of the Essenes. What is the meaning and origin of their name?
B. Write a short paragraph on each of the following:
  1. Hellenism
  2. Second Commonwealth
  3. Maccabees
C. Discuss the contrasts and parallels between the Pharisees and the Essenes.
  Describe the rites and doctrines of the Essenes.
E. Write about a two-page description of the Therapeutae.

XVII

THE MANUAL OF DISCIPLINE

One of the most controversial and important of the scrolls is the *Manual of Discipline*, its significance being mainly due to its bearing upon the background of Christianity and the New Testament. This work describes the doctrines of the sect and the rules and regulations by which its daily life was governed. The scroll discusses the three-stage probationary period through which each initiate had to pass, the initiation ceremony, the daily life of the members, and the disciplinary code for members of the sect. It will be interesting for you to compare these with what you have already learned in the *Thanksgiving Hymns* (Unit 6). If you wish to study the scroll thoroughly, you should obtain Wernberg-Moeller's work on the *Manual of Discipline*.

RECOMMENDED READING

Allegro, J. M., *The Dead Sea Scrolls*, pages 101-118

Burrows, M., *The Dead Sea Scrolls*, pages 227-272, and the translation of the document, pages 371-389

Burrows, M., *More Light on the Dead Sea Scrolls*, pages 285-296, 326-334, and 355-374

Gaster, T. H., *The Dead Sea Scriptures*, pages 33-60 (Introduction, pages 33-38, and translation of the document, pages 39-60)

Van der Ploeg, J., *The Excavations at Qumran*, pages 50-51

Vermes, G., *Discovery in the Judean Desert*, pages 36-42, and *The Dead Sea Scrolls in English*, pages 71-94

Wernberg-Moeller, P., *The Manual of Discipline* (The entire book is devoted to this Scroll.)

Yadin, Y., *The Message of the Scrolls*, pages 113-127

THE MANUAL OF DISCIPLINE

A. *Discovery and description*

1. The original title, if any, has been lost because of damage done to the beginning of the scroll.

2. Millar Burrows likened it to the Manual of Discipline of the Methodist Church, and therefore named it the *Manual of Discipline*—a title generally accepted by all writers.
3. This scroll was one of the seven scrolls first discovered in Cave One in 1947.
    a. It was found in jars which may well be Roman.
    b. It was probably deposited in the cave in the first century A.D.
4. The Manual, when discovered, was in two separate pieces:
    a. Many cracks in the brittle leather showed that it had been unrolled several times, so it is uncertain whether the two pieces were already separated when found.
    b. The two pieces are consecutive portions of what was originally a single scroll. They are made of five strips of coarse-textured leather or parchment sewn together.
    c. Together they are a little over 6 feet long.
        (1) The beginning is missing, but the original length must have been at least 7 feet.
        (2) The width is about 9 1/2 inches.
5. This scroll shows little evidence of hard wear, and has survived the ravages of time better than some of the other scrolls.

B. *Analysis of the text*

1. The Manual gives an account of a sect—probably the Essenes—who had withdrawn to the wilderness to lead a monastic life and to study the Law. (For the Essenes, see Unit 16).
2. The work describes the doctrines of the sect and the rules and regulations by which its daily life was governed.
3. This Manual appears in eleven fragmentary manuscripts from other caves, proving that it was regularly copied and worked over.
4. The lack of unity or logical order in the contents of the Manual suggests that it was compiled gradually in scrapbook fashion from various sources.
5. The first column begins in the midst of a passage that states what is expected of those who "enter into the covenant."
6. Then the directions for the ceremony of entering into the covenant follow.
7. At the middle of the third column a new section, dealing with the origin and future destruction of sin, begins.

8. The rules of organization and discipline occupy columns 5 to 10.
9. The document concludes with a beautiful devotional poem or psalm.

C. *Contents*

1. Before being admitted to the brotherhood, the initiate had to pass through a three-stage probationary period.
   a. The first, of unspecified length, was a matter of becoming acquainted with the spirit and practices of the sect.
   b. When he passed this, the candidate was promoted to the second stage, where he joined the Party of the Community, but without touching the Purity of the Many. This stage lasted for one year.
   c. In the third stage, also one year, he handed over all worldly wealth which was marked to his credit but not yet "mixed" for the common pool. He was still excluded from the Messianic Banquet, but was now apparently admitted to the Purity of the Many.
2. After the probationary period, each member had to pass through an initiation ceremony.
   a. The priests and the Levites pronounced their blessings.
   b. Then followed a recitation of the wondrous works of God.
   c. Those entering the covenant made a general confession of their former wickedness.
   d. This rite of initiation was probably accompanied by an initial baptismal ceremony (ritual purification by water).
3. The fully initiated members, called the *rabbim*, were each assigned a regular rank or place within three basic groups: priests, levites, and "the people."
4. The order in any activity—for example, in seating as well as speaking in the assembly—was prescribed according to rank.
5. Each year a solemn reunion took place at which the general condition of the community was discussed, and each member was assigned the place due him.
6. Members were "volunteers" who pledged themselves "to do what is good and right before God."
7. Members undertook the following:
   a. To separate themselves from the society of wicked men, to love all the Sons of Light, and to hate all Sons of Darkness.
   b. To practice in community truth and modesty, to act righteously and justly, to love mercy, and to walk humbly in all their ways.

8. The idea of unity was at the heart of the sect, and the members shared all the spiritual and material necessities of life. "They shall eat communally, bless communally, and take counsel communally."
9. Celibacy is implied but not definitely stated. In some Essene-like communities, members *did* marry.
10. Much of the time of the members was given to the study of the Law.
    a. This had to be carried out continuously, day and night, throughout the year.
    b. In every group of ten there always had to be at least one man studying or interpreting the Law.
    c. The membership was divided into three shifts to keep the reading and exposition of the Law going throughout the night.
11. In accordance with the basic desire to fulfill all the demands of the Law, there was a rigid insistence on ritual purity.
    a. Various forms of ritual ablution were prescribed.
    b. The idea of washing in a spiritual sense is characteristic.
12. The closing psalm of the Manual speaks of prayer at sunrise, at sunset, at the new moons, at festivals, and at the beginning of each year.
13. It is not clear whether these were periods of common prayer or private prayer.
14. The members celebrated a renewal of the covenant every year, presumably on the Day of Atonement. All the members confessed their sins and renewed their undertaking to live according to the will of God.
15. A strict disciplinary code applied to the members of the sect. (Cf. Allegro).
    a. Interrupting one's neighbor in a public session—ten days in isolation.
    b. Leaving a session of the Many "aimlessly and wantonly" as many as three times during one session—ten days, and in some cases, thirty days in isolation.
    c. Falling asleep during the session of the Many—thirty days in isolation.
    d. Spitting in the session of the Many—thirty days in isolation.
    e. Indecent exposure of parts of the body while moving the hands about—thirty days in isolation.
    f. Indulging in foolish laughter—thirty days in isolation.
    g. Acting fraudulently with the property of the community—he

shall make good the damage or loss. If he lacks means to do so—sixty days in isolation.
- h. Indulging in indecent talk—three months in isolation.
- i. Committing a fraud against one's neighbor—three months in isolation.
- j. Harboring a grudge against one's neighbor without a legitimate cause—six months in isolation. (A later scribe has inserted above the line "one year.")
- k. Taking personal revenge on one's neighbor in any manner—six months in isolation. (A later scribe has inserted above the line "one year.")
- l. Speaking in anger unintentionally against the priest—six months in isolation.
- m. Lying deliberately—six months in isolation.
- n. Speaking deceitfully to one's neighbor or intentionally praticing deceit upon him—six months in isolation. (If unintentionally—three months.)
- o. Exposing oneself in public, insufficiently dressed, not being poor —six months in isolation.
- p. Complaining or murmuring against one's neighbor without legitimate cause—six months in isolation.
- q. Deliberate lying in the matter of personal property—exclusion from the "pure thing of the Many" for one year and a fine of one fourth of his food allowance. (The person is placed in isolation for one year and regarded as outside the state of purity entailed in membership of the community.)
- r. Answering one's neighbor with arrogance or speaking to him with anger—one year in isolation.
- s. Speaking in anger deliberately against the priest—one year in isolation.
- t. Slandering one's neighbor unjustly and deliberately—one year in isolation.
- u. Cursing him who reads the Book or the blessings—banishment for life.
- v. Slandering against the entire community—banishment forever, "never to return."
- w. Murmuring against the entire community—banishment forever, "irrevocably."

D. *Doctrines in the Manual of Discipline*

See the section on the doctrines in Unit 13, "The Thanksgiving

Hymns," and Unit 14 on the doctrines and beliefs of the sect of the scrolls.

Topics for Study and Discussion

A. Describe the discovery and general contents of this scroll.
B. Discuss three of the following specific contents of the scroll:
   1. Initiation of novices
   2. "Rank" in the community
   3. Aims and activities of the members
   4. Some aspects of the disciplinary code
C. Discuss the importance of this scroll.

XVIII

THE ESSENES AND THE IDENTIFICATION OF THE SECT

This unit outlines some of the problems scholars have faced in identifying the sect of the Dead Sea Scrolls and explains why it is that most scholars today accept the identification of the sect with the Essenes. You will see who the Essenes were as described by Philo, Pliny, and Josephus, since we have no original Essene literature. In this unit, the descriptions of the Essenes are compared with the information we have about the Dead Sea sect from their own literature, and the information we have about the Essenes and the Dead Sea sect are compared for similarities and differences. While the similarities are numerous, many of the differences can be explained by the fact that there were several different sects of Essenes.

RECOMMENDED READING

Allegro, J. M., *The Dead Sea Scrolls*, pages 94-118
Burrows, M., *The Dead Sea Scrolls*, pages 273-298
Burrows, M., *More Light on the Dead Sea Scrolls*, pages 253-274
Cross, F. M., Jr., *The Ancient Library of Qumran*, pages 37-79
Milik, J. T., *Ten Years of Discovery in the Wilderness of Judaea*, pages 44-98
Van der Ploeg, J., *The Excavations at Qumran*, pages 45-52
Vermes, G., *Discovery in the Judean Desert*, pages 52-61, and *The Dead Sea Scrolls in English*, pages 16-33
Yadin, Y., *The Message of the Scrolls*, pages 160-189

ESSENES AND THE IDENTIFICATION OF THE SECT

A. *Problems in the identification of the sect of the scrolls*

1. No name is given in any of the documents.
2. We have no original Essene literature, only second-hand information written by Philo, Pliny, and Josephus. All three men lived around

the first century A.D. when the Essenes were flourishing and the community of Qumran was still studying and copying its manuscripts.
a. Philo was an Alexandrian philosopher, who was born about 20 B.C. in Alexandria, Egypt, and died after A.D. 40. Philo had visited Judea when he was a young man and may have been in actual contact with the Essenes, about whom he wrote in *Quod Omnis Probus Liber* in about A.D. 20.
b. Pliny (A.D. 23-79) was an historian and an officer of Titus in the Jewish War. He describes Judea and its neighboring countries and refers to the Essenes in his book *Historia Naturalis*, written about A.D. 70.
c. Josephus, a general and historian born in A.D. 37 or 38, died after A.D. 100. He came from an aristocratic family, and he describes himself when young as an ardent student of Jewish law and tradition, including the tenets of the Pharisees, Sadducees, and Essenes. According to his account he spent three years in the desert with a hermit, perhaps an Essene, as an ascetic. At the age of nineteen he became a Pharisee, and between A.D. 69-94 he wrote *Antiquities of the Jews* and *Wars of the Jews*.
3. There are only a few references to the Essenes in rabbinical literature.

B. *Major groups in Israel at the time of the Qumran sect*

1. Josephus, the New Testament, and rabbinical literature speak of Sadducees and Pharisees as the two major groups within Judaism.
2. The Qumran sect is not to be identified with the Sadducees.
   a. The Sadducees seem not to have been in reality a party but rather a class. They were in general the wealthy aristocracy of which the Temple priesthood was an important element. Thus, although they were probably not a party, they stood together on political and religious issues as social classes often do.
   b. The Qumran sect cannot be associated with this group, for in the *Habakkuk Commentary* we have a strong denunciation of the Jerusalem priesthood.
   c. The Sadducees also rejected the newly developed beliefs in resurrection and in angels to which the Qumran sect adhered.
   d. They accepted only the Pentateuch as Scripture, interpreted the law very strictly and rejected the Pharisaic system of oral tradition concerning the meaning of the law.
   e. The name *Sadducee* was probably derived from the name Zadok and is the equivalent of Zadokite. Sadducees were probably called

Zadokites, since they considered themselves the descendants and successors of the Zadok who was high priest under David and Solomon.

  f. When the *Damascus Document* was published, the prominence of the sons of Zadok in it led scholars to suspect an association between the Dead Sea sect and the Sadducees. Further study showed they could hardly be identical. To the reasons mentioned above, we can add the fact that the Dead Sea sect highly honored the prophets, and the Sadducees did not accept the prophetic books as scripture.
  g. To account for the term *Sons of Zadok* in the scrolls, Dupont-Sommer has suggested that before the Maccabean crisis of the second century B.C. there may have been devout priests who called themselves Sons of Zadok to signify their authentic priestly lineage and their attachment to the traditional faith and cult. They were not the same group as the covenanters, but there was probably a division within the Sons of Zadok when those who felt drawn to a higher religious ideal separated themselves from the rest and formed the sect of the new covenant.
  h. Such a connection with dissident members of the Zadokite priesthood is questioned by De Vaux. He suggest that in calling themselves Sons of Zadok the priests of the Qumran community were reclaiming a title that had been appropriated and abused by the Sadducees.

3. Some scholars have argued that both the Essenes and the Qumran sect were a branch of the Pharisees.
    a. The Pharisees accepted the beliefs concerning the angels and resurrection.
    b. They accepted as sacred the writings of the prophets and other writings in contrast to the Sadducees who accepted only the Written Law, rejecting the Oral Law developed by the Pharisees.

4. A few scholars have identified the Qumran Covenanters with the Hasidim, but the term *Hasidim* seems to designate conservative, devout Jews in general rather than a definite sect or party.

C. *Identification with other sects—such as the Samaritans, the Ebionites, the Karaites, the Zealots, and the Magharians*

1. Identification of the sect with the Samaritans.
    a. The manuscript fragments in the archaic Hebrew script naturally

recalled the continued use of a form of that script by the Samaritans to the present time.
  b. Affinities with the Samaritan dialect were noted in the language of the scrolls.
  c. Similarities in religious practices and beliefs were also detected.
  d. A comparison of the Samaritans and the Qumran covenanters has been made by John Bowman. He finds no indication of a connection between them, but points out that there are many similarities between the beliefs held by the Samaritans to this day and those of the Qumran sect.
     (1) The Samaritans consider themselves the Sons of Light; and they call the chief of forces of evil, Belial.
     (2) They look for a redeemer called the Taheb, who corresponds to the Messiah of Israel of the Qumran documents.
     (3) Their high priest is the anointed one (Messiah of Aaron).
  e. Bowman concludes:
     (1) These beliefs are survivals of the teachings of the ancient Samaritan sects.
     (2) The similarities between them and the Qumran sect do not indicate any direct contact but are to be explained by the fact that their backgrounds were similar—both arose out of the same situation of ferment and tense expectation.
     (3) There is even said to have been a Samaritan branch of the Essenes.
2. Identification of the sect with the Jewish-Christian sect called the Ebionites—a view maintained mainly by Teicher of the University of Cambridge.
  a. Teicher argues that the use of the word *Ebionites* (literally "the poor") several times in the writings of the Dead Sea sect proves that it members were Ebionites.
  b. The Ebionites were a Judaeo-Christian sect founded immediately following the crucifixion of Jesus. It is known that the members were Jews in all principles, customs, and beliefs except one—they believed Jesus to have been the Messiah.
  c. Many scholars feel that Teicher's theory is untenable on chronological grounds alone.
     (1) Teicher recognizes that the texts presuppose a well-developed, organized sect, and concludes that their composition must therefore be dated considerably later than A.D. 70.

(2) However, archaeological evidence makes A.D. 70 the latest possible date for the copying of the latest manuscripts, and the paleography compels us to date the oldest of the manuscripts earlier than that.
d. This does not mean that there was no connection between the covenanters and the Ebionites. The possibility of such a connection has been explored by O. Cullmann. In particular he has investigated the contacts between the Qumran texts and the early Christian documents known as the pseudo-Clementine writings, which are believed to be of Ebionite origin.
e. Cullman finds differences between the two groups:
  (1) The priesthood is held in high honor by the Dead Sea sect, and is radically rejected by the Ebionites.
  (2) The opposition to the temple that is evident among the Essenes and the Dead Sea sect has become much sharper in the pseudo-Clementine writings.
  (3) The Ebionites have a critical attitude towards the Old Testament which is lacking among the Essenes.
f. Cullmann finds many similarities. Both groups have the same ritual practices, the same prescribed ways of living, and at many points the same theology.
g. Cullmann concludes that the relationship is too close to be explained by supposing that the Ebionites merely preserved features of primitive Christianity that had been derived originally from sectarian Judaism.
  (1) He assumes a later, more direct influence upon the Jewish-Christians.
  (2) The Qumran community was destroyed during the war with Rome in A.D. 66-70, and it was at this time that the Jewish Christians left Jerusalem and withdrew across the Jordan.
  (3) Cullmann concludes that the remnant of the Qumran sect must have joined these Jewish Christians, and he claims that both the resemblances and the differences can be understood as a result of this fusion.
3. Identification of the sect with the Karaites
  a. Still more decisively than the Ebionites, the Karaite sect is excluded by archaeological evidence from being given credit for the Dead Sea Scrolls.
  b. The Karaite movement arose in the early Middle Ages in the

eastern part of the Arab empire. It rejected the traditional interpretations built up by the rabbis and acknowledged only the authority of the Scriptures.

c. Professor Zeitlin, however, believes that the scrolls are of a late date, as we discussed in the unit on the dating of the scrolls. As a result he feels that the scrolls might be products of the Karaite sect.

d. While most scholars feel it is impossible that the medieval Karaites could have produced the Dead Sea Scrolls, the parallels with Karaite literature which Zeitlin and Weiss have pointed out do have some significance.

d. Professor Kahle suggests that Benjamin al-Nihawandi, a leading Persian Karaite of the ninth century A.D., was acquainted with the books found in the ninth century in a cave near Jericho, and that these stimulated him to develop Karaite theology on a new basis, related to the theology of the Qumran sect.

(1) The manuscripts of the *Damascus Document* found in the Old Cairo Geniza, Kahle believes, were copies of older scrolls found in the cave at that time.

(2) Instead of supposing that the *Damascus Document* was composed under Karaite influence, Kahle maintains that the Karaites were influenced by the *Damascus Document* and the other scrolls found in the cave near Jericho about A.D. 800.

(3) Support for the historical connection between the Karaites and the Qumran sect can be adduced from the fact that bits of the *Damascus Document* have now been found in the Qumran caves.

4. Identification of the sect with the Zealots

   a. The Zealot movement was inaugurated by Zadok the Pharisee and Judas of Galilee about A.D. 6.
   b. Possibly some members of the Qumran community united with the Zealots in the last decade before the destruction of the Temple. However, the community of the Dead Sea scrolls is much older than the movement inaugurated by Zadok and Judas.

5. Identification of the sect with the Magharians

   a. The Magharians are a sect which may have appeared shortly before the Christian era.
   b. Barthélemy and de Vaux have suggested that the Magharians may have been the Qumran covenanters.
   c. It is quite possible that the Magharians were actually the Essenes,

and that they were given the name Magharian by later writers because their books had been found in a cave. (The Arabic word for cave is *magharah*).

IDENTIFICATION OF THE QUMRAN SECT WITH THE ESSENES GENERALLY ACCEPTED TODAY

A. *The differences between the Essenes (as described by Josephus, Philo, and Pliny) and the Qumran community (as reflected in its own literature) can be accounted for*

1. There existed several communities of Essenes—what was true of some may not have been true of others.
2. At least three different branches of Essenes are known to us:
    a. Celibates lived at Qumran.
    b. Married Essenes lived in isolated Jewish villages of southern Syria.
    c. The Therapeutae or the Egyptian Jewish Hermits are described by Philo and also Eusebius in *Ecclesiastical History* II : 17. It is believed that they are an Egyptian offshoot of the Essenes who lived in the vicinity of Alexandria. Each lived in his own house leading a celibate, ascetic life. They gave up their property and devoted themselves exclusively to prayer, meeting only on the Sabbath (See Chapter 16).
3. Other differences may reflect different stages in the history of the Essene movement; contrast for example, the militant spirit of the *War Scroll* and the extreme pacifism attributed by Philo to the Essenes.
4. G. Vermes feels that there were three evolutionary stages in the Essene movement:
    a. The Damascus stage resulted from a rupture within the ranks of the Jewish priesthood; it was characterized by a striving for the strictest ceremonial purity. Neither common ownership of property nor celibacy were entailed at this stage.
    b. During the Qumran stage, a separation from the bulk of Judaism is much more marked. A fully developed communal organization, an actual renunciation of private property, and celibacy are evident.
    c. The last stage of the community's evolution brings us to the middle of the first century A.D. Little change is found since the Qumran period according to descriptions by Philo, Josephus, and Pliny. Vermes suggests that such an evolution points to a relatively lengthy duration of the Essene movement.

5. The organization of the community at Qumran must have taken considerable time to develop.
   a. Some fragments found in Cave Four represent various recensions of the *Manual of Discipline*, the *Damascus Document*, and the *War Scroll*.
   b. There is a reference in the *Damascus Document* to many generations, afflictions, and years of sojourning.

B. *There are discrepancies among the accounts of Josephus, Philo, and Pliny*

1. Josephus and Philo describe mainly the Essene communities scattered in towns and villages of Palestine; Pliny alone mentions the settlements west of the Dead Sea.
2. The fact that nothing is mentioned by Philo and Josephus of the Teacher of Righteousness and the new covenant is explained by the supposition that the Teacher of Righteousness founded a schismatic group among the Essenes.

C. *Descriptions of the Qumran sect and of the Essenes lead scholars to identify the Qumran sect with the Essenes*

1. The scrolls were hidden in the very region where the Essenes are said to have had their headquarters. *Philo* (compare B, 1) locates the principal Essene settlement close to the Dead Sea.
2. Both groups had similar organization and discipline.
   a. The deeds and thoughts of both groups were guided by the law of Moses. They were most orthodox in adhering to the rules of the Torah.
   b. Among both the Essenes and the Qumran sect there was a period of probation preceding admission to membership. Further parallels can be seen in the limitations imposed upon those undergoing probation, in the instruction given them, and in the examination to which they were subjected before they were admitted.
   c. The taking of the oath by the candidate for membership and the oath of initiation were applicable to both groups.
   d. The people were divided into classes.
      (1) When the Essenes assembled, they were seated in classes according to age and rank.
      (2) The order of seating at the meetings of the Qumran sect was also strictly prescribed.

(3) There was a strict rotation of the order of speech in both groups.
  e. Great importance was attached to the common meal by both groups.
  f. Both groups prohibited spitting in the midst of the assembly.
  g. In both groups decisions upon questions of admission and discipline were made by the assembled members.
  h. Both groups had similar penalties for various offenses. (See Unit 17, The *Manual of Discipline*).
  i. One of the major concerns of both sects was the study and interpretation of the Law, and in both sects the members studied the Law in groups.
3. Moral and social practices—nowhere are the parallels more noticeable:
  a. According to Philo the Essenes were much more interested in ethics than in logic or metaphysics.
  b. The Essenes devoted themselves assiduously to moral philosophy under the guidance of the divinely inspired laws.
  c. Both Philo and Josephus pay tribute to the high reputation of the Essenes for sanctity.
  d. The Essenes were a strictly ascetic group, putting great stress on the control of bodily appetites.
  e. The *Manual of Discipline* also emphasizes self-control and a serious demeanor.
  f. Humility, patience, simplicity, obedience, fidelity, and purity are among the virtues most highly prized by members of the sect and Essenes alike.
  g. In both groups there was a strong attachment to one another and intolerance towards outsiders.
4. Economic life.
  a. According to Philo and Josephus, the Essenes lived primarily by agriculture and our accounts indicate that the members of the Qumran sect were probably also farmers.
  b. Community of goods was practiced by both groups.
  c. Philo's statement that the members received wages but put them into a common fund recalls the provision of the *Damascus Document* that a fixed portion of each man's wages must be given to the superintendent.
5. Theology.
  a. Both emphasized strongly the complete sovereignty of God as the source of all being.

b. The Essene belief in immortality seems to correspond quite closely to that held by the Qumran sect.
6. Ritual (There seems to be some divergence at this point.)
   a. Emphasis on the exact observance of sacred days is common to both, but the particular observances emphasized in our sources are not the same.
   b. Both groups emphasized public and private prayer. For the Essenes our sources indicate a strict regimen of daily prayer, work, and meeting for worship as well as for meals and study. No such definite order is specified in the extant portions of the *Manual of Discipline* or the *Damascus Document*.
   c. Special ablutions and lustrations are stressed in the descriptions of the Essenes; compare with this, for instance, the Qumran rites of baptism and the emphasis on purity.
   d. Philo and Josephus say that the Essenes did not offer sacrifices. The *Damascus Document* presupposes the practice of offering sacrifices.
   e. Strict dietary regulations are attributed to the Essenes by Josephus; no indication of any such extraordinary concern for correct diet is shown in the scrolls.
   f. Our lack of knowledge of Essene ritual may be due partly to the fact that the accounts of Jewish practices and ideas given by Josephus and Philo were intended for the gentile readers and consequently they minimized everything peculiar to Judaism.

TOPICS FOR STUDY AND DISCUSSION

A. Discuss the problems relative to the identification of the Qumran sect.
B. Why do the majority of scholars identify the Qumran sect with the Essenes or an Essene-like sect.
C. Give the reasons advanced by scholars who identify the Qumran sect with the Karaites.
D. Write a short paragraph on each of the following:
   1. Zealots
   2. Karaites
   3. Sadducees
   4. Pharisees
   5. Ebionites
   6. Samaritans

XIX

QUMRAN WRITINGS AND CHRISTIANITY

The relationship of the Qumran sect to Christianity has aroused a great deal of interest and discussion, and much has been written on the many facets of this topic. We can consider the relationship of the two groups under three main headings: literary, institutional, and doctrinal similarities and contrasts. It is notably with the writings of John and Paul that the greatest number of points of contact, both literary and doctrinal, have been discovered. Between the Synoptic Gospels and the Qumran texts there seem to be relatively few literary parallels.

As for institutional parallels, the organization of the early Church, as it appears in Acts and the Epistles of Paul, is similar in some ways to the organization of the Qumran community. Thus, in the summary in Acts 2 : 42-7 of the activities of the first Christians, reference is made to "community of property," "prayer," and "teaching." Parallels have also been made between the practices of celibacy, communal meals, and the rites of baptism existing in both groups, although there are also numerous contrasts in the organization of the early Church and the sect.

There are numerous similarities between the Qumran doctrines and the authentic early Christian doctrine, although there are, as you will see, numerous contrasts as well. Both groups had a strong belief in predestination, in the existence of the spirits of good and evil that are engaged in a struggle both in the cosmos and in the soul of each man, and in Messianic concepts. Both believed that they were the elect, and that they had in this life a foretaste of the blessedness that the end of days would bring about. Both also held the eschatological concept of the true Israel as ruled by twelve leaders, and in both systems the believer shared in the life of the angels.

However, in early Christianity, all these features, and many others, are taken up into a new doctrinal structure; the integration of these elements with the central beliefs of the new faith transforms them. The Messianic figure for the Christians is embodied in a single person, whereas for the Qumran sect the Messianic concept is embodied in several figures. The Qumran community might have hoped for resurrection, but for the Christians it was a fact. Both groups believed in the sinfulness of human nature, but for the Christians it was so radicalized that a merely human mediation of the New Covenant and a merely human Messiah would no longer seem effective, as it would have been for the Qumran sect.

Furthermore, although there definitely are links of ideas and practices between the sect of the scrolls and the early Church, many of these ideas and practices were not unique to the sect, but were current in the first century B.C. It is now certain that the sect of the scrolls was a far less dynamic group than the Church of the New Testament, and as we mentioned before, the sect's expressions and ideas may have been taken up but they were invested with a new and deeper meaning and content.

In conclusion we may say that the paramount importance of the scrolls to New Testament studies is that they add to our knowledge and understanding of the immediate pre-Christian era and give us a more precise insight into the life and faith of one of the sects living in the second and first centuries B.C. The Dead Sea Scrolls provide us with the setting in which Christianity was born and show us the roots of some of its ideas and also its unique and distinct character.

Recommended Reading

Allegro, J. M., *The Dead Sea Scrolls*, pages 134-167
Burrows, M., *The Dead Sea Scrolls*, pages 326-345
Burrows, M., *More Light on the Dead Sea Scrolls*, pages 56-132
Cross, F.M., Jr., *The Ancient Library of Qumran*, pages 146-173 and 181-184
Danielou, Jean, *The Dead Sea Scrolls and Primitive Christianity*
Gaster, T. H., *The Dead Sea Scriptures*, pages 1-28
Howie, C. G., *The Dead Sea Scrolls and the Living Church*
Milik, T. H., *Ten Years of Discovery in the Wilderness of Juaea*, pages 140-143
Van der Ploeg, J., *The Excavations at Qumran*, pages 189-224
Vermes, G., *The Dead Sea Scrolls in English*, pages 53-68.

John the Baptist and Qumran

A. *It is possible that there was contact between John the Baptist and the sect*

1. About the year A.D. 27, according to Matthew, John the Baptist was in the wilderness of Judea.

2. John lived beyond the Jordan River about ten to twelve miles from the Qumran monastery. It is believed he was aware of the existence of the monastery and the library, and some say the sect may have influenced Christianity through John.
3. John tells of being in the wilderness till the day of his manifestation to Israel. He also tells of going forth to baptize in the Jordan River.
4. John tells his interrogators, "I am the voice crying in the wilderness," but John's wilderness and the wilderness of Qumran are not necessarily the same.

B. *There are contrasts between the sect and John's ascetic way of life and his monastic ideals*

1. Qumran texts say nothing of eating honey and locusts.
2. Abstinence from wine and strong drink are characteristic of other earlier sects as the Nazarites and Rechabites, as well as the Qumran sect.
3. The tight organization of the Qumran community does not correspond to the freedom of life of the disciples of John.
4. John went among the common man but the Qumran sect members were exclusive and kept to themselves.
5. John speaks of a single baptism; the Essenes practiced continual ritual washing.

QUMRAN WRITINGS AND CHRISTIANITY

A. *The relationship of the Gospel and Epistles of John to Qumran writings*

1. Scholars feel that the writings of John are closer to Qumran writings than other parts of the New Testament.
    a. The fourth Gospel of John contains phrases and expressions found in the Dead Sea Scrolls.
    b. The manner of thinking and the literary style of the Gospel and Epistles of John seem to be similar to those of the Qumran texts.
2. Principles of dualism and antithesis of light and dark, are evidenced in both writings.
    a. For John, the light of the world has appeared and the victory over darkness is won.
    b. Both Qumran and John recognize that without God nothing was made. There is a verbal parallel between the *Manual of Discipline* and John 1 : 3 (although this does not necessarily indicate a direct connection).

c. Qumran especially stressed that God created the two spirits of light and darkness.
3. On predestination John differed from the sect.
   a. John emphasized faith as a decision by which men determine their own judgment.
   b. Determinism was stronger in Qumran thought. Human will was negated and the omnipotence of God was asserted: that man can look only to God's grace and will for predestination.
4. For the Qumran sect the Messiah's coming was imminent whereas for John the "visitation" had taken place: the Messiah was already there and the Spirit was abroad (Luke 1 : 58, John 1 : 32-33). John's mission was to designate Jesus as being the realization of the expected event.
5. Strong parallels exist between John and the Qumran sect.
   a. One of the key words in both the Fourth Gospel and the Qumran writings is the word *truth*.
   b. In both we have the concept of the eternal life as a present possession of the believers.

B. *Jesus and the Qumran sect*

1. Possibly there was contact between Jesus and the sect.
   a. Qumran is only a few miles from familiar places in the life of Jesus —Jericho, Bethlehem, and Jerusalem.
   b. Edmund Wilson suggests that the unknown years in the life of Jesus (ages 12-30) might have been spent with the sect, but there is no reference to this in the texts.
2. There is a contrast between Jesus and the Teacher of Righteousness and the Qumran Messianic idea.
   a. In the New Testament we have the idea of the pre-existence of Christ before his life on earth. In the Qumran texts there is no hint of the pre-existence of the Teacher of Righteousness or of the Messiah.
   b. There is nowhere any suggestion of the miraculous in the death of the Teacher of Righteousness.
      (1) The New Testament portrays Christ as suffering for the sins of others. No such meaning is ascribed to the death of the Teacher of Righteousness.
      (2) The Teacher's death is left obscure in the Qumran texts. The story of Jesus' death and resurrection is told many times in the New Testament.

c. The New Testament and the Qumran writings reveal differing Messianic expectations.
   (1) The Qumran sect expected two or three Messiahs. If the Teacher of Righteousness was expected to come again, it would be as one of two or three Messiahs and not as *the* Messiah (See below F 2).
   (2) In the New Testament Christ comes again as the only Messiah and His coming is the culmination of all hopes for the early Christians.
   (3) The term which Jesus used most commonly in reference to himself—"the son of man"—is one that does not occur at all in Qumran literature as a Messianic designation.
d. There is no indication that the Teacher of Righteousness was considered divine in any sense—he is never called Messiah, Son of Man, or Son of God, and he is never called Lord.
e. Relatively few of the texts refer to the Teacher of Righteousness whereas it would be impossible to describe primitive Christianity without naming Christ.
f. We know more about Jesus than about the Teacher of Righteousness, but the lives of the two figures seem to have little in common.
   (1) The Qumran sect was ascetic; Jesus was not.
   (2) The Qumran sect was an exclusive community, whereas Jesus lived and went among the common men.
   (3) Jesus lived mostly in Nazareth and his disciples did not resemble the strict organization of life at Qumran.
   (4) The Qumran sect members were strict legalists. Jesus went back to first principles. For example, Jesus would say about the Sabbath that the Sabbath was made for man and not man for the Sabbath. The Qumran sect would not agree.
   (5) The Qumran sect placed a great deal of emphasis on rituals, placed importance on times and seasons, exalted the dignity and prerogatives of the priests, and looked forward to the resumption of sacrificial cults. There is little indication of any of this in the teachings of Jesus.
g. The closest resemblance between Jesus and the sect is in the degree to which their thinking was dominated by the conception of a cosmic struggle between good and evil, and their sense that a decisive crisis in this conflict was at hand.

C. *Other New Testament writings and the writings of the Qumran sect*

1. Several scholars have seen connections between the Epistles to the Hebrews and the Dead Sea Scrolls. It is possible that the use of the Old Testament in this letter is much more like that in the Qumran commentaries than that in the Gospel of Matthew.
2. Gaster points out several expressions in the Epistles of James which seem to him to be the echoes of the language of the Dead Sea Scrolls, but there is not necessarily a direct connection between the two.
3. Minor parallels in terminology have been seen in other books of the New Testament.
   a. The explanation in II Peter 3 for the delay in Christ's return and the final judgment recall to some scholars the effort of the *Habakkuk Commentary* to meet the same difficulty.
   b. The idea of the destruction of the world by fire expressed in the same chapter also appears in the Dead Sea Scrolls.
4. In the Revelation of John there are points of similarity with the Qumran texts.
   a. We find some of the Old Testament passages quoted or echoed in Revelation and in the *Manual of Discipline* and the *Damascus Document*.
   b. The most remarkable parallel is the symbol of the woman giving birth to the child in Revelation 12 : 1-6, which is similar to 1QH iii. The force of the parallel has to do with the birth of the Messiah.
   c. The war in Revelation, in which Michael and other angels take part, has a remote relation to ideas in the *War Scroll*—both draw on the Old Testament idea of an eschatological warfare, though there is no suggestion in Revelation that the saints on earth are to be armed in physical combat with the Sons of Darkness.
   d. Both drew heavily on earlier biblical apocalyptic literature, as well as on common sources in nonbiblical writings.
   e. Both recognized a season when God would allow evil to run rampant upon the earth and a time when He would utterly destroy that evil.

D. *Parallels between Christianity and Qumran life and doctrines*

1. Elements of the organization of the sect have parallels in the early Christian church.
   a. The Qumran communal meal is often likened to the Last Supper. Milik feels that the Qumran sacred meal is connected with what we learn from Paul and the *Didache* about the ordinances for liturgical gatherings (the *eucharist* and the *agapê*).

b. Both groups seem to have sat at meetings and to have spoken in turn according to rank. Also both groups were organized into companies and ranks.
c. Parallels have been made between the authority of the leaders of each group within the Qumran sect and the later authority of the Christian bishops.
d. Both groups held the eschatological concept of the true Israel as ruled by twelve leaders, and we find that Christ established a group of twelve Apostles, while at the head of the Qumran community there was a council of twelve members and three priests. We do not know if the three priests were higher in authority than the twelve, but if so the resemblance would be even more striking because among the twelve Apostles there was a privileged group of three—Peter, James, and John.

2. There are other parallels between the two.
   a. Both groups faced the prospect of persecution.
   b. Both held similar views on the importance of the Book of Isaiah and other canonical writings in Hebrew (especially Psalms and Deuteronomy).
   c. Both believed that they were living in the last days of the world, and each believed it was the community of the elect.
   d. Both groups believed that man is a sinner who can be saved only through the grace of God.
   e. Both believed that they were interpreting the law through a new direct revelation.
   f. The two groups believed that the spirits of good and evil are engaged in a struggle both in the cosmos and in the soul of each man, and in both systems the believer shared already in the life of the angels.
   g. Both groups had a deep sense of personal devotion to God as exemplified for the Qumran sect in the *Thanksgiving Hymns*.
   h. The Sovereignty of God was upheld by both groups.
      (1) The belief in God's sovereignty was a major aspect of Qumran doctrine. God, they believed, was the maker of all things, the giver of all gifts, and the director of the destinies of men. God was at the very center of life and history. The prologue to the Fourth Gospel also states that the word of God was the creator of all things and that without this word nothing was made.
      (2) Both the Christians and the Essenes were rooted in the Scriptures and hence emphasized the sovereign power of God.

Expressions concerning the sovereignty of God as they appeared among the Qumran sect and the Christians are but variant developments of a major theme of Old Testament religion. Both communities undoubtedly drew from the same source, with neither being directly dependent upon the other.

E. *Similarities overemphasized*

1. Some scholars feel that there is no need to suppose the early Church borrowed material from the sect; both groups of writings reflect ideas current at the time and for some time.
   a. Some of the parallels are only superficial and others decrease upon a closer investigation of both groups of writings.
   b. In addition, some of the ideas and practices which seem similar and which Christianity seems to have borrowed from the sect often change within the context of Christian doctrine and organization.
2. Many scholars feel the material is simply a further illustration of the Jewish background of Christianity of which New Testament scholars have always been aware.
   a. As you have seen and will see below, there are great differences between the ideas of the sect and the early Christians.
   b. Any comparison of first-century Judaism with Christianity would produce similarities, as the latter emerged from the midst of Judaism.
   c. There is no proof that John the Baptist, Paul, or Jesus were ever members of the sect or were influenced more by Qumran than by other Jewish sects.

F. *Contrasts between the sect and Christianity*

1. The Church and the Qumran community lived in the expectation that the Age would soon end, ushering in the Kingdom of God with power. However, the Qumran community was almost all expectancy and for them the New Age was coming sometime in the indeterminate future. Paul and others in the early Church anticipated the glorious fulfillment of the Kingdom at any moment.
   a. The Christians expected Jesus, who had ascended from the earth, to return in "clouds of glory" and establish the New Israel forever.
   b. The Qumran sect looked for the advent of a Messiah whose presence would beget the same result, but their expectations were not embodied in a specific figure who had lived amongst them. There is absolutely no evidence that the Teacher of Righteousness

was the Messiah who had been put to death, had risen, and would return in glory. The Qumran sect was looking for the first coming of a Messiah with the advent of the New Age.
   c. An air of expectancy seems to have been part of the attitude in many religious sects of the day, both Christian and Jewish. Here again the Qumran sect and the Church are but two pieces in the pattern of the times.
2. There is a difference in the concept of the Messianic figure.
   a. The Messiah is a single figure for the Christians, whereas for the Qumran sect the Messiah is embodied in two, or possibly three, figures.
   b. The Qumran sect expected the Messiah to restore the political kingdom of Israel. Jesus rejected the idea of such a Messiah and the concept of such a warfare.
   c. In Jewish tradition the Messiah is not a divine being—simply the finest of the human race, the chosen of his nation.
3. The Qumran sect may have hoped for resurrection; for the Christians it was a fact.
4. The Dead Sea Scrolls veil dates and persons. The Gospels are as explicit as possible.
5. Salvation by faith in the Teacher of Righteousness had a completely different meaning from what was described by salvation through faith in Jesus Christ.
   a. The Teacher of Righteousness taught that salvation came by adherence to the Law in a law community. Keeping apart from the world, swearing allegiance to the law of Moses, participating in the life and knowledge of the community—these were the means of salvation. Faith in the Teacher of Righteousness meant acceptance of what he stood for and adherence to the principles which he laid down as the true ways.
   b. For the Christians, salvation was to be achieved through faith in the resurrected Lord whom God sent to redeem the world. Jesus enunciated a broad motivational base for the good life rather than a particularistic interpretation of the Law, and salvation for Paul resulted when a man put his trust in the work which Christ accomplished in the death-resurrection event.
6. Qumran teaches to hate those outside the sect, whereas Christianity's special mission is love of all fellow men.
7. A world vision was foreign to the sect. Christ, on the other hand, was called the "Redeemer of the world."

8. There were differences between the way of life of the Qumran sect and that of Jesus, John, and the Disciples:
   a. Qumran's exclusiveness versus Jesus' emphasis on going out among the common men.
   b. The rite of baptism for the sect was a daily practice, self-administered, whose purpose was to maintain ritual purity. For John, and the Christian, it was a personal initiatory act.
   c. Emphasis on ritual and the importance of the priests in the Qumran community versus a nonemphasis in the New Testament.
   d. Emphasis on the letter of the Law in the Qumran community versus Jesus' emphasis on the primacy of charity over strict observance of the Law (Matthew 12 : 1, 7).
   e. Emphasis at Qumran on legal purity, particularly in regard to meals, versus Jesus' breaking bread with publicans and sinners. (Luke 7 : 39 relates the story of Christ's dining at the house of Simon the Pharisee and of Magdalene's approaching him.) By contrast, in the Qumran community to be admitted to the communal meals, one first had to go through a novitiate lasting for two years; even then each meal was to be preceded by a ritual ablution in pools that have been discovered, and by a change of clothing.

G. *General inferences*

1. The tradition behind the Gospels and the Epistles seems to be related to Qumran thought, but it is a thought taken up and radically reinterpreted in the light of Jesus.
2. It is true that there are links of ideas and practice between the sect of the scrolls and the early Church, but it is becoming clear that Christianity took ideas and practices already current.
3. It is now certain that the sect of the scrolls was a far less dynamic group than the Church of the New Testament. The sect's expressions may have been taken up but they have been invested with a new and deeper meaning and content.
4. The paramount importance of the scrolls to New Testament studies is that they add to our knowledge and understanding of the immediate pre-Christian era and give us a more precise insight into the life and faith of one of the sects of the time.

Topics for Study and Discussion

A. Discuss the relationship of the Qumran sect and the early Christians as shown in the literature of the two groups. Compare ideas and practices.

B. Discuss the possible contact between John the Baptist and the Qumran sect.

C. Discuss the parallels and contrasts between New Testament writings and those of Qumran.

D. Discuss the significance of the scrolls to New Testament studies and to the background of Christianity.

XX

DISCOVERIES PERTAINING TO BAR KOCHBA'S REVOLT

The Jewish revolt against Rome in A.D. 132-135 was not recorded by any second-century historian, and yet it was an extremely interesting and important event in Jewish history. It was the last fight for Jewish independence that took place in Palestine until the recent War of Independence in 1947-1948. The only information we had until now about the revolt and its leader Simeon Bar Kochba was the information given us in the Talmud, and it is possible that much of what is legend has been woven in with the facts.

In 1951 and 1952 the first actual physical evidence of the revolt was found. The evidence consisted of several bundles of papyrus and leather which contained contracts and documents dating from about A.D. 132. Especially interesting was the discovery of two letters sent by Simeon Bar Kochba, one of which is believed to have been written in his hand and to contain his signature. In 1953 a letter sent to Bar Kochba was found. All these discoveries were made in the Wadi Murabbaat caves in Jordan, about 18 kilometers (some 10 miles) south of Qumran, where the first Dead Sea Scrolls were discovered in 1947. (See Unit 5, above.) Some of the drama of the discovery of the documents from the period of the second revolt was lost because the major involvement by the public and scholars was still with the Qumran Dead Sea Scrolls, and in 1951 and 1952 important discoveries were still being made in the Qumran area.

After the discovery and excavation of the Murabbaat caves, the area south of Qumran and further inland near Ein Gedi was explored further. Expeditions were made to this area in 1953, 1955, 1956, 1960 and 1961, in which the archaeologist uncovered numerous manuscripts, tools, household articles, war articles, and many skeletons dating from the period of the Jewish revolt against Rome. The finds in 1960 and in 1961 were the first manuscripts from the first century to be uncovered in the Israeli part of the Judean desert. The 1960 expedition yielded fifteen letters written to or from Bar Kochba (second century A.D.), as well as two parchment fragments from Exodus which were part of texts inserted in phylacteries and dated from the first century. The expedition in 1961 yielded a great deal of material. A waterskin cache was found containing thirty-six letters and documents on papyri. In another leather pouch, five papyri documents were also found. In the 1960 and 1961 expeditions some sixty-five papyri and parchment documents were found. Although it would be some time before the contents of all the documents could be deciphered, there was no doubt that they contained some of Bar Kochba's orders, his activities, the life of the time, and some history of the revolt. So the material found will shed much light on what has hitherto been obscure.

RECOMMENDED READING

The discoveries relating to the period of Bar Kochba discussed in this unit and the two following units have been made mainly in 1960 and 1961. Only articles and pamphlets have so far been published on the subject. For this reason, unusually detailed outlines are provided in these units.

However, it is strongly recommended that you read at least one of the following articles by Yadin. The article in the *Atlantic Monthly* should be available at your local library.

Yadin, Y., "The Secrets in the Cliffs. The Discovery of the Bar-Kochba Letters," *Atlantic Monthly*, November, 1961, pages 129-135

"Cache in a Cave," *Life*, May 26, 1961 (for pictures)

Yadin, Y., "New Discoveries in the Judean Desert," *The Biblical Archaeologist*, Vol. XXIV, May, 1961, and September, 1961

The Israel Exploration Journal, Vol. XI, 1961, is entirely devoted to this discovery.

If you can read Hebrew, you are strongly advised to read *Mahanayim*, edited by I. Alfasi, August, 1961.

You should also read the articles on Bar Kochba in one of the encyclopedias, preferably the *Jewish Encyclopedia*, the *Universal Jewish Encyclopedia*, or the *Encyclopedia Britannica*.

HISTORICAL BACKGROUND OF THE BAR KOCHBA REVOLT

A. The basic causes of the uprising of the Jewish people led by Bar Kochba against the Romans in A.D. 132 can be easily surmised.
   1. Roman rule was harsh and oppressive and Judea's poverty made the severe burdens imposed on the people even more unendurable.
   2. The unshakeable faith of the people in a speedy, miraculous deliverance and the certainty of a life hereafter robbed war of its terrors. Such a situation needed but a spark and a capable leader to bring about an inevitable explosion.

3. Strangely enough, the Roman Emperor Hadrian began his reign with the best intentions towards the Jews, granting them various concessions and even promising to permit the rebuilding of the Temple which had been destroyed by the Romans in A.D. 70.
4. Influenced however, we are told, by Samaritans who always regarded the Temple of Jerusalem with disfavor, Hadrian decided not to implement his promise. A few years later the prohibition of circumcision caused relations between Jews and Romans to become severely strained until they reached the breaking point with Hadrian's decision to rebuild Jerusalem as a heathen city to be renamed *Aelia Capitolina*.

B. The leader of the revolt was Simeon Bar Kochba, whose real name we learn from the new letters was Simeon ben Kosiba. Nothing is known about his antecedents.

C. He was proclaimed Messianic King by Rabbi Akiba and was henceforth called Bar Kochba ("Son of a Star"), no doubt with reference to Numbers 24 : 17—"There shall step forth a star out of Jacob."

D. Not all the rabbis shared Rabbi Akiba's enthusiasm towards Bar Kochba. Rabbi Jonathan ben Tortha told him: "Akiba, grass will grow on your cheeks and the Messiah will still not have come."

E. Rabbi Akiba's role in the revolt is somewhat obscure. It has been surmised that his numerous journeys abroad were designed to gain support for the projected uprising. There is, however, no substantial evidence for this view. If it were true, Rabbi Akiba would undoubtedly have been put to death by the Romans, who employed large numbers of spies. In fact, Rabbi Akiba was imprisoned and subsequently executed for an entirely different offence—teaching in public—which was prohibited by the Romans after the suppression of the rebellion.

F. In its early stages the uprising was completely successful.
1. Romans were driven out of the whole of Judea.
2. Jerusalem was captured.
3. The sacrificial cult was apparently restored.
4. The "Freedom of Israel" was officially proclaimed, and Jewish coins were once again struck.

G. In 133 the Romans counterattacked with an army of thirty-five thousand under Hadrian and the commander Julius Severus. Talmudic extracts suggest that they first entered Galilee, then fought for the valley of Jezreel, Ephraim, and the Judean hills, eventually retaking Jerusalem. In 134-135 the Romans invaded Bar Kochba's last stronghold, Bethar, and gradually reduced the remaining hill and cave strongholds.

H. Bethar fell to the Romans soon after, either through Samaritan treachery or through the failure of the water supply, as archaeological evidence tends to show. Bar Kochba was killed, reportedly by a poisonous snake, though a Samaritan claimed to have slain him. Virtually the whole population of Bethar was slaughtered, including school children who, according to an eyewitness account, were wrapped in their study scrolls and burned to death.

I. Records speak of the destruction of 50 fortresses and 985 villages during the war, and of 580,000 Jewish casualties besides those who died of hunger and disease.

J. As a result of the revolt, Judea fell into desolation, its population was annihilated, and Jerusalem was turned into a heathen city barred to Jews.

DISCOVERIES PERTAINING TO THE SECOND JEWISH REVOLT
—A.D. 132-135

A. *Early discoveries*

1. The first discoveries were made in 1950 by the Bedouins of the Ta'amireh tribe.
2. In 1951 they brought to Jerusalem a group of manuscripts they had found the preceding summer in caves in the Wadi Murabbaat. In addition they brought other fragments which were described by scholars as coming from an "unknown source." It is now known that the material which was announced as coming from this unidentified source did in fact come from a cave north of Masada in Israeli territory. It was later found that most of the documents from Wadi Murabbaat and the "unknown area" dated from the era of the second revolt.
3. On the basis of the information given by the Bedouins, Father R. de Vaux and G. L. Harding, two archaeologists who had been working with the Dead Sea Scrolls from the very beginning, excavated the Wadi Murabbaat area in 1952.
4. Wadi Murabbaat can be described as follows:
a. It rarely figures on Palestinian maps.

b. It is the name given to a section of the great Wadi which begins south of Bethlehem, where it is called Wadi Taamre, and falls into the Dead Sea some 8 miles south of Ein Gedi, under the name of Wadi Daraje.
c. The Wadi Murabbaat caves are situated 25 kilometers east of Jerusalem (about 15 miles) and 18 kilometers south of Qumran (about 10 miles).
d. The Wadi Murabbaat caves are situated at sea level or above, while the Qumran caves are situated below sea level.
e. The caves are all difficult of access.

5. Letters were found in Wadi Murabbaat pertaining to the second Jewish revolt. (See also Unit 5 for other finds in this area.)
   a. In 1952 two letters were found adressed by Simeon ben Kosiba to Yeshua ben Galgola.
   b. In 1953 a letter was found that was written to Bar Kochba from two officials of a Jewish community.
   c. A letter addressed to Yeshua ben Galgola was found. It was written by several leaders of the community in a village called Beth Mashko, and ben Galgola is addressed as the Head of the Camp, that is, commander of the army.
   d. Other fragments were found coming from the period of the revolt —documents dealing with real estate transactions, a bill of divorce, and contracts concerning the renting of fields and guaranteed by the authority of Bar Kochba. These finds are discussed in Unit 5. Many of the documents found there have been published in *Discoveries in the Judean Desert*, Volume II (Oxford University Press). This unit discusses only the Bar Kochba letters found at Murabbaat.

6. Description of letter addressed to ben Galgola (or ben Gilgula) from the leaders of the community of Beth Mashko.
   a. The following is a translation of this letter:
   "From the headmen of Beth Mashko, from Yeshua and from Elaazar to Yeshua ben Gilgula, chief of the encampment, greeting: That it be known to thee that (as for) the cow which Joseph ben Ariston is taking from Jacob ben Judah, that Beth Mashko certifies it that she is his by purchase. And also, if it were not that the Gentiles are approaching us, then I would go up. So disperse. And I have advised thee concerning this, that it may not be said (it is) because of disrespect (that I have not gone up to thee). May I fare well, and the House of Israel.

Yeshua ben Elaazar wrote it. Elaazar ben Joseph wrote it. Jacob ben Judah, concerning its essence, Saul ben Elaazar witness, Joseph ben Joseph, witness, Jacob ben Joseph, attestant".

b. Some scholars feel that the main problem in the interpretation of this document is to account for the dual character of it contents: it is simultaneously a legal attestation and a message. Isaac Rabinowitz suggests that the problem is soluble on the basis of such a reconstruction of the immediate context as follows:

"Joseph ben Ariston has bought a cow at Beth Mashko from Jacob ben Judah and is taking her home with him. As his homeward journey will take him past the military installation of which Yeshua ben Gilgula is the commanding officer, he is asked to take a message to this officer from one of the headmen of Beth Mashko. Joseph is reluctant: he fears that Yeshua may confiscate his cow on the pretext that she is not legally his. His reluctance is overcome when the headman causes his own message to be prefaced by a certification of Joseph's legal ownership of the cow, properly endorsed, witnessed and attested, and Joseph accordingly delivers the document to Yeshua ben Gilgula."

7. Description of letters relating to the Bar Kochba period that were found at Murabbaat:
   a. One of the letters addressed by Simeon Bar Kochba to Yeshua ben Galgola was probably written in his own hand, as there is a resemblance between the script in which the text is written and that of the signature. The letter is signed "Simeon, son of Kosiba," as Bar Kochba was the name later adopted by him. (The significance of his name is discussed later.)
   b. The letter believed to have been signed by Bar Kochba runs as follows:

   "Simeon, son of Kosiba, to Joshua, son of Galgola, and to the men of Kephar Habbaruk, greetings. I take Heaven as witness against me (that) if anyone of the Galileans who are among you should be ill-treated, I will put fetters on your feet as I did to Ben-Aphlul. Signed, Simeon, son of Kosiba . . ."
   c. There are many lacunae in the letter. The second sentence has also been translated as follows, "I call Heaven to witness against me (that if) of the Galileans, who are at your place, there should be missing (even) a single one, I will put fetters on your feet, as Akiba (did) to Ben Aphlul."

d. There is speculation as to who the Galileans were—Christians, or members of a Galilean sect that lived in the neighborhood of Khirbet Qumran itself. Some scholars feel that the term Galileans seems to refer to Jewish refugees from Galilee rather than to Christians, who, according to St. Justin and Eusebius of Caesarea, were persecuted by Bar Kochba. The ill treatment the Galileans suffered can easily be explained on the assumption that, as the food shortage (of which other documents inform us) grew greater, non-Judeans received a biased treatment.
e. This document shows us that Bar Kochba was in the habit of issuing direct and short orders to his subcommanders; that he demanded absolute discipline and was ruthless towards those who disobeyed him.
f. If the letter can be translated as referring to Rabbi Akiba, it tells us of his active participation in the war. But this is doubtful.
g. This letter is one of the few first Hebrew letters in the original not written on ostraca. It acquaints us with the original form of the name on which the Bar Kochba of our sources is based. It confirms the fact that Simeon was his first name, which till now had only been inferred from the name Simeon on certain coins. The letter also shows that Hebrew was used, at least for official letters, and it demonstrates the influence of Aramaic on this Hebrew. Finally, the letter demonstrates the use of papyrus for letter writing in the second century and gives us an initial formula "From X to Y, Greeting" employed at the time; provides a specimen of a private—that is, nonscribal—hand of certain date; and of course provides a direct piece of contemporary evidence in connection with the revolt.

TOPICS FOR STUDY AND DISCUSSION

A. Discuss the historical background of the Bar Kochba revolt.
B. Discuss briefly the contents, importance, and date of the finds at Wadi Murabbaat. (You may also refer to Unit 5 before answering this question.)
C. Give the contents of the letters found in Wadi Murabbaat, and discuss their significance.

XXI

DISCOVERIES PERTANING TO BAR KOCHBA'S REVOLT (CONTINUED)

RECOMMENDED READING

See observations in "Required Reading" for Unit 20. The article published in the *Atlantic Monthly*, November, 1961, is highly recommended. (For study notes see the introduction to Unit 20).

BACKGROUND OF DISCOVERIES RELATING TO THE JEWISH REVOLT DURING THE 1960 EXPEDITION

A. There were suspicions that Jordanian Bedouins, lured by the fantastic sums paid by western scholars in the Old City for scroll fragments, had helped themselves to the contents of caves in Israel. These suspicions were strengthened when new finds of Hebrew documents were published in the Old City and their origin indicated as "an unknown area."

B. To check these suspicions, Y. Aharoni of the Hebrew university set out with a unit of paratroopers in 1953. The discoveries being made in Wadi Murabbaat were a further spur to this trip. The paratroopers discovered a number of caves at a height of over 1,000 feet above sea level. In these caves the they found bat droppings, cigarettes, and shreds of Bedouin clothing and firearms, in addition to some documents.

C. Anxious to forestall further depredations, and convinced that there were still many valuable documents in both unfound caves and caves that had been rifled by the Bedouins, the University was determined to make another expedition.

D. In 1955, Aharoni led a new expedition which discovered the "Cave of Fears" in the Hever Valley. This area was slightly south of the finds made at Wadi Murabbaat.

1. The expedition found dozens of well-preserved skeletons of adults and children. Other finds in this and nearby caves made it clear that this was one of the hideouts of the Bar Kochba rebels after they had been driven into the mountains by the Roman legions.

2. It turned out that many of the caves had been rifled by the Bedouins, but they had overlooked many items which the trained eye of the Israeli archaeologists managed to perceive.
3. The tools, inscriptions, and documents found in 1955 showed that rather than surrender to the legionaries who were besieging them, the rebels slowly starved to death in the caves after their supplies had given out. The Romans, on the other hand, were unable to storm the caves on the forbidding mountain slopes. The remains of the Roman siege camp were found on the top of the mountain.

E. In March, 1960, Y. Yadin, N. Avigad, Y. Aharoni, and P. Bar-Adon of the Hebrew University, under the sponsorship of the Hebrew University, the Israel Exploration Society, and the Government Antiquities Department, led an expedition to the Judean desert to follow up the expedition in 1955. Among other important items discovered were fifteen letters dispatched by Bar Kochba. The time elapsing between the two expeditions was so great because of the following:

1. The expedition is a difficult and expensive one, and the caves are extremely hard both to enter and to explore.
2. Once in the desert the expedition could progress only in four-wheel-drive jeeps at a top speed of about three miles per hour.
3. In the mountain area they could proceed only by foot.
4. The area is within easy shooting distance from Jordan, and no expedition is possible without an armed escort and helicopters ready to rush in reinforcements in case of emergency.
5. From the Israeli side the caves are accessible only with enormous difficulty. The area is crisscrossed with rugged mountains and fissured with steep precipices, where one false step can hurtle the unwary digger to a stony death hundreds of feet below. Most of the caves must be entered through small holes in almost vertical cliff faces. The digger must lower himself from the peak on a rope ladder, or from a helicopter, and slowly maneuver himself towards the cave, suspended in mid-air.

F. Details of the expedition in March, 1960
1. The expedition began on March 23 and lasted for two weeks.
2. The army provided the expedition with scouts and engineering and liaison units, in addition to equipment. To this force were added some tens of students and an equal number of kibbutz members, many of whom were veterans of other archeological expeditions.

3. The expedition worked in four teams under the leadership of Avigad, Aharoni, Bar-Adon, and Yadin, and each of the four teams carried on its work independently.
4. The area was divided into four strips running south to north, in accordance with the peculiar topographical conditions governing the terrain. The total area covered was about twenty miles as the crow flies.
5. Prior to the expedition, helicopters took pictures of the area, as the caves are in canyons as deep as 300 to 400 yards and the caves along the cliff faces are not visible to one standing on top of the canyons. From the films, the leaders of the expedition were able to decide which openings might be the mouths of caves.
6. The first cave explored by Yadin's group was the "Cave of the Vulture"[1] which disappointingly proved to contain nothing but a white sock that had the name on it of a member of Kibbutz Ein Gedi, and a Bedouin headcloth. This cave was extremely difficult to enter. A volunteer was lowered on a rope and directed by a man with a walkie-talkie situated below the cave. When the volunteer reached the mouth of the cave, he was suspended 300 yards above the ground. The face of the cliff was overhanging and there was no place for the man to put his feet—the only way he could enter the cave was to swing back and forth like a pendulum and at the right moment hurl himself inside.
7. While the Cave of the Vulture was being explored, another group had been exploring the large cave of Nahal Hever and had discovered a burial niche in the depths of the cave.
   a. This cave was situated in a steep, brittle slope that led down from the ruins of a Roman camp at the top of the cliff.
   b. The descent ended at a one-foot ledge to the right of which was a steep slope. This ledge ended some 50 feet below the cave. A rope ladder was constructed, and one end was fastened at the entrance to the cave by a member of the squad who had climbed up barefoot at the risk of life and limb.
8. The cave of Nahal Hever was difficult to explore for several reasons.
   a. The mouth of the cave consisted of a kind of corridor about 25 feet deep with a low roof. One then crawled through a narrow, black passageway to find the entrance to the first chamber covered by blocks of large stone, rising about 6 feet in height.

---

[1] So called because of the large nest of vultures at its entrance.

       After he had climbed them, the first chamber came into view.
- b. The first chamber was large, measuring about 40 by 30 yards and about 15 to 20 yards high at the center. Fallen stones covered the floor, and a huge mound of dirt rose in the center. From this chamber one again crawled through a winding passageway to reach the second hall, which resembled the first in size and appearance.
- c. The third, innermost chamber was the longest of all and was also covered by heavy stone falls. Breathing was extremely difficult here; apart from its depth—some 150 yards from the cave entrance—the chamber was infested with thousands of bats and their dung, and the stench was unbearable.

9. The burial niche was found in the third chamber of the Nahal Hever Cave.
    - a. The opening to the burial niche was completely concealed by a heavy fall of stones and one could get through only by crawling through a heavy slit. The man who discovered the burial niche went in alone and managed to squeeze through the slit.
    - b. From there he found it difficult to go forward, a problem made no easier by the sight in front of him. Along the right-hand wall of the chamber, which was several yards long and two yards wide, there was a collection of baskets overflowing with skulls. In the far corner was layer upon layer of large mats covering human bones. Between the mats and the bones were a great many fragments of colored cloth. In the center of the niche was another burial basket covered by large pieces of colored cloth.
    - c. Yadin speculates that these were the remains of Bar Kochba's fighters who had met their death in some unusual way, and their bones were later gathered up; perhaps those who came after could not distinguish between the various skeletons and put away the skulls and bones separately. Yadin also speculates that the fighters died from famine or thirst with the Roman soldiers besieging them above; but he says there can be no definite answer unless a clue is forthcoming from the examination of the skeletons, which is now going on under Dr. Nathan of the Hebrew University.
    - d. Thanks to the extreme dryness of the cave, the cloth was in an excellent state of preservation, as were the baskets and the mats.
10. Several days went by without any more discoveries and then one of the students found a small coin on the ground in front of the cave.

a. On one side was a palm tree and the inscription *Simeon.*
b. On the other side was a bunch of grapes and the words *Leherut Yerushalayim*, "for the freedom of Jerusalem."
c. It was easy to suppose that this coin from the Bar Kochba revolt had rolled to the foot of the cave when it fell from the hand of one of Bar Kochba's men as he climbed to the cave.
d. It was decided to clean the small entrance hall to the cave, and almost immediately the searchers found an almost intact arrow, its triangular metal head still imbedded in a wooden stick. This was probably one of the last arrows of Bar Kochba's men in this cave, and it was never used.

11. The coin and the arrow led the searchers to believe that other metal objects might still be buried in the cave, and the army offered the group a mine detector. The detector reacted in the first chamber, about 30 feet from the entrance, along the left wall.
    a. A woven basket, similar to the one in which the skulls were found, was imbedded in the earth at a depth of about 20 inches.
    b. The basket was lying on its side with both handles tied together with a rope.
    c. The members of the expedition removed large and small jugs, completely intact, some of them engraved near the handles with head of birds, others with palm-like motifs. They then removed three incense shovels, and at this point it was clear to them that the items in the bag were Roman cult objects.
    d. One shovel was large, one medium-sized, and the third small. Of special interest was the first shovel which had two goblets on either side of the handle; no shovel of this kind was known to the archaeologists from any other source. The goblets revealed the circles known to them from pictures of shovels that had been been found and which were inexplicable until now. Similar finds had been discovered in Pompeii.
    e. After the shovels they found a large pan—a fine work in craftsmanship. At the top of the handle was a ram's head. Together with the handle it resembled the Roman battering ram. In the center of the pan was a *bas relief* taken from Greek mythology, a kind of Triton, a figure half man and half fish. On the back of the dolphin was the figure of a woman: Thetis and the Triton.
    f. The next object found was a five-pronged key typical of the Roman period. From the bottom of the basket came two large bowls,

one of them unusually well preserved. On the handle of the second bowl was a rope woven from palm leaves. This was the rope that led out of the basket to tie the two handles of the container. The entire basket was packed beautifully.
12. The total cache found in the basket was twelve jugs, three incense shovels, a cult pan, bowls, and a key. Some of the figures of the Roman deities stamped on the handles appeared to have been deliberately rubbed out, and filed to a point where the faces were scratched. It was clear that the objects were originally Roman cult apparatus; and Yadin feels that they are possible booty taken by Bar Kochba's fighters from a Roman camp before they were forced to flee to the caves, since it is known that the Roman legions went into battle carrying all the equipment needed for ritual purposes, for sacrifices, and libations. It is possible that while the Bar Kochba men were fleeing, the articles were damaged, and it is also possible that they were used by Bar Kochba's men for their own purposes.
13. In the last few days of the expedition several of the most important finds were made in a cave known as "Cave of the Scrolls."
14. The first of these finds was a scroll fragment from the Book of Psalms. It was a small fragment made of nicely worked animal hide, but inferior in quality to parchment. The writing resembled that of all the scrolls found until then but it was very clear, and chapter 15 and the beginning of chapter 16 of Psalms could be discerned.
    a. Yadin, from the type of script employed, dated this manuscript to some sixty or seventy years before the Bar Kochba revolt—in other words, in the second half of the first century A.D. This would place it in time between the Qumran scrolls and the Bar Kochba period.
    b. Further work is necessary before more details can be ascertained; if the scroll had been found in its entirety, the work would be easier. It seems probable, however, that the remainder of the scroll was removed by Bedouins.
    c. J. T. Milik's list of documents and fragments now in Jordan includes "from an unknown source" fragments of the Book of Psalms from Chapters 7 to 31. Those fragments and the ones found by the 1960 Israeli expedition may possibly have formed the same original scroll.
15. In the innermost cave was one of the most valuable finds. A water bottle made of goatskin, which was torn in the middle, yielded many items.

a. First to be discovered were large bundles of colored raw wool wrapped in cloth and skeins of wool in many colors. Then followed strings of beads, a bone spoon, metal beads, and a spindle.
b. A number of large pieces of cloth together with some packages were also found. Each packet contained something different: a salt stone, a peppercorn, sea shells, and other materials which could not immediately be identified. It seemed quite clear that these were women's treasures that had been intentionally concealed at the farthest end of the cave.
c. A small package tied with cords was discovered next. It contained a collection of papyri tied with two cords, one thick and one thin. Between the papyri, slats of thin wood containing written inscriptions could be discerned. This small package proved to be one of the most startling discoveries of the expedition—fifteen letters from Bar Kochba.

G. The Bar Kochba letters found in the 1960 expedition are of the following nature:
1. All fifteen of the Bar Kochba letters found in 1960 have now been opened. Nine are in Aramaic, four in Hebrew, and two in Greek.
2. The letters are in varying states of preservation, some in extremely good condition.
3. One of the letters is inscribed on four wooden tablets; the rest are on papyrus.
4. The letter written on wood consists of orders given by Bar Kochba to his adjutants.
   a. Two of the four wooden tablets were entirely separate, and the other two were folded and joined at the edges. The four slats constitute one board about 17.5 centimeters wide and 7.5 centimeters long. (One inch = 2.54 centimeters.) It is covered by two columns of writing which read from right to left. Nine lines were preserved in the right column and eight in the left. The ink inscription was very clear except in a few places where the ink had not been properly absorbed because of knots in the wood.
   b. This is the first discovery in Israel of inscriptions on wood that date to this period, although wood as a writing material had been in widespread use in the ancient East due to the high cost of papyrus.
   c. It was obvious that the wooden slats had been too wide and too

long to be packed into one bundle with the papyrus. Therefore, before it was inserted, the board was cut down and across to make four slats, of which the lower two were still linked. At the right-hand corner, at the connecting point of the upper and lower slats, an "x" had been written in across the break by the person who folded the packet to indicate where the slats should be joined.

5. Contents of the letter on wood are as follows:
    a. The letter stated that it was from "Simeon ben Kosiba, *hannasi al Yisrael*" (Simeon Bar Kochba, prince, or president, over Israel). Although there are contracts which bear this title of Bar Kochba, this is the first time it had been found on a letter.
    b. The letter is an order from "Simeon ben Kosiba" addressed to "Yehonatan and Masabala" instructing them to confiscate wheat belonging to one Tahnun Bar Yishmael and to send it to him (Bar Kochba) under guard. He threatens punishment for non-fulfillment of the order.
    c. The two men must further deal with some people from the city of Teqoah (in the desert of Judea) in connection with the repair of houses, an injunction again followed by a warning lest the order not be carried out.
    d. The third appointed task is the most interesting. The two men are ordered to seize a certain Yeshua Bar Tadmoraya (Tadmor-Palmyra) and to send him to Bar Kochba under guard. Bar Kochba adds that they must not neglect to relieve their captive of his sword. The letter is signed Shmuel Bar Ami. As the signature is in a different handwriting from that employed in the body of the letter, we may assume that the signatory was not the writer of the letter but rather served as Bar Kochba's adjutant or secretary, dictating letters to a scribe on his chief's behalf.
6. James Biberkraut of the Hebrew University undertook the task of opening the papyri.
    a. To open, dry folded papyri must be softened by dampening the material and then spread out flat.
    b. The main difficulty with these papyri was that the wide pages had been folded several times lengthwise, and if they were still too long for the basket, were folded once crosswise.
    c. As the packet contained a large number of papyri, they were pressed together tightly and the folds were torn in place.
7. The first four papyri opened by Biberkraut turned out to be more letters from Bar Kochba. The first of them unfortunately was written

on papyrus that had been used before. The original writing had been rubbed out with a wet sponge and the surface used again. This custom, arising from the need to save papyrus, was widespread throughout the East during this period.

8. The third of the opened papyri, which measured about 8 by 12 centimeters, contained inscriptions written in a fine and still distinct hand. In it, Simeon commands Yehonatan Bar Baaya to do whatever Elisha commands him to do.
    a. It is not known yet who Elisha was. Simeon goes into no details, perhaps because the matter was secret.
    b. We do learn from this letter the nature of the chain of command by which Bar Kochba transmitted orders. It also contains a clear example of the way he formulated orders; they are marked by simplicity, directness, and brevity.

9. Other letters opened after the first four are these:
    a. One letter orders both Yehonatan and Masabala Bar Simeon to send him "immediately Elazar Bar Hittah," and to reap the benefits of the property of this man. This letter is signed "Simeon Bar Yehudah has written this"; since the handwriting of this Simeon Bar Yehudah is different from the body of the letter, we see that again a secretary of some kind dictated the letter to a scribe who wrote it. And again, as on the wooden block, the letter is written in the first person as though from Bar Kochba's hand.
    b. Another letter tells Yehonatan and Masabala "to harvest the ripened wheat of the winter" and to send it to a specified person.
    c. One of the letters, giving instructions to the same two men, confirms Yadin's belief that the letters belong to the period before the rebels took refuge in the caves, since it deals with such matters as crops, fields, and houses, as do most of the letters of this period—both those from Israel and from Jordan. This letter also establishes that rebel headquarters were at Ein Gedi, about 4 miles north of Nahal Hever where the letters were found. Ein Gedi is the oasis of the entire region of the Dead Sea. In this letter Bar Kochba writes:
        "You, Yehonatan Bar Baayah and Masabala Bar Simeon, and people of Ein Gedi, are sitting in comfort, eating and drinking the property of the house of Israel, and are not concerning yourselves about supplies for your fellow soldiers."
    Yadin assumes then that these letters were written while Yeho-

natan and Masabala ruled over an area which contained fields of wheat, and that upon taking refuge in the caves, brought with them this packet of documents containing the letters of their commander, Simeon Bar Kochba.

d. Another letter, giving instructions to the same two men in regard to the loading and unloading of supplies from a boat "at your port" also underlines the importance of Ein Gedi at that time. According to Yadin these supplies must have come from the southern shore of the Dead Sea or from one of the other fertile areas on its banks, and were to be transported from Ein Gedi overland to the troops, since there were roads from Ein Gedi inland.

(1) Those who lived there were apparently charged not only with strictly military duties but also with matters concerning supplies.

(2) This letter also mentions "the people of Tekoah," who, it is indicated, were creating difficulties for Bar Kochba by not complying with his orders. This would seem to bear out the belief that Tekoah (also mentioned in another letter and said to be situated some 11 miles southeast of Jerusalem) was within the jurisdiction of Yehonatan and Masabala (who were at Ein Gedi).

e. Another letter points to the existence at the time of a very learned man who was obviously held in high esteem, since he was called *rabenu* ("Our Master," par excellence). This title, when used together with a first name, was conferred only in very rare and exceptional cases.

(1) The *Rabenu Botniyah* mentioned in the letter has so far not been identified.

(2) This letter also refers to one Thirsus Bar Tinius, of whom Bar Kochba says, "keep him with you because we need him." The name is very probably that of a non-Jew, and gives support to the view of some historians that non-Jews joined Bar Kochba's forces because of the war booty they hoped to receive.

f. Another letter is addressed by Bar Kochba to Yehuda Bar Menasha, at Kiryat Arvayah. It states:

"I sent you two donkeys for you to dispatch with two men to Yehonatan Bar Baayah and Masabala Bar Simeon in order they might load and send to the camp in your direction palm branches (lulav) and citrons (etrog)... You send others from your end to collect myrtle and willow branches, and arrange for them to be tithed, and send them to camp. Peace be with you." The *lulav* and *etrog* are two items used in celebrating the holiday of Succot (Tabernacles).

(1) This letter, according to Yadin, shows clearly that Bar Kochba considered Yehonatan and Masabala to be "unreliable" and could not be depended upon to do the tithing (that is, apportioning a tenth of the harvest for the priests) correctly.

(2) It is also apparent that Bar Kochba at this stage was living in a camp. The "Kiryat Arvayah" mentioned does not appear in any of the known sources, but the theory has been advanced that it can be identified with the spring of Ein el-Arrub, just south of King Solomon's pools and south of Beitar where, tradition has it, Bar Kochba fell. From this it may be deduced that his camp was then possibly situated near Jerusalem.

(3) The dating of this letter dealing with the *lulav* and *etrog*, articles needed for the impending Festival of Succot, strongly suggests that all the letters were written in the year before the defeat of the Jewish rebels, that is, A.D. 134. Since according to tradition the war ended on the 9 of Ab in 135, and since Succot falls two months later, it would seem that this was the last Succot Festival to be celebrated in freedom by the rebels.

g. There are two letters in Greek, which were not written by Bar Kochba but were addressed to the same recipients as the letters mentioned above. Bar Kochba is mentioned in these letters, the first time that his name has been found anywhere in a Greek inscription. The Greek and Aramaic letters also show that even in the most nationalistic circles both languages were widely current.

h. All the letters in Hebrew are in different handwriting and bear the signature not of Bar Kochba but of other persons, indicating that they were dictated to a scribe.

10. These letters shed much light on what has hitherto been obscure.
   a. We learn that the real name of Bar Kochba was Simeon ben Kosiba and that he assumed the title of Nasi (prince or president).
   b. The letters confirm the rabbinical stories that Bar Kochba was a stern and ruthless commander.

c. We learn about some of the people involved in the revolt and also about what their life in Judea was like.
d. We learn about some of the villages involved and are given actual names and places which will help historians to reconstruct more of the story of the revolt.
e. Ein Gedi was one of the military and economic bastions of Bar Kochba.

H. Other discoveries in the same area in 1960 pertain to the revolt and to life from about A. D. 132-135.
1. In February, 1960, parchment scroll fragments written almost two thousand years ago—about the same time as the famous Dead Sea Scrolls—were found in two caves overlooking the Dead Sea, about 3 miles north of Massada. They are the first written documents dating from this period to be found in the Israeli part of the Judean desert.
   a. The discovery was made by a ten-day expedition headed by Aharoni.
   b. The caves in which the discoveries were made are extremely difficult of access and are believed to have served as a refuge for rebels following the defeat of the Bar Kochba revolt.
2. This expedition also brought back coins of this period and arrows used by the rebels against the Roman army.
3. The expedition discovered near the mouth of the Nahal Tseʻelim canyon a group of caves high upon a 300-meter cliff, barely accessible, which they succeeded in reaching with the aid of ropes. The larger among the caves revealed signs of fairly recent diggings by Bedouins, as well as various articles left behind by them which proved that they had come across the border.
4. The expedition found two small caves that had not been touched by the Bedouins. Operations were extremely difficult owing to the accumulation of the debris of centuries, the slightest disturbance touching off choking clouds of dust.
5. Among the first objects discovered were two small strips of parchment, which on closer examination proved to be the text of Exodus 13 : 1-10, 11-16. This is one of the biblical texts inserted in the "tefillin" (phylacteries) and the assumption that the strips formed part of a phylactery is strengthened by their size and shape. The script is similar to that of the famous Dead Sea writings and the writing was executed by an expert hand. (Tefillin are two small

leather cubicles containing biblical inscriptions from Exodus or Deuteronomy. The cubicles are attached to the arm and forehead during morning prayers.)
6. The discovery of a coin dating from the time of Emperor Trajan, who died in the year A.D. 117, points to the fact that the caves had been occupied by rebels.
7. This is substantiated by another important discovery, that of a store of eleven iron arrowheads, together with numerous wood and cane shafts, as well as sinews by which the heads were bound to the shafts.
   a. Wooden arrow-shafts of such antiquity had never been found before—hitherto only the arrowheads had been found.
   b. These articles have been preserved only because of the absolute dryness of the climate in this region.
8. Another important find was several sections of papyrus scroll, covered with square Hebrew writing of the same period. The scroll has been sent to an expert for treatment so that it can be opened and read. Apparently it is part of a letter or perhaps some deed or similar document.
9. Other objects found were remnants of linen and leather articles, wooden and clay utensils, and food remains, such as date and olive stones.
10. A few clay implements discovered in the caves date back to the Chalcolithic period, that is, the fourth millenium before the common era.
11. Two additional coins found in the same cave date back to the Emperor Severus Alexander, of the year A.D. 230. This gives ground to the assumption that rebel pockets continued to exist for almost a hundred years after the Bar Kochba revolt and that these caves served as headquarters and places of refuge for the Jewish insurgents.
12. The very factors that made it so difficult for the expedition to find the caves, including a tortuous ascent up a canyon overlooking the sea, would serve to make it attractive to refugees in hiding.
13. Many skeletons were found in this expedition, as well as in earlier (1955 and 1959) expeditions and in the latest one, 1961. The accepted belief that the rebels were observant Jews for the most part seems to be borne out by an examination of colored garments found on the skeletons of the warriors.
    a. An investigation by the Government Fiber and Forest Products Institute has revealed that the gowns were made entirely of woolen

material, instead of a mixture of wool and flax as was common in the east.
   b. They thus observed the religious precept forbidding a garment to be made of a combination of various materials, known as *sha'atnez*. (Leviticus 19 : 19).
14. Avigad's group, which explored the southern bank of Wadi Tse'elim and vicinity, found that only two of the caves had ever been inhabited during the Chalcolithic period some five thousand years ago. Avigad concluded that Bar Kochba's men, seeking a refuge in the area, kept their distance from the Roman fortress of Massada, 2 1/2 miles away.
15. Aharoni's group covering the northern part of the Wadi Tse'elim and Wadi Harduf found items from the Chalcolithic period.
16. Bar-Adon's group, exploring Wadi Mishmar and southern Wadi Hever, found Bar Kochba period relics of glass, pottery, remains of food, and a fragment of papyrus not yet opened but showing a few letters in Greek.

Topics for Study and Discussion

A. 1. Give some of the reasons why the Hebrew University, the Israel Exploration Society, and the Government Antiquities Department wanted to sponsor another expedition to the Dead Sea in 1960.
   2. Describe the initial difficulties the expedition faced, who participated, how the group was organized, and what area they covered.
B. Describe the Nahal Hever cave of the three chambers, the burial niche, the Roman cult vessels found in it, and the coin and arrow found outside.
C. Discuss the contents of the Bar Kochba letters.
   1. The language of the letters
   2. The wooden letter
   3. The two papyrus letters
   4. Some of the information we learn from these letters about Bar Kochba and the Jewish revolt
D. Evaluate the results and significance of the 1960 expedition.

XXII

DISCOVERIES PERTAINING TO BAR KOCHBA'S REVOLT (CONCLUDED)

RECOMMENDED READING

See observations in "Required Reading" for Unit 21. The article published in the *Atlantic Monthly* of November, 1961, is highly recommended.

DISCOVERIES OF MATERIALS RELATING TO THE JEWISH REVOLT IN THE 1961 EXPEDITION

A. The expedition in 1961 was lead by the same four archaeologists who headed the 1960 expedition, and they explored approximately the same area. This was the largest expedition so far carried out by the Israelis; some two hundred people including kibbutz members, students, journalists, and soldiers took part. A full account will of course have to wait until all, or at least most, of the items found have been studied more carefully. However, according to Yadin, the new discoveries constitute the largest collection of historic documents ever unearthed in the Holy Land.

1. As a result of the 1960 and 1961 expeditions, the world of Bar Kochba and his times is steadily being reconstructed and we are now able to catch vivid glimpses of everyday life both before and during the time the Bar Kochba rebels took refuge in the caves. It is now clear from the documents found that the revolt led by Bar Kochba lasted three and a half years.

2. It was reported that altogether sixty-four documents were found, written on both papyri and parchment. By May of 1961, ten documents had been opened. All ten deal with administrative and legal matters, indicating that Ein Gedi was an important administrative center for the region. These papyri belong to the period before the rebels entered the caves, and were most probably

taken there for safekeeping. The documents are carefully dated, according to Yadin, from A.D. 88 (biblical texts) to A.D. 135. Most of the documents related to a group of Judeans who fled to the caves after the Roman Emperor Hadrian crushed their revolt in A.D. 135. They were besieged by the Romans and eventually died of hunger, trapped in the caves.

3. It seems certain now that the cave in which the papyri were found both in 1960 and 1961 served as a refuge for the survivors of the Ein Gedi garrison (formerly a rebel stronghold) after it had been overpowered by the Romans.
   a. The rebels took with them to the cave their archives, the remnants of which were found, in addition to household articles, and some farming tools—although they were never to use them anymore.
   b. Most interesting was the discovery of women's cosmetics, a mirror, cotton, wool, and jewelry, in addition to a large collection of coins, beautifully fashioned vessels and many other utensils in bronze, glass, and wood.
4. The parchment documents were found in the same cave in which the fifteen Bar Kochba letters had been discovered in the previous expedition.
   a. Further search in that cave or another yielded skillfully made wooden tools, a lacquered box of trinkets, a quantity of household utensils in black wood and copper, and a hand mirror shaped like a table tennis paddle.
   b. Kitchen knives, undamaged women's sandals of fashionable design, a scythe, and five door keys, one of them, particularly large, were also found. It is now believed that these were the keys of the Ein Gedi fortress which the rebels had had to abandon.
   c. A further discovery was the first complete undamaged parchment scroll from the Roman period ever found in Israel. Only fragments had been found prior to this discovery.
5. The documents found by Yadin's group have been opened and deciphered.
   a. In a decorated leather bag were five papyri, all of which have been opened. Three of the documents, written in elegant Mishnaic Hebrew in a script far superior to that of any of the secular documents which have so far been found either in Israel or in Jordan, are contracts covering the leasing of land

in Ein Gedi by Bar Kochba through "Yehonatan ben Machnaim, administrator of Simeon Bar Kochba, prince over Israel in Ein Gedi."
b. These three documents are dated in the third year of Simeon ben Kosiba, prince over Israel, one "on the twenty-eighth of Marcheshvan" and another on the "second of Kislev." The lessees were residents of Ein Gedi or its environs.
c. The contracts detail the manner of payments in both Roman and Jewish money, in accordance with the formulas found in the Mishna ("sixteen dinars which are four selas"). All of them end with the signatures of those who are principally concerned, and of the witnesses. One of the witnesses is "Masabala ben Simeon," who is known from the Bar Kochba letters found in 1960.
d. The documents give place names such as Haluhit "which is in the coastal district, Aglatain" (on the eastern side of the Dead Sea), and shed light on the development of the spoken and written language used in the country at that period.
e. The other two documents in this bundle of five consist of a receipt for payment of a lease of land from Bar Kochba and a contract for the sale of property in Ein Gedi—also through the medium of Bar Kochba's administrator. Both of these are written in Aramaic.

6. The remaining four documents that have been deciphered as of May, 1961, are written in Greek and are being deciphered by H. Polotsky of the Hebrew University. These documents include a summary and signatures in Aramaic and date back to the last years before the revolt. It is possible to date them exactly since they mention the dates according to the year of the Emperor Hadrian's reign and note the day and the month according to both Roman and local usage.
   a. One of these documents is a marriage contract between members of families from Zoar at the south of the Dead Sea, and Ein Gedi. The name of the bride is Shlomzion. This is the first document of its kind to be found in such remarkably complete condition.
   b. Another document is a contract regarding the guardianship of the orphan Yeshua, the son of Babata, who was the daughter of Simeon. There were two guardians: one a Jew and the other a Nabatean. Each signed his name in his own

language. The contract is dated the ninth year of the Emperor Hadrian, that is, A.D. 125.
- c. The third document—a very large one—deals with the lease of a palm grove in Zoar by the widow Babata to Simeon ben Yeshua. The lessee undertakes to pay to the lessor forty-two talents of dates of a certain kind, and smaller amounts of other kinds; the balance he is to keep for himself "for labor and expenses." The details given establish the date of the contract as September 11, 130 (A.D.).
- d. The fourth document comprises a request from the widow Babata to one of the guardians of her son Yeshua that he give her the sum of six dinars that are due to her for three months. The date of the document is A.D. 132.

B. Skeletons, skulls, and human bones were found in all the caves.
In the cave explored by Aharoni, about forty skeletons were discovered, most of them of women and children, which seems to indicate that the majority of the men were killed in battle outside the caves. Many graves were revealed in certain of the caves, and in some cases wooden coffins. One coffin was of a type never before found in Israel. It was made of bone and red wood, and decorated in a geometric design.
- 1. A skeleton covered in canvas was found, the face still clearly defined, with some hairs left on the head. The way in which this skeleton was covered and preserved has led the Israeli archaeologists to assume that he was one of Bar Kochba's senior commanders, who was therefore given special burial.
- 2. It was not certain, and still may not be, whether all the skeletons found were those of Jewish warriors who took part in the Bar Kochba revolt. In the meantime, however, steps have been taken to honor these rebels. Ben-Gurion has given orders to Chief of Chaplains Shlomo Goren to arrange a proper burial with military honors in the cemetery on Mt. Herzl in Jerusalem for the remains of the rebels.
- 3. One report has it that Avigad and Aharoni together found about two hundred skulls.

C. The following articles from the Chalcolithic period were found in the 1961 expedition.
- 1. Avigad's group found remains of three periods of settlement in one of the caves, called the "cave of the well"—Chalcolithic,

biblical, and postbiblical. Among the finds were intact wooden bowls, a thin leather sheet apparently used for writing, and several sarcophagi.

2. Eight miles from Yadin's finds, Bar-Adon made a sensational find of objects from the Chalcolithic period. The objects date from about 3500 B.C. and predate Abraham by about fifteen hundred years. This find has been described by experts as of first-rate, worldwide importance, and as providing a link with the civilizations of the same period in the Caucasus and Anatolia.
3. Bar-Adon found 439 objects mainly of bronze and copper, including six beautifully fashioned ivories, six objects made of hematite, and one of limestone.
4. The objects range in size from 3 to 15 inches, and the collection is ornamented with geometric patterns, herringbone and rope designs, and beautifully sculpted ibexes and deer.
5. The artifacts are distinguished by extraordinary technical perfection and beauty, and reveal a very high standard of art and technology.
6. The study of the finds is not yet completed, and while certain of the objects can be identified—for example, mace-heads, chisels, axes, adzes, and hammers—many are of a kind never before found in Israel or in other countries of the Middle East, and even their purpose is unknown.
    a. It is possible that the hoard came from a temple or palace, and had either been hidden in the cave during a time of emergency or brought there as the spoils of battle.
    b. Bar-Adon feels the discovery will make a significant contribution to our knowledge of the history of human culture and art in ancient times. It will also cast new light on the history of life in this period, which constituted a transition period between the Stone Age and the Bronze Age and about which much is still obscure.
7. Also found by Bar-Adon's group was a quantity of cereals, from the Chalcolithic period. It is now being examined by David V. Zaitschek, a Hebrew University botanist interested in prehistoric and archaeological botany and especially in the origin of cultivated plants.
    a. Zaitschek has already arrived at the conclusion that the wheat found in the cave is the "missing link" between the wild two-

grained wheat (*Triticum dicoccides*) discovered in Israel by A. Aaronsohn fifty-five years ago and the primitive hard wheat cultivated by the Arabs in Israel for hundreds of years. This missing link, the *emer* wheat (*Triticum dicoccum* or cultivated two-grained glume wheat, the biblical "kussemet") has never before been found in Israel and was probably supplanted already in antiquity by the more successful naked, hard wheat species.

b. As a result, the history of the cultivated wheat species was not properly understood until now.

c. The recent finds include, for the first time, not carbonized remains of cereal grains such as were found in other excavations, but whole spikelets with perfectly preserved glumes and palae (husks and chaff), making it possible to determine the species and even the variety concerned. In the arid conditions of the desert caves only the color of the plant material underwent a change, so that further histological and microchemical investigations can now be carried out.

d. Other cereal finds, not less important for an understanding of the origin of cultivated plants, relate to spikelets of einkorn, a primitive cultivated wheat species found for the first time in Israel, and to spikelets (and even a whole spike) of cultivated barley, the ancestral wild species of which has even till now grown in the valley of the Judean desert.

8. Avigad found a plastered pool, 5 meters long and 1.20 meters wide, built at the entrance to one of the caves for the purpose of collecting water. The pool proves that the Bar Kochba followers prepared well ahead for the days of emergency and siege.

D. Here is a summary of finds and their importance:

1. Archaeologists have reconstructed the habitation of the Dead Sea caves explored in the 1960 and 1961 expeditions and in all the previous expeditions as follows:

   a. Many thousands of years ago in the area of the Dead Sea the earth convulsed. Cliffs 1,500 feet high suddenly appeared. Over the ages, abrasive rains trickling through the limestone scratched cracks into the rock. The cracks widened slowly into caves. By about 4000 B.C. an unknown people found these caves, lived in them and left behind traces of their habitation.

   b. King David (about 1000 B.C.), running away from jealous and

wrathful King Saul, saved his life by taking refuge in the roomy caves.
   c. Still later, at the northern end of the Dead Sea, not far from Jerusalem itself, an ascetic group of men believed to have been the Essenes, lived a monastic life and used the caves to deposit their writings. The discovery of these Dead Sea Scrolls in 1947 made archaeological history.
2. Now archaeologists have found a vast treasure trove indicating habitation of these caves from the period A.D. 132-135, the period of the Jewish revolt from Rome, and now for the first time we have actual documents from that period, whereas before we had many legends but a paucity of historical information.
   a. We know now for certain that the Emperor Hadrian's troops, under the leadership of Julius Severus, wiped out the Jewish rebels after the rebels had successfully captured about fifty towns from the Roman legions. Severus pushed the Jewish rebels into the last refuge among the caves of the Judean wilderness hard by the Dead Sea.
   b. The caves were well stocked with food and natural cisterns. The Romans, knowing this, sat down at either end of the valleys leading into and out of the cave areas and waited. Rather than surrender, the rebels stayed put and died of starvation. This uprising was the last major revolt by the Jews against an established authority throughout eighteen centuries until the Warsaw Ghetto revolt against the Nazis in 1943.
3. The Bar Kochba letters reveal much information.
   a. Eleven were decipherable and the letters were written in Hebrew, Aramaic, and Greek. This was the first real indication that all three languages were in common and equal use during that period.
   b. We learn from the letters that Bar Kochba's authority might have been a little weak in the provinces, and that he probably had his headquarters in the vicinity of Bethlehem. We also learn the importance of Ein Gedi as a port. Supplies must have come from the southern end of the Dead Sea or from the eastern bank to Ein Gedi on the western bank, then transferred inland to troops fighting the Romans.
   c. We learn of the religious fervor of the rebels—in their preparation for the holiday of Succot and in the fact that the garments found were made entirely of wool, since in strict Jewish ob-

servance it is forbidden to mix animal and vegetable fibers in a garment.
    d. We learn of a new and unknown figure in Jewish history, Botniya Bar Miasa, who is called *Rabenu*, a name given in existing sources only to Moses and Judah. Bar Miasa must have been a great spiritual leader, about whom all records have been lost.
    e. Yadin feels that the letters were written before the flight to the caves because some of them deal with the village of Teqoah, which at the time of the last stand in the caves was already in Roman hands. Also the fact that some of the letters concern grain harvest indicates that the Jews still possessed some land.
    f. The collector of the letters must have prized them highly, since he or she took the trouble of carrying them along on the flight to the caves and deposited them among the women's belongings where they were not likely to be found by Roman captors.
4. The documents give new information about Bar Kochba.
    a. The Greek spelling of his name is ben Kosiba, or Kozba.
    b. His existence is no longer in doubt. He was a terse, tough commander who gave his orders in a clear, simple, concise style. The documents establish the authenticity of Bar Kochba (hitherto believed to be a legendary figure in Jewish history), whose existence had been questioned.
    c. He was undoubtedly a pious man concerned with religious observance just as much as with his fight for independence against the Romans.
    d. He described himself as "Prince over all Israel."
    e. Bar Kochba would suffer no breach of discipline if he could prevent it; he gave orders for punishment and seizure of property of those not obeying his commands.
    f. The documents have established that the Bar Kochba rebellion was not just political; it was also religious.
5. The many household items (clothes, furniture, textiles, and cooking utensils), personal items, war items, and documents found give us much new and valuable information as to how the people lived in Palestine during the Bar Kochba revolt, some 1,800 years ago. This was a period of Jewish history which until now contained many gaps for the historian and the archaeologist.
6. The finds from the Chalcolithic period are unparalleled to a great extent and are extremely important. They will provide much in-

formation about the life of a people in that era that was unknown to us before.

TOPICS FOR STUDY AND DISCUSSION

A. Describe some of the items found in the caves in the 1961 expedition.
B. Describe the four documents written in Greek found in 1961.
C. Discuss the general significance of the Bar Kochba finds.
D. Describe some of the Hebrew papyrus documents found in the 1961 expedition.
E. Evaluate the importance of the Chalcolithic finds.

XXIII

THE TEMPLE SCROLL

INTRODUCTORY OBSERVATIONS

Any study of the Temple Scroll needs to be carried out in the context of the broader background of the Dead Sea Scrolls. There are substantial connections between the Temple Scroll and the Qumran community that produced the Dead Sea Scrolls, as will be outlined later in this chapter.

Generally speaking, the Temple Scroll and the Dead Sea Scrolls show the same priestly and ascetic view of life, as well as agreement in specific areas such as their use of the religious calendar. And like the Dead Sea Scrolls, the Temple Scroll is an important addition to our understanding of late Intertestamental history and Christian origins.

It is interesting that Yigael Yadin, who purchased the Temple Scroll during the Six Day War, is the son of the late E. L. Sukenik, who purchased three of the most important Dead Sea Scrolls twenty years earlier.

It is due to the dedicated effort of Yadin that the Temple Scroll has now been published in four volumes of careful photographic reproduction, translation, and research. This achievement is all the more remarkable in view of his ongoing academic and governmental responsibilities as Israel's deputy prime minister.

ACQUISITION OF THE SCROLL

In 1960 Yadin received a letter from a resident of Virginia, and then on September 16 of that year purchased from him a fragment of Psalm 16 from Cave Eleven of Qumran. In the course of several letters Yadin was told by this "Virginian" (whose identity is not known to this day) that he represented a man in Jerusalem who had access to a number of Dead Sea Scrolls and would sell them for $1 million each, for a total of $15 million.

It turned out later that there was only one scroll (the Temple Scroll), which the Jerusalem owner agreed to sell to Yadin for only $100,000.

Yadin was sent a portion of the Temple Scroll for verification. At that time no real confirmation could be made of its value because of the small size of the fragment and the short time available for inspection. Nevertheless, Yadin began to raise the $100,000 and hired a New York attorney, Barney Barnett, to continue negotiations.

The Virginian, however, backed away from his previous asking price, stating that he had other offers amounting to $1.25 million but would accept $750,000 from Yadin as a gesture of good will. Yadin refused, but later they both agreed to a six-page legal contract stipulating a selling price of $130,000, with $1,500 for travel expenses and $10,000 as a down payment for the Virginian.

Despite the legal contract, the Virginian sent Yadin a letter saying that the owner now demanded $200,000. Yadin refused, and the Virginian vanished with his $10,000 and traveling expenses.

For a while it seemed as if any chance of obtaining the scroll had vanished. But then came the Six Day War in 1967, and it suddenly occurred to Yadin that the scroll might now be within reach, since East Jerusalem along with other Arab areas was now under Israeli control.

This, in fact, did turn out to be the case, and the scroll's owner, after initially asking $1.25 million for it, finally parted with it for $105,000.

The owner had hidden the scroll in a shoe box under a tile floor and wrapped it in layers of paper, towels, and cellophane. Next to the shoe box was a cigar box filled with many fragments and wads of several columns which had fallen off the scroll.

Description and Unrolling of the Scroll

Yadin believes that keeping the Temple Scroll and its fragments in boxes under a tile floor contributed to the scroll's deterioration. Excessive humidity is very destructive to ancient materials such as parchment scrolls, and when the Temple Scroll was finally found, it was in various stages of humidity-related decomposition. The top of the scroll was affected the most, so that segments of it were completely lost or reduced, as Yadin says, to "melted chocolate." The lower part, however, was in relatively good condition and, on the whole, retrievable.

While the fragments found in the cigar box were eventually pieced together like a jigsaw puzzle (along with other fragments from the Rockefeller Museum), the real challenge was the restoration of the scroll itself. In addition to the damage at the top of the scroll, the retrievable lower parts did not unroll easily. Special techniques were necessary.

The first technique attempted was the usual practice of exposing a scroll to 75-percent humidity in order to soften the brittle parchment so that it can be unrolled. In the case of the Temple Scroll, the parchment was of extremely delicate gazelle skin less than 0.1 millimeter in thickness. Its length of 28 feet (the longest of the Dead Sea Scrolls) was rolled up tightly to a diameter of only 2 inches.

Exposing the scroll to humidity was not completely successful. The layers of parchment at times continued to stick to one another. In these cases Yadin and his associate, J. Shenhar, used a "shock treatment" in which the difficult sections were exposed to an extreme amount of humidity for a few minutes and then put into a freezer for about the same time.

Some sections, however, did not respond even to this shock treatment. Infrared, ultraviolet, and x-ray photography were used to read the contents of these undetachable sections.

In some cases, as the scroll was unrolled, the organic-ink letters from a section's layer would adhere to the back of the section against which it had been rolled. This would produce a reversed, mirrored image of the script. In these cases Yadin simply photographed the backs of the sections to which the ink letters had adhered and printed them in reverse.

The Temple Scroll, as mentioned previously, is the longest of the Dead Sea Scrolls at approximately 28 feet. It consists of nineteen sheets, each of which is 10 inches in height. They average 18 inches in width. Parts of sixty-six columns of text have been preserved. Most of the columns contain twenty-two lines, and perhaps 65 to 70 percent of the scroll is legible to the naked eye.

The scroll had been rolled from its end, so the beginning was on the outside. A part of this, then, was lost, although Yadin thinks that it was relatively little. He believes that none of the end was lost, since connected to it was a blank sheet, apparently marking the scroll's termination.

Authorship and Date of the Scroll

In Yadin's opinion, the style of writing or calligraphy in the Temple Scroll is Herodian and therefore indicates the scroll was composed at the latest in the second half of the first century B.C. or the first half of the first century A.D. He believes that there are good reasons for dating the original composition of the work at the end of the second century B.C.

It is doubtful that the original composition was much earlier than this. Although the author tried to follow a biblical style, his writing is beset with anachronisms and slips into late Hebrew and rabbinic style, vocabulary, and syntax.

An example of a slip into rabbinic vocabulary would be the author's reference to a pregnant woman as אשה מלאה ("a full woman"). This term is found only in rabbinic literature. The biblical term would be אשה הרה ("a pregnant woman").

An example of an anachronism would be the law of the King regarding hanging. Hanging was not practiced until later.

As to the author of the Temple Scroll, Yadin is convinced that he must have been a member of the Qumran community. This would further support a date of composition between the second half of the second century B.C., when the Qumran community first arose, and the end of the Second Temple period, when it was destroyed (along with the rest of Palestine) by the Romans.

As Yadin notes, there is ample proof of the author's connection to the Qumran community on the basis of paleography and spelling peculiarities as well as the author's support for the Qumran calendar and the rigorous Essene view of life. Both the author of the scroll and the Qumran community championed the imposition of the priestly rules for the Temple upon the city of Jerusalem and all Israel.

Their agreement in three cultic details is also interesting: they refrained from anointing themselves with oil, provided themselves an area outside of Jerusalem for disposing of their bodily waste, and celebrated an unknown feast called the Festival of New Oil.

Contents of the Scroll

A. *General contents*

The Temple Scroll deals basically with four groups of subjects: a large collection of Halakhot or religious rulings, relating especially to ritual cleanliness; the enumeration of sacrifices and offerings according to various festivals; a detailed description of the Temple; and the statutes of the King and the army.

One of the most striking aspects of the scroll is its apparent claim to be on the same level of authority as the Pentateuch itself. There seems to be no comparable example in the Qumran literature. The commandments of God, for example, are given in the first-person singular, and even in lengthy quotations from the Bible the author regularly changes third-person singulars to first-person singulars.

A very strong indication that the author wanted people to believe he was writing Holy Scripture is this use of the Tetragrammaton. The practice of that day was to avoid the Tetragrammaton if possible in non-biblical texts or to use only the paleo-Hebrew script in representing it. Only in a biblical text was the Tetragrammaton written in normal characters, but in the Temple Scroll this restraint is openly challenged. The author consistently writes the Tetragrammaton in the common script.

It is interesting to note that in his quotations of the Pentateuch the author sometimes follows Septugintal and even independent readings in addition to the Massoretic text.

B. *The Halakhot or religious rulings*

A basic characteristic of the Halakhot, or religious rulings, in the Temple Scroll is that they are grouped together topically from dispersed sources in the Pentateuch. Their most interesting feature, however, is the addition of laws not found in the Pentateuch, many of which appear to be of a polemical nature.

In some cases, for example, a law or practice in the Temple Scroll unknown to the Pentateuch can be found in the Mishna in a less severe form. This is especially true of rules of cleanness and uncleanness. An example would be the scroll's ruling that a pregnant woman with a dead embryo within her is unclean. The Mishna maintains that she is clean until the child comes forth.

Another example of strictness in ritual purity is in the limitation of one cemetery to every four cities. This apparently is to protect the land from defilement.

A special area of severe regulation in the Temple Scroll as compared to "normative Judaism" of that time is the legislation pertaining to activity within Jerusalem itself. An example of the author's rigorous viewpoint would be the prohibition of all sexual intercourse within the city. Anyone who had engaged in intercourse, or who had even experienced a nocturnal emission, had to purify himself for three days. Only then would he be allowed to enter Jerusalem's gates.

Other such regulations pertaining to activity within Jerusalem deal with the lepers and the maimed, and the nature of the vessels in which offerings were to be brought to the Temple; and there is even a law which bars from the city the hides of animals which have been slaughtered in an incorrect way.

Everything was to be strictly controlled by an ascetic male priesthood, a priesthood which firmly barred women from all sacred precincts.

One of the most interesting stipulations of the Temple Scroll is that public toilets were not to be allowed within the city but were to be placed about 1,500 yards northwest of the Temple. This particular location would place these facilities in a most inconspicuous position outside the walls and away from sacred areas—and in a favorable relationship to prevailing winds.

Perhaps the most interesting fact in this connection is that the Temple Scroll forbids the use of all public toilets on the Sabbath.

C. *Sacrifices, offerings, and festivals*

As mentioned previously, there are significant links between the Temple Scroll and the Qumran community in their strict priestly views of life. They both had definite views as to how sacrifices and festivals were to be carried out, and one of the most central concerns was for a faithful adherence to the proper calendar in celebrating these festivals.

It is almost an understatement to say that the choice of a calendar during the Second Temple period was a fundamental source of conflict between rival religious communities.

The Temple Scroll goes into great detail on the proper way to conduct various festivals and sacrifices on the basis of the calendar it shared with Qumran and other Essene groups. Several issues brought this calendar into conflict with almost all other rival groups.

First of all, in contrast to the somewhat irregular calendar of normative Judaism, the calendar of Qumran and the Temple Scroll had a substantially regular division of each month into 30 days with 1 extra day at the end of every three months, making a year of 364 days.

Secondly, the Temple Scroll introduced into this year two new festivals, the Festival of New Wine to be celebrated fifty days after the raising of the Omer (a ritual connected to Passover), and the Festival of New Oil to be celebrated in turn after another fifty days. This festival, as previously noted, is known to have been celebrated also in Qumran.

Finally, in addition to these differences, there was a variant interpretation of Leviticus 23 : 15-16, which states that Pentecost is to come fifty days after the "raising of the Omer," and that this ritual is supposed to occur on the "morrow after the Sabbath."

The key word here is "Sabbath." The Pharisees interpreted this "Sabbath" as the first day of Passover (i.e., simply a day of rest); other groups (such as the Sadducees, Boethusians, and Samaritans) interpreted it as the first Saturday after the beginning of Passover; but the

Temple Scroll and Qumran interpreted this "Sabbath" as the first Saturday after the end of the Festival of Unleavened Bread.

It is interesting to note that Easter is always on a Sunday. In this case the Christian church has been influenced by the calendar of Qumran and the Temple Scroll.

D. *The Temple*

Because almost half of the Temple Scroll deals with the building and furnishing of a Temple, Yadin first provisionally named it the "Temple Scroll," a name it has held since. The primary message of this large section is to command those who are faithful to God to build a proper Temple; it also provides detailed instructions on how to do this.

It is interesting that there are no instructions in the Old Testament on how the first temple was to be built. There is only the allusion in I Chronicles 28 : 11-19. In passing plans for the building of the temple on to Solomon, David notes that he had received these instructions in writing from the hand of God. Perhaps this account of a missing Torah on the temple may have prompted a desire on the part of the author of the Temple Scroll to "supply it."

The most interesting aspect of the section on the Temple's construction, however, is that its measurements do not correlate with descriptions of temples known from other sources. It differs from the first and second temples, Herod's temple, and Ezekiel's temple.

Perhaps the most significant fact historically is that the scroll's Temple differs from Herod's temple. The scroll's Temple was to be built in the present age rather than the eschatological future, so anyone accepting the authority of the scroll would have to oppose Herod's temple as a present offense against God himself. The Qumran community, of course, would welcome such an attitude.

The scroll calls for a rectangular main Temple building surrounded by three concentric square courtyards of about 250, 500, and 1,600 cubits each, the square shape being a symbol of perfection.

The middle and outer courts of the Temple were each to have twelve gates, three on each side, and each gate was to be named for one of the twelve tribes of Israel.

This is of interest because both in Ezekiel and in the New Testament Book of Revelation (chapter 21), gates are named for the twelve tribes, although these are the gates of Jerusalem itself and not of the Temple as in our scroll. That the gates were named after the tribes is significant. The whole apocalyptic literature and that of Qumran were occupied with the concept of uniting the twelve tribes of Israel as ordained by God.

An interesting aspect of the scroll's description of the Temple is its terminology. It is especially here that the scroll slips into terminology which indicates its origin in the later part of the Second Temple period (second and first centuries B.C.). Later terminology is used especially wherever the Bible lacks an architectural term; this terminology is most often supplied from vocabulary found only in the Mishna and Qumran literature.

E. *The statutes of the King and the army*

The last section of the scroll deals with the statutes of the King of Israel and, more specifically, his bodyguard and mobilization plans should the country be faced with external military threat.

On God's direct instruction, the scroll prescribes that the King's bodyguard should consist of twelve thousand men, one thousand from each tribe, soldiers who should be without blemish in their dedication to God and country. They were to protect the King from falling into the hands of the Gentiles.

Of an especially timely nature are the scroll's instructions for mobilization under a foreign military threat. Yadin notes that when he read this section immediately after the Six Day War, he "could not help remarking the parallel to actual phases of mobilization preceding the conflict."

The scroll states that as soon as the King becomes aware of a foreign threat, he is to mobilize a tenth of the nation's force. If a full-blown military confrontation is imminent, one-third of the force is to be called out while two-thirds protect the nation's frontiers and cities from attacking enemy bands. If the actual conflict is severe, the King is to mobilize half of the fighting force, but the other half is to remain in the cities to protect them.

Yadin notes that these rules realistically reflect the political and historical time in which they were written. They differ basically with the rules found in the Qumran document "War of the Sons of Light against the Sons of Darkness." This is because the Temple Scroll is dealing with a defensive war envisioned in the present era while the Qumran document is dealing with an offensive eschatological war.

The scroll places an interesting restriction on the King's married life: "From his father's house (the King) shall take unto himself a wife . . . and he shall not take upon her another wife, for she alone will be with him all the days of her life." This is the earliest prohibition of royal polygamy or divorce; Jewish kings were traditionally allowed up to eighteen wives.

The scroll also enjoins the King to appoint an advisory council of twelve priests, twelve lay leaders, and twelve priestly attendants. Israel was to be a country permeated with priestly influence, from the highest political decision-making to the control of even the types of animal hides allowed to enter Jerusalem.

The Scroll and Christianity

As with the other Dead Sea Scrolls, it is apparent that the Temple Scroll shows significant links between the Essenes and Christianity. Although some of the ideas which they both share, such as similar views on marriage and divorce, could be coincidental or transmitted through a third source, there is an indication of a more direct contact through John the Baptist, who lived within a few miles of Qumran.

At least one scholar believes that the Temple Scroll adds weight to the old argument that Jesus was strongly influenced by the Qumran community through John the Baptist or even through direct contact.

The majority of scroll experts, however, are cautious. Granted, there are similarities between the scrolls and early Christianity, perhaps even through direct contact in some cases, but the differences between the two are now even more obvious in the Temple Scroll.

For example, the Qumran sect was, if anything, hyperlegalistic. The Temple and sacrifices were central to the sect. Although they rejected the Temple worship in Jerusalem, they had no intention of abandoning this aspect of their faith. They awaited divine intervention to establish a new Temple in Jerusalem where their own priests would officiate.

The Temple Scroll makes clear for the first time that Qumran intended to build an earthly, not a heavenly, Temple. It suspended temple worship and sacrifice only temporarily, but Christianity made this suspension permanent on the basis of its own unique theological views.

As Yadin has pointed out, there seems to be a link between Christianity and Qumran on the issue of celibacy. But even here there are some biblical scholars who, while applauding Yadin's reconstruction of the second-century-B.C. text, still feel that a celibate priesthood arose from motives fundamentally different from those of the Essenes.

For example, Paul's motive for celibacy was to keep one ready for the work of the kingdom of God, whereas Qumran was extending the ritual purity required to every detail of the life of its community, including marital issues.

A religious aspect, however, which does form a fundamental link between early Christianity and the Qumran community and probably lies at the basis of much of their thinking was the feeling of being in an eschatological era.

Whatever the outcome of the ongoing debate on the relationship between the scrolls and Christianity, it is certainly true that the Temple Scroll will make a vital contribution in filling the gap between biblical and rabbinic Judaism. By shedding additional light on the development of sectarianism at the close of the pre-Christian era, it will further enlighten our knowledge of the background of Christianity.

XXIV

MASADA

Physical Characteristics of the Site

A. Masada is a large plateau on the western edge of the Dead Sea about two-thirds of the way down its coast.

Masada's eastern edge drops about 1,300 feet to the shore of the Dead Sea, and the western cliff dropping to the Judean desert is approximately 400 feet in height. The length of the plateau running north-south is about 1,900 feet and the breadth at its widest point is about 650 feet. It is roughly rhomboid in shape.

B. There are two ways of access to the top of Masada. One way is on the eastern side via the "snake path," which involves approximately one hour of climbing. The other is on the western side, and involves only about ten minutes of climbing along a path over a ramp which the Roman general Silva had constructed in assaulting Masada.

Silva's ramp did not reach quite to the top of the plateau, but engineers under Yigael Yadin erected a bridge over the remaining distance. It was this path which Yadin's expedition used to and from their campsite on the western side of Masada.

C. Masada, which is normally dry, at times during the winter can experience torrential rains and high winds. After one of these rains, the expedition witnessed, along with puddles of water in various places, flowers and other vegetation springing up almost immediately on the plateau.

This striking event gave some credibility to reports by Josephus, received with skepticism by some scholars, that a band of men who had sought refuge at Masada were dying of thirst when a rainstorm saved them and that Herod used the plateau for agriculture.

D. The plateau of Masada is not uniformly level, but there are hollows and mounds. The structures were consistently built on the higher ground.

Short History of the Site

A. During the years 36-30 B.C. Herod built up Masada into a formidable fortress. Josephus writes that Herod put a double casemate wall around the top, constructed a watercourse to catch the winter rains in a large number of cisterns he had hewn out of the rock, and also built a winter luxury palace hanging on a precipice on a northern shaded cliff and equipped with large storerooms, baths, and even a luxurious swimming pool.

B. In the beginning of the Jewish revolt of A.D. 66, a group of Zealots destroyed the Roman garrison at Masada and held it to A.D. 73, three years after the fall of Jerusalem.

For over two years, a force of less than one thousand used Masada as a base to harass the Romans, until Silva marched against Masada with the tenth legion, a force totaling five thousand soldiers and over nine thousand slaves and prisoners of war.

C. To take Masada, Silva established nine camps and with his huge force constructed a ramp of beaten earth and stones. Under covering fire from the top of a siege tower he had erected, he moved a battering ram up the ramp. Finally in April, A.D. 73, he succeeded in making a breach in the Zealots' fortifications at the top of Masada.

Silva planned a frontal attack on Masada for the following day.

D. During the night after the breach was made and before the Romans attacked, the Zealot leader, Eleazar ben Ya'ir, convinced the group that suicide was preferable to Roman capture.

E. According to Josephus, the deaths of all took place systematically by lot, except for two woman and five children who had escaped the notice of the leaders and lived to tell the story.

Excavation Under Yadin

A. Yadin, an archaeologist with a detective's flair, is a former Israeli chief of staff as well as an outstanding scholar. With this unique background Yadin was able to organize an excavation with military-like operations, using helicopters, mine detectors, walkie-talkies, and other such equipment.

B. The expedition, which lasted only eleven months, covered the two seasons of 1964 and 1965. Yadin used hundreds of volunteers who worked for no pay and yet labored with a dedication and devotion which no wages or money could buy. This enabled Yadin to run 23 two-week shifts throughout the two seasons of excavations, averaging three hundred workers each shift. The volunteers sifted 50,000 cubic yards of earth and accomplished what normally would have been the work of twenty-five archaeological seasons.

INSTALLATIONS AND ARTIFACTS FOUND

A. *The northern palace-villa*

Due to some inaccurate information in Josephus, the northern palace-villa was previously confused with a larger administrative palace on the west side of the plateau. However, it is clear to Yadin that most of the details of Josephus' account fit this northern structure.

The palace is basically composed of three terraces. The bottom terrace is supported by walls up to 80 feet in height, which were necessary for providing an adequate foundation, since the plateau is so narrow at this point.

Within this terrace were found wall paintings and a small Roman bath, but perhaps the most arresting find of the whole expedition was the discovery of three skeletons—a man in his twenties, a child, and a young woman with plaited hair still attached to her scalp. The purpose of this lower terrace seems to have been for rest and relaxation.

The middle terrace, like the lower terrace, seems to have been used for relaxation. The structure of the middle terrace is somewhat odd, since it has two concentric walls, an inner and outer one, with a space between them large enough for statues or other objects of worship, as some scholars have suggested. It appears to Yadin, however, that the inner wall was an attempt to take structural pressure off the outer wall caused by the unevenness and narrowness of the rock foundation.

The upper terrace appears to have served as the living quarters for Herod and perhaps one of his wives at most. This is the only part of the palace with living quarters. It originally had only four rooms. Here the oldest mosaics ever found in Palestine were uncovered.

The northern palace-villa seems to have been built primarily because it offered the best shelter from the sun and south wind, and commanded the best view of the surrounding countryside.

B. *The large bathhouse*

The bathhouse, 33 by 36 feet with walls 6 feet thick, was thought previously by scholars to be a defence tower or an administrative center for the Masada storehouses. As the structure was excavated, however, it became clear that it was a caldarium—the hot room of a Roman bathhouse of the kind that were found at Pompeii and Herculaneum. Clay pipes for carrying heat were found in the walls, and a specially built floor with a second floor directly underneath with tiny pillars separating them was unearthed. The caldarium turned into a steam room as a furnace forced hot air between the two floors, heating the top floor enough to create steam as water was poured over it.

Three other buildings associated with a Roman caldarium were also found. These were a cold room (frigidarium), built to be strictly functional and therefore austere in design, a tepid room (tepidarium), and a disrobing room (apodyterium), both of which were richly designed with wall paintings and black and white tiling on the floors.

C. *The storehouses*

Just south of the palace-villa in the northeast section of the plateau are large rectangular structures which were previously identified by scholars with storehouses said by Josephus to have been built by Herod. During the excavation under Yadin this identification was confirmed. There is evidence that these storehouses contained large supplies of food stockpiled by Herod and used by the Zealots.

During Masada's final hours it appears that much of the food supply was destroyed by the Zealots, but in a few storerooms there is evidence of no destruction at all. This may be partial redemption for Josephus' statement that the Zealots decided not to destroy their food supply in order to show the Romans that death was not from lack of food. After Masada's fall, the Romans probably found these few rooms full of supplies and used them.

In connection with the storehouses, an administrative building was found—a large rectangular building with a number of rooms situated around a central court.

As the excavation progressed and much of the debris was removed, Yadin discovered that originally the only access to the storehouses, as well as to the bathhouse and northern palace-villa, was through a Herodian gate uncovered near the administrative building. A single guard could control access to all these sensitive areas.

During the excavation the decision was made to leave some storehouse areas untouched while restoring the others as much as possible. The visitor today, therefore, can obtain some idea of what the unrestored site was originally like.

D. *The garrison building*

The garrison is the only building on Masada which was originally built as a dwelling place. It is to the south of the storehouses and consists of a number of living quarters built around a large central court, with each living quarter itself divided into a court and two small rooms.

During Herod's day the garrison may have held court officials or even troops, but it became clear with a number of finds that some of the most important Zealot leaders lived in these rooms during the revolt. The evidences for this are numerous alabaster vessels and cosmetic ware and especially a number of silver shekels and half-shekels found in this building. These coins constitute the largest group of shekels ever found in one location.

E. *The Byzantine chapel*

Southwest of the garrison Yadin excavated a Byzantine chapel, which was structured basically as a long hall with an apse at its eastern end.

The principal discovery here was a complete fifth-century Byzantine mosaic floor. It is one of the most beautiful of its period and its designed with a series of round medallions with representations of various fruits and plants. A small cross is part of a design in one of the medallions.

F. *The western palace*

The western palace is the largest building on Masada. It was not mentioned by Josephus, perhaps because he was more impressed by the unique northern palace-villa. Nevertheless, the western palace appears to be the most important building on Masada for official royal purposes.

The palace is composed of three main wings: (1) a southeast wing, which served as the dwelling quarters, with a number of rooms around a central court; (2) a north wing, which seems to have been a service area, with rooms surrounding a central court; and (3) a west wing, which contained the storeroom and administrative quarters.

An exciting discovery in the west wing was a colored mosaic floor from Herod's time, one of the most ancient and beautiful ever discovered in Palestine. It was designed with representations of plant life and geometric patterns rather than of people or animals, as was customary in Herod's day, and so shows that Herod was reluctant to offend Jewish religious sensibilities.

Also found was a small private bathhouse in the northeastern section of the residential (southeastern) wing. This bathhouse was similar to the other baths found at Masada except that it was heated directly by a furnace immediately behind its rear wall.

As the storerooms in the western wing were excavated, it was discovered that they held more costly materials than the main storerooms to the north. It was evident also that these storerooms were well enough supplied that the western palace was able to operate independently from the other installations.

G. *The casemate wall*

The casemate wall as Yadin first discovered it was very much a pile of rubble, although aerial photographs taken beforehand did show outlines of a wall. It took almost half the manpower of the excavation eleven months to clear the ruins and uncover the important living areas between the outer and inner casemate walls.

The wall turned out to be 1,400 yards in length with 4½ yards between the outer and inner wall, but it was probably less than the 12 feet in height claimed by Josephus. Also, the wall was made of plastered dolomite stone rather than the "white stone" reported by Josephus. His report probably arose because of the appearance of the plaster from a distance.

The space between the walls was divided into 110 rooms ranging in length from 6 to 38 yards. In the larger chambers the Zealots had built partitions, further dividing the available space into living areas.

Since the rooms in the casemate wall were used for living areas by the Zealots, they offered exciting discoveries once they began to be uncovered. For the most part the rooms had not been fired, although some families had collected their personal effects and burnt them in a corner of a room.

Hundreds of coins were discovered from the period of the revolt, some in groups of two to three hundred. Also found were cosmetic items such as a wooden comb and a box for eyepaint, kitchen items such as pots and pans and stone measuring vessels, and one of the most extensive textile finds from the Roman period. Stones weighing about 100 pounds each, which were kept at strategic points to be hurled against the enemy, were also found.

H. *The ritual bath (mikve)*

One of the most exciting discoveries at Masada for the orthodox Jewish community was the ritual bath or *mikve* in the southern section of the casemate wall. A second, almost identical ritual bath was discovered afterward on the northern end of Masada in the northeastern corner of the administration building just west of the main storehouses.

The baths basically consisted of three pools: a large one for collecting and holding rainwater, a medium-sized pool to serve as the actual ritual bath, and a small pool for the physical cleansing of the hands and feet before entering the actual ritual bath.

The ritual baths were significant to the orthodox community because their construction helped to shed light on some obscure passages on *mikve* regulations in the Talmud. The legal conformity of these baths goes a long way in showing how eager the Zealots were to preserve their religious traditions in the face of very difficult circumstances.

I. *The synagogue*

A very important architectural discovery is the synagogue on the northwestern section of the casemate wall. This find is of great significance primarily because it is the only synagogue to have survived from the Second Temple period. Other synagogues in Palestine date from no earlier than the late second century A.D.

The structure is situated toward Jerusalem as required by Jewish law, with the entrance facing east. In addition to an ostracon inscribed as a "priestly tithe," two pits were found in this building containing the Books of Ezekiel and Deuteronomy. These discoveries led to an even greater certainty that this was indeed a synagogue with a geniza.

The synagogue is basically a rectangular structure with rows of plastered stone benches around its walls. As one enters it, there are five pillars in the main area, three to the left and two to the right, which originally supported it, and a large back room in the northwest corner.

The structure was originally built by Herod with a somewhat different design, perhaps as a synagogue, but it was modified by the Zealots. For example, they constructed the benches partly from broken stone columns from the lower and perhaps upper terraces of the northern palace-villa.

J. *The cisterns*

From an engineering standpoint, Herod's cisterns were an amazing accomplishment. He had two rows of cisterns hewn out of solid rock on the northwestern side of the summit and a set of cisterns hewn at the top. Each cistern had a capacity of about 140,000 cubic feet with a total capacity of about 1,400,000 cubic feet.

Herod's engineers found a way to dam two nearby wadis so that their water during the rainy season could be channeled into the two rows of cisterns on the side of the plateau. Herod's work force would then carry the water from these to the cisterns at the top of the summit.

This ingenious system solved the problem of Masada's water supply, which was perhaps its greatest drawback as a fortress.

K. *The cave*

Besides the three skeletons found on the lower terrace of the palace-villa, the only other remains of the Zealot defenders were found in a small cave near the top of the southern cliff.

Twenty-five skeletons were found: fourteen of men between the ages of twenty-two and sixty and one over seventy; six of women between fifteen and twenty-two; four of children between eight and twelve (there was also one of an embryo).

These skeletons are probably the remains of Zealot defenders, since the other two possibilities, that they are to be associated with the Romans or the monks who later inhabited the site, seem to be unlikely.

L. *Roman installations*

The Romans built a large circumvallation or wall around Masada more than 3,800 yards long and 6 feet thick. This was built to prevent the Zealots from either escaping or mounting surprise attacks on the Roman camps at the base of the plateau. Twelve towers were also built along the eastern section of the wall at intervals of 80 to 100 yards.

Of special interest are the two major Roman camps to the east and west of Masada, respectively, and seven other smaller camps. Not only did these camps house and defend the Roman troops, but they were all strategically placed to guard against any possible escape route and to confine the Zealots' movements as closely as possible.

A major feat of the Romans was their assault ramp. It is still in a good state of preservation and measures about 215 yards in length. The width of its base at the foot of the plateau is about the same. On this ramp the Romans built their siege tower, from which a battering ram and catapults could assault the fortress.

Once the ramp was built, the end of Masada was strategically inevitable.

EPIGRAPHICAL MATERIAL FOUND

A. Fragments of Psalms 81-85 were found in one of the rooms in the casemate wall (room 1,039). Archaeologically their date could not be later than A.D. 23 and probably they should be dated thirty years earlier. The special significance of this find lies in the fact that these are the first parchment fragments of the Second Temple period found outside of a cave, and their text is almost identical to the traditional Hebrew text used today.

B. A scroll fragment dealing with liturgy in relation to Sabbath sacrifice was found in the same room (1,039) in a stratified layer dated to A.D. 73. This fragment is very significant because it contains sectarian material identical to a text discovered in Qumran's Cave Four. This further confirms a previous scholarly consensus that the Dead Sea Scrolls were written before the fall of the second temple.

C. An important find which settled an old controversy was the discovery of a part of Ecclesiasticus in casemate room 1,109. This appears to be an early-first-century-B.C. copy of the Hebrew original of Ecclesiasticus, which was first composed about 200 B.C. and later in that century translated into Greek.

It was believed that the original Hebrew text of Ecclesiasticus had been completely lost until the appearance of several Hebrew fragments in the Cairo Geniza in 1896. Even then some scholars forcefully argued that these geniza fragments were themselves translations of the Greek or Syriac versions. Now, however, in comparing the Masada fragments with the geniza fragments, it is evident that they both reflect the text of the Hebrew original.

D. A small but important fragment of the original Hebrew text of the Book of Jubilees was found in one of the wall towers to the west of the western palace.

Jubilees was preserved only in various translations, so the discovery of only a small fragment of a Hebrew copy is very important. Furthermore, the Book of Jubilees is also associated with the sectarian calendar of Qumran and so provides another link between Masada and Qumran.

E. The only scroll found outside the casemate rooms or Zealot lodgings was a copy of Leviticus, Chapters 8-12. It was found in a small heap of debris on the upper terrace of the northern palace-villa. This scroll is significant in that its text is identical to the traditional text, and even the traditional divisions into "open" and "closed" sections are the same.

F. Two important scrolls were discovered in two different pits in a room which the Zealots had modified to a synagogue. The pits served as a kind of geniza. One contained a scroll of Ezekiel whose parchment was badly gnawed, although parts of it could be easily read. The other pit contained the final two chapters of Deuteronomy. Both scrolls reflected the Massoretic textual tradition.

The special significance of the discovery of these scrolls lies in the fact that the use of the synagogue at Masada for geniza purposes would hardly have occurred after its fall in A.D. 73. These scrolls, therefore, which are very close to the traditional text, are almost certainly to be dated before the fall of Masada on archaeological grounds alone.

G. Altogether portions of fourteen scrolls were found at Masada containing biblical, sectarian, and apocryphal material.

H. Of special importance are the pottery inscriptions found at Masada, almost seven hundred in number. Most of them were short, containing only names or even single letters signifying, perhaps, codes of various kinds.

Among the more important names discovered were *Herod* and *ben Ya'ir*. The ben Ya'ir inscription was found with ten other ostraca, and Yadin has speculated that these eleven ostraca were the very lots cast in determining the order of the Zealots' death.

Of special significance to the paleographer is the fact that many of the ostraca inscriptions can be precisely dated, unlike a scroll whose date of writing could be many years previous to the stratum in which it is found.

Important also to the pottery expert were sherds of wine jars bearing the exact date of use. These absolute dates greatly enhance the relative dating by pottery.

SIGNIFICANCE OF THE EXPEDITION

A. Yadin believes that Josephus' account of the events at Masada is basically substantiated by the archaeological finds.

B. A noted writer, Trude Weiss-Rosmarin, argues that Josephus fabricated the events at Masada.

She gives three basic reasons: (1) heroic self-annihilation is contrary to basic Jewish doctrine; (2) on personal and political grounds Josephus is not reliable as a historian; and (3) the story of two women and five children reporting verbatim the words of Eleazar ben Ya'ir is very improbable.

The majority of scholars, however, tend to accept the basic credibility of Josephus on Masada.

C. Archaeologically, Masada has great significance. Knowledge of Herodian architecture and even the character of Herod himself has been significantly expanded, and the many artifacts found have shed light on the daily life and history of the Second Temple period.

Of great importance is Masada's synagogue (the only one discovered from the Second Temple period).

Of even more importance to the paleographer and biblical scholar are the biblical and sectarian texts and especially the precisely dated sherds with their various inscriptions.

According to Yadin, the most important discovery was the eleven small ostraca each of which was inscribed with a single name, including that of the leader, ben Ya'ir himself. Yadin feels that these may be the very lots cast which determined the Zealots' order of death.

XXV

THE CASE OF SHAPIRA'S MISSING DEAD SEA (DEUTERONOMY) SCROLL OF 1883

INTRODUCTION

One of the most fascinating stories in recent history is about a nineteenth-century manuscript collector, Moses Wilhelm Shapira, and some manuscript fragments obtained by him in 1878. A short time after Shapira presented these fragments for sale to the British Museum in 1883, they were rejected by the museum and the academic world as forgeries.

Many scholars now believe, however, that Shapira may have actually acquired manuscript fragments which belong in the same general category as the Qumran manuscripts. Both share many of the same characteristics, although the Shapira fragments are written in the paleo-Hebrew script and may be older than anything found in Qumran and, according to Shapira's report, his fragments were found in the southeastern region of the Dead Sea.

Although the question of whether Shapira's fragments were genuine has not been satisfactorily resolved even to the present day, there are strong reasons for including them among the kinds of writings found in the Dead Sea area since the late 1940s.

NATURE AND CONTENT OF SHAPIRA'S FRAGMENTS

A. *Physical characteristics*

The Shapira fragments consist of sixteen strips of dark brown leather on which were written portions of Deuteronomy with interpolations from Numbers and Exodus, including a unique rendition of the Ten Commandments. They were between 7.6 and 9.7 centimeters in width and 15 to 18 centimeters in length. Some strips (from two to five) were connected end to end so that a connected group could reach almost 90 centimeters in length. There were also several smaller pieces.

A physical characteristic of the fragments which was very much like some of the Qumran scrolls was its illegibility until rubbed by spirits or wine. The leather was so black that the inscription could not be read by Shapira without each time subjecting the fragments to this process. "I found the manuscript very hard for my eyes," wrote Shapira. "The ink is nearly indestructible—either by rubbing or by washing with water or spirits—which is unusual in oriental manuscripts."

B. *Content*

Shapira's fragments were written in a compressed manner in the paleo-Hebrew script, occupying less than a third of the space taken up by the corresponding text in the Old Testament. They also contained the same text twice.

The text of the Old Testament corresponding to the Shapira fragments is as follows: Deuteronomy 1 : 1, 5, 7, 8-9, 19, 20; Numbers 14 : 21ff; Deuteronomy 1 : 34ff; 2 : 24-37; 3 : 1a; 2 : 17-23; Numbers 21 : 31-33; Deuteronomy 3 : 1b, 2-11; Numbers 25 : 1-8, 16-18; 31 : 1-20; Deuteronomy 4 : 3, 14, 2, 23, 39-40; 6 : 4-9; 5 : 2, 5-19; Exodus 20 : 19; Deuteronomy 5 : 25; 9 : 1; 7 : 17-19; 9 : 3; 7 : 20; 9 : 6-11, 22; 10 : 1-4; 9 : 23-25; 10 : 15-17, 21-22; 11 : 22-29; 27 : 11-14; 28 : 1-13; 27 : 14-26; 20 : 15-20, 25, 37, 43-44, 63; 31 : 1-6.

The general content of the above texts is as follows: Moses reviews the events of Israel's desert wanderings, including an occasion at Beth Pe'or after Israel's victory over Midian, at which time he had been commanded by *Elohim* to teach Israel the laws to be followed in the Promised Land; the Decalogue follows; then there is a series of blessings and curses; and finally Moses indicates that Joshua will be his successor in leading the people into their land.

The Shapira fragments, then, form a skillfully abridged manual compiled from Deuteronomy, with Moses' last speech to Israel as its central theme, together with relevant interpolations from other parts of the Pentateuch. Biblical texts with these kinds of interpolations are found also in the Qumran writings.

One of the most interesting and controversial elements in the fragments was their rendition of the Decalogue. Instead of using the Tetragrammaton in the usual manner of the canonical Decalogues (i.e., "I am the Lord, your God"), the Shapira Decalogue had "I am God, your God." Although it is not true that the Shapira Decalogue eliminated the Tetragrammaton entirely, some scholars were so upset at its frequent omission that they used this as an argument against the authenticity of the fragments in general.

History of the Shapira Manuscripts

A. *Shapira's background as an antiquities dealer*

Although Shapira's reputation suffered severely after his fragments were pronounced a forgery (one English publication called him "Mr. Sharp-eye-ra"), it is apparent that these attacks were really not justified in the light of his previous work. His life was dedicated to the legitimate acquisition of antiquities, and with this as his goal he worked as an agent for the British Museum in an antique shop in Jerusalem. Through him the British Museum obtained many valuable ancient manuscripts which it still has.

Shapira was not a professional scholar. He was a Polish Jew, converted to Christianity, who had an immense interest in antiquities. He was a respected collector with a substantial background of important finds, which he sold not only to the British Museum, but also to the Royal Library in Berlin. One such manuscript, for example, is the commentary of Maimonides on the Mishna. This is of special interest since through it the editing of the whole work of Maimonides was made possible.

The *Jewish Chronicle* of London (August 10, 1883, p. 10) described Shapira as a pillar of the London Mission and a leading antique dealer in Jerusalem.

Although it is true that Shapira was involved in selling forged Moabite pottery to the British Museum in 1872, he was subsequently cleared of all responsibility at that time. He was a collector, not a scholar who was capable of verifying everything he saw. When he was denounced for trying to sell his Deuteronomy fragments, however, the severity of the charge at that time so overwhelmed him that he committed suicide in a Rotterdam hotel on March 9, 1884.

B. *Shapira's account of his acquisition of the fragments*

According to Shapira, he first heard of the fragments while talking to some Bedouin in the house of Sheikh Mahmud of Arakat. One of them told him that he and some others came upon the fragments in a cave while seeking to hide from enemy forces. They found several bundles of old rugs in the cave, and thinking that these bundles might contain gold, they took them apart only to find the dark-brown leather fragments.

The fragments were wrapped in either linen or cotton, and the cave was high up on a rock facing the Arnon River. One immediately sees the resemblance to the Qumran discovery at this point, since the Qumran scrolls and fragments were also found in dry caves near the Dead Sea and some scrolls had been wrapped in linen. Shapira reports that he marveled at the dryness of the place. With the help of Sheikh Mahmud, an Arab brought Shapira these fragments over a period of time during 1878. After he received all the fragments, Shapira had copies sent to Constantine Schlottmann, a professor of Old Testament at Halle. Schlottmann denounced the fragments as forgeries and began to take steps to prevent Shapira from making them public, so Shapira put them in a Jerusalem bank for safekeeping.

Shapira writes that sometime before Easter of 1883 he began a reexamination of the fragments, and by the end of July he was in Leipzig to have them photographed. He relates that at that time the fragments were favorably received, especially by Professor H. Guthe, who intended to write about them.

C. *The role of German scholarship*

The first academic community to get a good look at the fragments was the leading scholars of Germany, including such notables as August Dillmann, Eduard Sachau, Adolf Erman, and Moritz Steinschneider, who met at the house of Richard Lepsius, the chief librarian of the Royal Library of Berlin. There is some question as to their real views at that meeting.

According to a report made by a London *Times* correspondent in Berlin, the group unanimously pronounced the fragments a "clever and impudent forgery." The accuracy of this report can be questioned on a number of grounds:

1. The report was never published by the *Times* until after the tide of scholarly opinion turned strongly against Shapira (August 28), more than a month and a half after the meeting occurred (July 10).
2. The most thorough investigation was completed by the German scholar H. Guthe on July 6, yet even after this date Lepsius (the Berlin librarian) was willing to buy the fragments. It seems almost certain that if Guthe had any reservations about the fragments, he would not have hesitated to share them with his colleague Lepsius.
3. During the weeks after the July 10 meeting, when the fragments were being investigated by the British Museum, the German scholars remained silent. Although they were reading every day in Ger-

man and English newspapers about the sensational impact of Shapira's manuscripts in England, there was no word of warning or caution from them.
4. Perhaps the most curious fact in all this is that a number of Berlin scholars were trying to buy the fragments as Shapira was negotiating with the British Museum.

D. The role of English scholarship and the catalytic effect of C. S. Clermont-Ganneau

The main English scholar to examine the fragments along with several other experts on behalf of the British Museum was the well-known Hebraist C. D. Ginsburg. He had the fragments under intensive investigation for almost three weeks and during that time he was unable, even with the aid of his colleagues, to come to any firm conclusions.

It is perhaps this period of delay which is most embarrassing to the subsequent opinion that the fragments are a flagrant forgery. When academic opinion fell like an avalanche on Shapira with so much dogmatic certainty after August 28, a number of internal inconsistencies were created which remain with us to the present day.

1. If the fragments are a patent forgery as it was claimed, why was the sale price of one million pounds not rejected by the British Museum even after several days of examination, not only by Ginsburg, but also by a group of experts who met at the office of the Palestine Exploration Fund for the sole purpose of examining the fragments?
2. Why were a number of these fragments put on prominent display at this time in the museum?
3. Why did William Gladstone, the British prime minister, pay a special visit on August 13 to look at the fragments and discuss them favorably with both Shapira and Ginsburg present?

If one event had not occurred, perhaps the academic world would have come, at the very worst, to no real conviction regarding the authenticity or inauthenticity of the fragments. Perhaps there would have been a stalemate. If that had happened, Shapira might not have collected his one million pounds from the British Museum, but he probably would have obtained a substantial sum from somewhere, and most important, the fragments, now lost, would have been preserved for modern research. An event fatal to this possibility did happen, however, and that was the arrival of the well-known French scholar C. S. Clermont-Ganneau.

Clermont-Ganneau must be regarded as the catalyst of the hostility which quickly swept the academic world against Shapira's manuscripts. It was an unfortunate situation. There was hostility from the beginning between Clermont-Ganneau and Ginsburg, and even before Clermont-Ganneau saw the fragments he confessed that he was prejudiced against them. He took no more than five minutes to examine the fragments which other scholars had investigated for weeks, and with no hesitation he branded them as forgeries.

Clermont-Ganneau felt certain that the ancient leather strips which served as the writing surface were taken from the bottom margins of ancient synagogue manuscripts (since the bottom margin is the widest). The London *Daily News* sent its own expert afterwards, who reported that the fragments were too thick to come from such a source.

Such was the influence of Clermont-Ganneau, however, that the academic world almost overnight adopted his skepticism. Shortly afterward Ginsburg published a number of arguments against the fragments, all of which we now know to be in error (see pp. 221-224).

E. *The location of the fragments since 1883*

Presently no one seems to know where the Shapira fragments are located or even if they still exist. It is highly unlikely that they still exist somewhere in the British Museum.

With the information at hand it is known that the fragments were examined once again by a number of scholars (including Clermont-Ganneau, as related in his book *Les Fraudes archéologiques en Palestine* [Paris, 1885], pp. 254ff) in January of 1884, but the sources for the subsequent history of the fragments are somewhat contradictory. It seems fairly certain, however, that Bernard Quaritch, a well-known bookseller, came into possession of the fragments by July 16, 1885, and allowed them to be part of the Anglo-Jewish Historical Exhibition at the Royal Albert Hall from April to June of 1887.

It would have been fortunate had Quaritch and his firm retained the manuscripts. As it was, however, he sold them to an unknown source and apparently made no record of the sale; at least the present-day firm of Bernard Quaritch cannot find any trace of the transaction.

One source maintains that C. D. Ginsburg purchased some of the Deuteronomic fragments. But among the manuscript collection that Ginsburg left to his friend, William Addis Wright, vice-master of Trinity College, Cambridge, there is no trace of the Shapira fragments.

ISSUES ON THE AUTHENTICITY OF THE SHAPIRA FRAGMENTS

With very few exceptions the kinds of criticism offered against the Shapira fragments in the nineteenth century are the kinds of criticism offered today. They fall roughly into two broad categories: external and internal evidence.

A. *External evidence*

External evidence against the fragments is perhaps the weaker, especially in the light of new knowledge. There were strong doubts, for example, that any manuscript could last for two thousand years in Palestine, much less the linen in which it was supposed to be wrapped. The circumstances of the Dead Sea Scrolls, of course, are complete proof of the opposite.

It is interesting that the orthography of the fragments favorably impressed the nineteenth-century scholars who had direct access to them. Recently, however, objections have been made that the script as it appears from the nineteenth-century reproductions imitates *monumental* letters (e.g., letters formed on coins and other hard surfaces) rather than *written* letters (e.g., in manuscripts). However, it is apparent especially in Hebrew scripts that a dogmatic distinction cannot be drawn between monumental and written orthography. There are numerous cases in which there is simply no distinction.

B. *Internal evidence*

If the original fragments of Shapira's Deuteronomy should ever appear today, perhaps the *external* evidence would be more decisive in proving or disproving the fragments' authenticity. In the Dead Sea Scrolls, for example, external evidence has been perhaps the more important and decisive factor in establishing their date and provenance.

In the nineteenth century, however, *internal* evidence was the single most important area in forming scholarly opinion. Internal evidence against the fragments was cited more often than external evidence. Despite the fact that many of these internal arguments are based on inaccurate or inadequate information, they are still often uncritically cited by scholars today.

Without entering into too much detail, we note that the internal evidence falls into three main categories: (1) words and phrases which supposedly are not to be found in the Old Testament; (2) words and phrases thought to reflect late or rabbinic Hebrew; and (3) spelling errors which seem to betray the author of the fragments as a person who had learned Hebrew in northern Europe (e.g., Poland—the implication here, of course, being that Shapira himself may have been responsible for forging the manuscripts).

1. Words and phrases used in the fragments but not in the Bible

It should be pointed out first that a rare word or phrase has by itself little bearing on a document's authenticity. If it had substantial bearing, many writings in the Old Testament itself and many authentic extrabiblical writings would fall under suspicion.

Adolf Neubauer's argument, therefore, that the precise term החרתך ("I liberate thee") is not found in the Old Testament or in any other Hebrew source really has no bearing at all on the authenticity of the Shapira fragments, even though the statement is correct in itself. Other statements made by Neubauer, Ginsburg, and others of the nineteenth century (many of which are still defended by some scholars today) are simply inaccurate from the start, quite apart from their application.

An example of the kind of scholarship the Shapira fragments have had to endure at the hands of otherwise careful scholars can be seen in the treatment of the phrase, "you shall not kill the *person* [נפש] of your brother." Neubauer reports that when he and Dillmann read this expression, they considered it "quite sufficient for the recognition of a forgery." This is unfortunate, since the phrase, although not common, definitely belongs to biblical Hebrew (cf. Deut. 22 : 26; II Sam. 14 : 7).

Other hasty criticisms of the fragments are the contentions that הן (written with the vowel as הון), meaning "wealth" in the fragments, never has this meaning in the Old Testament (despite contrary evidence in twenty-four cases in the Old Testament); and that "God, our God" never occurs in the Old Testament as it does in the fragments (but cf. Pss. 45 : 7 [8]; 48 : 14 [15]; 50 : 7; 67 : 6 [7]; and that the fragments betray their inauthentic character by using רע ("friend") and אח ("brother") as synonyms (despite the fact that this occurs scores of times in the Old Testament).

One can give other examples of hasty and impatient scholarship of this nature, which span almost a hundred years of investigation of the fragments.

2. Words and phrases in the fragments thought to reflect late or rabbinic Hebrew

The same kinds of inaccurate criticisms noted in the above section can also be seen here. Neubauer maintains, for example, that the phrase

לנשא שמי לשקר, which is found in the fragments, is rabbinic Hebrew. Classical Hebrew would have לאיש אשר ישא. Neubauer is correct that the former expression is rabbinic, but it is also clearly an option for classical Hebrew (cf. Deut. 5 : 9-10).

One of the more accurate charges against the fragments since Neubauer's time is the observation that עדות ("testimony") is never used biblically in the phrase "false testimony" as it is in the fragments. This is correctly recognized as a rabbinic expression. However, it needs to be mentioned that the versions uniformly translate Deuteronomy 5 : 20 (the verse corresponding to the fragment in question) in a way that assumes the meaning of עדות rather than the corresponding word עד ("witness") which appears in the text. Yet even if the phrase "false testimony" (with עדות instead of עד) could be pressed as definitely non-classical Hebrew, the evidence of the versions would still caution against the view that the phrase עדות שקר *must* have its origin in late rabbinic circles.

3. Spelling errors which indicate a North European origin of the fragments

Perhaps one of the most incriminating attacks against Shapira himself has its origin in Ginsburg. On the basis of the way in which two words were spelled, Ginsburg was confident that the author of the fragments was "a Polish, Russian, or German Jew, or one who had learned Hebrew in the North of Europe." This would, of course, immediately point to Shapira as a forger, since he was a Polish Jew.

Ginsburg based his assertions on rather tenuous evidence. He noted, for example, that the word for "frontlets," לטטפת, was spelled לתתהת in the fragments, and he felt that this was "inexplicable" except as proof that a North European Jew, whose community pronounced the ת and the ט alike, had unwittingly made this slip.

It is hard to understand how Ginsburg, who had such an extensive knowledge of textual-critical problems, could base so much certainty on this point. There is evidence that the oriental Samaritan community occasionally confused ת and ט, as well as evidence within the Massoretic text itself of this kind of error. It is also significant that the greatest area of weakness for North European Jews, the guttural letters, is virtually untouched by problems of spelling. The same cannot be said of many texts in the Old Testament itself.

Another misspelled word which indicated to Ginsburg a Polish or German Jewish author was the spelling כבל for חבל in Deuteronomy

3 : 4, since these Jewish communities pronounce ח like כ without the dagesh.

The validity of this argument is dubious. The letter כ at the beginning of a word must assume a hard *k* sound, and it is therefore unlikely that the scribe will erroneously write כ when the consonant ח is pronounced. The true cause of the confusion may be seen in Shapira's text itself, in which the letters כ and ג look very much alike. It is possible to read כבל as גבל (for גְבוּל—"border," "territory"), which would make perfect sense in the context.

Conclusion

It is truly unfortunate that the Shapira manuscripts have too often suffered from hasty and impatient scholarship since their introduction to the scholarly world in 1883. This is not to say that the present writer believes that the Shapira fragments of Deuteronomy are definitely authentic documents of more than two thousand years of age. We simply maintain that there appears to be no internal or external evidence yet published which conclusively proves that the Shapira fragments are a forgery, and we are convinced that there is more than enough reasonable ground for a thorough reexamination of the Shapira case by the scholarly world.

GENERAL REVIEW

Answer ALL questions.
A. Give the contents of the following:
   1. The Manual of Discipline
   2. The Bar Kochba letters
   3. The Thanksgiving Hymns
   4. The Copper Scrolls
B. What is the significance of the Qumran scrolls to the following:
   1. Biblical studies
   2. The background of Christianity
C. Evaluate the importance of the Bar Kochba finds.
D. Write briefly on the following:
   1. The dating of the Qumran texts
   2. Mird finds
   3. The Genesis Apocryphon
   4. The Essenes

TOPICS FOR FURTHER STUDY

The following are suggested topics for further class or group study discussion:

1. The Essenes
2. Pharisaic Judaism
3. The Contents of the Habakkuk Commentary and its Significance
4. The Dead Sea Scrolls and the New Testament: Contrasts and Parallels
5. Doctrines of the Qumran Sect
6. The Theological Doctrines in the Thanksgiving Hymns
7. Significance of the Scrolls to Biblical Studies
8. The Identification of the Qumran Sect
9. The Teacher of Righteousness
10. The Dating of the Qumran Texts
11. Life and Times of Bar Kochba
12. The Septuagint and the Biblical Scrolls
13. The Massoretic Text in the Light of Qumran
14. The Talmud
15. The Apocrypha
16. Religious Ideas in the Apocrypha
17. History and Origin of the Septuagint
18. Jewish History During the Intertestamental Period
19. The Significance of the Discoveries Relating to Bar Kochba
20. Contents of the Genesis Apocryphon and its Significance
21. Contents of the War Scroll and its Significance
22. The Midrash
23. Contents of the Manual of Discipline and its Significance
24. The Contents of the Copper Scrolls and Their Significance
25. The Excavations at Qumran
26. The Commentaries
27. The Making of the Hebrew Bible
28. Josephus as Historian
29. The Life and Works of Philo
30. Pre-Christian Jewish Sects
31. The Role of Masada in Jewish History
32. Forged Palestine Manuscripts and Artifacts

GLOSSARY OF TERMS AND PROPER NAMES

Apocalyptic Writings A type of literature that flourished in Judaism and early Christian thought (165 B.C. to A.D. 120) with the purpose of encouraging the faithful to stand firm under persecution. The encouragement was in the form of a promise of speedy deliverance from current evils by the intervention of God, and the end of the present world order, the resurrection, and the eternal reward of the righteous and damnation of the unrighteous (compare Daniel and Revelation).

Apocrypha "Hidden" or "stored away." It refers to the fourteen books found in the Greek Septuagint but not among the canonical Hebrew Scriptures. The Apocrypha is important for a knowledge of Jewish religious development between the Old and New Testaments.

Aramaic The language, in various dialects, spoken by the Arameans of Syria and other northwestern Semitic peoples before and during the time of Jesus. Certain passages in the Old Testament are written in Aramaic: Jeremiah 10 : 11; Ezra 4 : 8-6 : 18, 7 : 12-26; Daniel 2 : 4-7 : 28.

Bar Kochba Later name for ben Kosiba, also spelled Koseba, Kosebah, Kosibah, Kozibah, or Kozba. This man led the Jewish revolt against Roman rule in Palestine in A.D. 132-135. Recent discoveries throw direct light on his place in Jewish history.

Codex A leaf book, as distinguished from a roll or scroll, invented and used first by the Romans. Handwritten manuscript in book form.

Dead Sea An inland body of water, extremely rich in salt and other minerals, between Israel and Jordan, covering an area of 370 square miles and being 1,290 feet below sea level.

Ebionites "The Poor Ones," name of a first century A.D. sect whose members were Jews who had been converted to Christ but who continued Judaistic practices.

Eschatology This is the study of the doctrine of "last things", that is, the nature of such future events as the end of the present world order, the final judgment of all men, and the future state of both the just and the unjust.

Essenes — A Jewish sect which flourished during the Second Commonwealth, and whose members lived an ascetic and sometimes mystic life in monastic communities.

Eusebius — Bishop of Caesarea for a quarter of a century, Eusebius (A.D. 263-ca. 340) was also an eminent scholar, the father of Church historiography and Christian apologist. His greatest work was the *Ecclesiastical History*.

Gemara — The rabbinic commentary on and interpretation of the Mishna; with the Mishna it comprises the Talmud.

Geniza — One of the rooms of a synagogue used exclusively for permanently storing discarded and worn Holy Writings. Such a room full of ancient scrolls was found in Cairo, Egypt, just prior to the start of the twentieth century. It yielded thousands of manuscripts and texts.

Hadrian — Roman emperor from A.D. 117 to 138. Jewish patriots, led by Simeon Bar Kochba, revolted during the last years of Hadrian's reign and this revolt led to their near extermination in Judea in A.D. 135.

Hagiographa — The Greek (Christian) term for all the canonical books of Jewish Scripture which are not included in the Law or in the Prophets; Hebrew—Kethubim. "Writings."

Halakhah — Used as a general name for authoritative law, which is a way of life to the Jewish people; refers also to those portions of the Talmud which deal with any phase of Jewish law.

Hasidim — Literally "the pious ones" or "the saints," referring to a group of Jews formed during the fourth century B.C. for the purpose of promoting the observance of Jewish ritual and study of the Law. The Pharisees developed largely from this group.

Hieroglyphics — An ancient method of writing which used pictures, rather than an alphabet, for signifying a syllable, a word or a concept. Although other ancient cultures employed this method, Egypt is best known for it.

Hellenism — The language and ideas of ancient Greek culture as absorbed by various peoples in the Near East and around the Mediterranean Sea after the conquests of Alexander the Great (d. 323 B.C.). Jewish thought and life was affected most by Hellenism at Alexandria, Egypt.

Hyksos — A loose confederation of western Asian people which dominated Egypt between the 12th and 16th dynasties. About 1580 B.C. Amosis I finally expelled them, and inaugurated a new empire. Some feel Joseph may have served under a Hyksos Pharaoh.

Josephus (Flavius) — Jewish historian and writer (ca. A.D. 37-100) who was well educated in Jewish lore and Greek disciplines. His most important works are *Wars of the Jews*, *Antiquities of the Jews*, and *Autobiography*. Though not always accurate or reliable, these are often our sole source for his period of history.

Karaites — A Jewish sect which flourished in the Near East, principally in Babylonia, from the ninth to the twelfth centuries A.D. These men adhered exclusively to the Hebrew Scriptures, rejecting the Talmud. Some twelve thousand Karaites are still supposed to exist, most of them in Russian Crimea.

Khirbet — An Arabic word meaning "the ruin of."

Maccabees — Also called Hasmoneans, or Asmoneans; the ruling family of the Jewish nation of the second and first centuries B.C. which led the opposition to Syrian domination and Hellenizing tendencies. They worked for the restoration of Jewish political and religious life.

Magharians — Arabic name of a Jewish sect called "men of the caves". The sect is so called because its books were found in a cave. It is believed to have originated during the first century B.C.

Massorah — A Hebrew word meaning "tradition". It refers to the body of Jewish tradition of the Hebrew Bible. (See "Massoretic Text.")

Massoretic Text — The traditional Hebrew text of the Old Testament which was given vowels and copious marginal notation by the Massoretes mostly between ca. A.D. 500 and 900. This group of men preserved, remarkably well, the text of the Hebrew Scriptures from before the Christian era.

Midrash — The collection of rabbinical homiletical interpretations of the Scriptures verse by verse, the purpose of which is to popularize the essence of Scripture in its particular and universal application.

Mishna	The digest and compilation of Jewish laws made by Rabbi Judah the Patriarch (ca. A.D. 135-200), although in the form in which it has been transmitted it contains many additions and modifications by other scholars. This work constitutes part of the Talmud.
Nabateans	Arabian people first living in the northwestern part of the Arabian peninsula with the Moabites and Edomites and later in the southern part of that area. Under Trajan their country was included in the Roman province of Arabia.
Nash Papyrus	A piece of papyrus from Egypt containing mostly the text of the Ten Commandments. It is generally considered to date from the second or first century B.C.
Origen	Christian scholar, teacher, and philosopher, Origen (A.D. 185-251) was educated in Alexandria and later taught in Caesarea. His works include the *Hexapla*, *De Principiis*, *Contra Celsum*, and *De Oratione*, much of which contains valuable historical material as well as theology.
Ostracon	A piece of pottery on which has been written such various things as contracts, bills, letters, documents, etc. Used extensively in ancient times.
Paleography	The study of describing or deciphering ancient writings with the purpose of placing each inscription in its proper cultural and chronological context.
Papyrus	A water plant, most abundant in Egypt, whose pith was cut into slices, laid side by side and pressed together into a 10- or 12-inch square sheet. When dry, these sheets were glued together and constituted 25- to 30-foot rolls used for writing, usually only on one side. This was the regular material used by the Greeks in antiquity, a roll of which they called a "biblion."
Parchment	The skin of an animal, usually a sheep or goat, prepared as a surface for writing and then usually rolled into scroll form. It was used extensively, along with papyrus, for documents and manuscripts in ancient times.
Pentateuch	The first five books of the Old Testament, also referred to as the Torah or the Five Books of Moses.
Pesher	A commentary or interpretation of the Scriptures.
Pharisees	Emerged as a distinct group during or after the

GLOSSARY OF TERMS AND PROPER NAMES 231

Maccabean Revolt (ca. 165 B.C.). They believed in the authority of the Written Law, along with the Sadducees; but they also held the Oral Law to be authoritative. As the latter was an interpretation of the Written Law from the viewpoint of each successive generation, the Pharisees represented the mass of Jewish people in religious and social outlook, and Pharisaism became the foundation of later rabbinical Judaism.

Philo Judaeus   Jewish philosopher and writer of Alexandria, Egypt, Philo (30 B.C.-A.D. 45) attempted to reconcile, in true Diasporic style, Greek philosophy and Jewish faith. His most important work was an interpretation of Hebrew Scriptures allegorically so as to transform history into abstract principles universally applicable; and his writings have much historical value also.

Phylacteries   Two small boxes of leather containing parchment slips on which are inscribed Deuteronomy 6 : 4-9, 11 : 13-21, and Exodus 13 : 1-10, 13 : 11-16. These were worn on the forehead and left arm all day by the Pharisees and rabbis, but today in present Orthodox practice are limited to morning worship on weekdays by adult males.

Pliny   Called *the Elder*, Pliny (A.D. 23-79) was a famous Roman naturalist and writer. He wrote, among other works, a thirty-seven volume *Natural History* which is highly valuable for historiography.

Pseudepigrapha   A collection of writings fictitiously claiming the authorship of great men of the past. These books are noncanonical and nonapocryphal Jewish works dating from between 200 B.C. and A.D. 200.

Rabbi Akiba   Lived ca. A.D. 50-135. He systematized the accepted Halakah; he also influenced the Haggadah (allegorical religious interpretations), philosophy, and contemporary politics. He is considered the "father of rabbinic Judaism," as he was perhaps the greatest Palestinian Tannaim or early teacher of the Law.

Recension   A revision of a text based on a critical examination of sources.

Sadducees   Tracing their ancestry back to Zadok, high priest during the time of David, this Jewish sect, in the Second Commonwealth period, was composed of the Jewish aristocracy, prosperous merchants, and Tem-

GLOSSARY OF TERMS AND PROPER NAMES

	ple priesthood. In their conservatism they accepted as religiously authoritative only the Written Law, refusing all oral tradition of the Pharisees. They also rejected the doctrines of the resurrection of the dead and the existence of angels.
Samaritan Pentateuch	The first five books of the Hebrew Scriptures, written in ancient Hebrew only on scrolls and used by the Samaritans who established themselves as a religious community separate from the Jews about 432 B.C. This version of the Torah differs in approximately six thousand passages from the traditional (Massoretic) version.
Scarab	An image of a black dung-beetle, held to be sacred by ancient Egyptians, cut from a stone or a gem and often engraved with symbols on the flat underside. This cut stone was worn as a charm and often served as a seal to identify its owner's signature.
Scriptorium	A room used exclusively by scribes for the purpose of transcribing, translating, and studying manuscripts; especially found in monasteries.
Scroll	A roll of parchment or paper used as a book in the form of a rolled manuscript.
Second Commonwealth	The period in Jewish history from the successful Maccabean revolt for independence (165 B.C.) to the fall of Jerusalem (A.D. 70).
Second Temple	The period of time in Jewish history during which the Second Temple stood, 516 B.C. to A.D. 70.
Septuagint	The Greek translation of the Hebrew Scriptures done in Alexandria, Egypt, between the third and first centuries B.C.
St. Justin (Martyr)	Born about A.D. 100, Justin became a Christian and with his philosophic background traveled around the Roman world lecturing on the truth of the Christian faith. He was martyred between A.D. 163 and 167.
Talmud	An encyclopedic collection of interpretation, oral tradition, and teaching related to the Hebrew Scriptures, this body of literature is the most important spiritual document of the Jewish people after the Bible. Summarizing more than six centuries of cultural and religious growth (150 B.C.-A.D. 500), the Talmud is made up of the Mishna and the Gemara.
Tefillin	See "Phylacteries."

Therapeutae	A group of Jewish ascetics, both men and women, having their center near Alexandria, Egypt, around the first century B.C. They spent their entire time, according to Philo, studying the Scriptures and contemplating divine realities.
Vulgate	Between A.D. 382 and 385, Jerome (A.D. 347-420) revised the Latin New Testament from Greek manuscripts and later, in Bethlehem, translated the entire Old Testament from Hebrew. This resulted in the Latin Vulgate, which became the standard biblical text for the western world throughout the Middle Ages. As many as eight thousand manuscripts exist today.
Wadi	An Arabic term for "valley," or "dry stream bed."
Zealots	A group composed of fanatic Jewish patriots who opposed all foreign political rule and who were zealous for literal and particularistic fulfillment of religious laws. They were most active against Rome from 37 B.C. to A.D. 70.

LIST OF MAIN SCROLLS DISCOVERED IN THE DEAD SEA REGIONS

I. Texts from the Old Testament *in Hebrew*

Parts of all the books of the Hebrew Bible, with the exception of Esther, have been discovered. Some fragments are very small and some have several columns of text.

The finds include fragments from:
Exodus—(Cave 4)
Numbers—(Cave 4)
Deuteronomy—(Cave 4)
Isaiah A—complete (Cave I)
Isaiah B—incomplete (Cave I)
Leviticus, in late paleo-Hebrew script—(Cave II)
Important fragments from the Books of Samuel (Cave 4) and numerous chapters from Targum of Job—(Cave II)
Psalms—(Cave II)

The most popular books, according to F. M. Cross, are Deuteronomy (14 MSS), Isaiah (12 MSS), and Psalms (10 MSS). Also found were (8) incomplete copies of the Book of the Twelve Minor Prophets.

II. Fragments from the Apocrypha and Pseudepigrapha
Tobit, in Hebrew and Aramaic
Enoch, in Aramaic
Jubilees, in Hebrew
Testaments of Levi and Naphtali, in Aramaic
Apocryphal Daniel literature, in Hebrew and Aramaic
Psalms of Joshua

III. Commentaries

Not complete scrolls; all fragmentary except the Commentary on Habakkuk, which is the largest.
Commentary on Genesis
Commentary on the Second Book of Samuel
Commentary on Psalms 37 and 68
Commentary on the Book of Isaiah
Commentary on the Book of Micah
Commentary on the Book of Nahum
Commentary on the Book of Habakkuk
Commentary on the Book of Hosea
Midrash on the Book of Moses

LIST OF MAIN SCROLLS

IV. The nonbiblical sectarian scrolls, hitherto unknown, discovered in Cave I
   The Thanksgiving Hymns
   The War Scroll
   The Manual of Discipline
   The Genesis Apocryphon (Aramaic)
   The Temple Scroll (location of discovery unknown)

V. Miscellaneous
   The Damascus Covenant (also known as the Zadokite Documents) is the same book as that found in the Cairo Geniza
   Testimonium of the Messianic Era
   Benedictions
   Copper Scrolls—(Cave III)
   Description of the New Jerusalem—(Cave II)

VI. Fragmentary texts from the New Testament at Khirbet Mird

   A. In Greek
      Mark
      John
      Acts

   B. In Syro-Palestinian
      Matthew
      Luke
      Acts
      Colossians

VII. Finds pertaining to the Bar Kochba Revolt (For details see Chapters 20, 21, and 22.)

N.B. It is estimated that about forty thousand fragments have been found. The above lists are obviously incomplete and refer only to main documents mentioned in this work.

Designation of some of the Qumran Scrolls

The first numeral refers to the cave in which the scroll or fragment is found; Q stands for Qumran, while the following letter(s) designates the Hebrew name of the scroll or the Book of the Bible.

1QS	—	The Manual of Discipline
1QA	—	The Thanksgiving Hymns
1QM	—	The War Scroll
1QIs^a	—	The complete Isaiah Scroll
1QpHab	—	The Habakkuk Commentary
1QApoc	—	The Genesis Apocryphon
4QpNah	—	The Nahum Commentary
4QSam	—	The fragments from I and II Books of Samuel

RECOMMENDED BIBLIOGRAPHY ON THE SCROLLS

The following books are recommended texts for this work
Allegro, J. M., *The Dead Sea Scrolls* (Penguin Books, 1956)
Avigad, N., and Yadin, Y., *A Genesis Apocryphon* (Jerusalem, 1956)
Black, M., *The Scrolls and Christian Origins* (London, 1961)
Burrows, M., *The Dead Sea Scrolls* (New York, 1955)
——, *More Light on the Dead Sea Scrolls* (New York, 1955)
Cross, Frank M., Jr., *The Ancient Library of Qumran & Modern Biblical Studies*, rev. ed. (1958, 1961; repr. ed., Grand Rapids, 1980).
Danielou, J., *The Dead Sea Scrolls and Primitive Christianity* (Baltimore, 1958)
Dupont-Sommer, A., *The Jewish Sect of Qumran and the Essenes* (London, 1954)
——, *The Essene Writings from Qumran* (Oxford, 1961)
Fritsch, C. T., *The Qumran Community* (New York, 1956)
Gaster, T. H., *The Dead Sea Scriptures* (New York, 1956)
Gilkes, A. N., *The Impact of the Dead Sea Scrolls* (London, 1962)
Israel Exploration Journal, Vol. XI, 1961. (The entire issue is devoted to the Bar Kochba discoveries.)
Mansoor, M., *The Thanksgiving Hymns* (Leiden, 1961)
Milik, J. T., *Ten Years of Discovery in the Wilderness of Judaea* (Naperville, Ill., 1958)
Rowley, H. H., *The Dead Sea Scrolls and the New Testament* (London, 1959)
Schubert, K., *The Dead Sea Community* (London, 1957)
Van der Ploeg, J., *The Excavations at Qumran* (London, 1958)
Vermes, G., *Discoveries in the Judean Desert* (New York, 1956)
——, *The Dead Sea Scrolls in English* (Penguin Books, 1962)
Wilson, E., *The Scrolls from the Dead Sea* (New York, 1955)
Yadin, Y., *The Message of the Scrolls* (New York, London, 1957)
——, "The Discovery of Bar Kochba Letters", *Atlantic Monthly* (November, 1961)

CHRONOLOGICAL TABLE OF MAJOR EVENTS

B.C.

586	Destruction of Jerusalem by Babylonians; "Second Captivity"; End of the Kingdom of Judah
586-538	Exile in Babylonia
539	Conquest of Babylonia by Cyrus the Persian; End of Babylonian Empire
538	Cyrus's edict permitting the return of Jews to Judea; Beginning of the Jews' return to Jerusalem
445	Nehemiah rebuilds the walls of Jerusalem; Priestly theocracy in Jerusalem
333	Alexander the Great overthrows the Persian Empire and establishes Greek rule throughout the Near East
323	Alexander dies and his newly founded empire breaks up into a series of rival Greek kingdoms. The Ptolemies rule in Egypt, the Seleucids in Syria, and the Antigonids in Macedonia
320	Ptolemy I conquers Jerusalem
285-246	Reign of Ptolemy II Philadelphus. Beginnings of the Septuagint (translation of the O.T. into Greek)
223-187	Antiochus III (The Great) of Syria annexes Palestine and makes it a province of the Seleucid Empire
200 B.C.-A.D. 100 (approx.)	Apocryphal and Apocalyptic Literature
187-175	Seleucus IV, beginning of Hellenistic infiltration, resisted by the Zadokite High Priest, Onias III
175-163	Reign of Antiochus IV (Epiphanes)
168	Antiochus begins his persecution of the Jews
165	Judas Maccabeus rededicates the Temple (Feast of Hanukkah)
163	Demetrius I reigns as King of Syria
160	Death of Judas Maccabeus. Independent Maccabean Kingdom established

238   CHRONOLOGICAL TABEL OF MAJOR EVENTS

B.C.

160-142	High Priesthood of Jonathan
145	Demetrius II reigns as King of Syria
142-134	High Priesthood of Simon
134-104	High Priesthood of John Hyrcanus (opposed by Pharisees)
104-103	Aristobulus I, High Priest and King
103-76	Alexander Jannaeus, High Priest, King, and conqueror
76-67	Salome Alexandra (widow of Alexander Jannaeus) rules as regent
67	Alexandra's two sons, Hyrcanus II and Aristobulus II, fight over succession
63	Romans intervene and occupy Jerusalem. Roman rule begins, Hyrcanus made high priest
37-4	Herod the Great; End of Hasmonean Dynasty
c. 30 B.C.-A.D. 45	Philo
27 B.C.-A.D. 14	Emperor Augustus
c. 38 B.C.-A.D. 100	Josephus
4 B.C.-A.D. 6	Archelaus, ethnarch of Judaea and Samaria

A.D.

—	Birth of Jesus
6-15	Annas, High Priest
26-36	Pontius Pilate, procurator of Judea
40-50 (approx.)	The beginning of the New Testament
66	First Jewish revolt against Rome started by Eleazar Ben Hannaih. Masada seized by Menahem. Murder of Menahem on Ophel
68	Destruction of the Essene community in the Dead Sea region by the Roman armies

A.D.

70	The Romans led by Titus destroy Jerusalem and the Temple
73	Capture of the last stronghold, Masada, by the Romans
90	Synod of Yabneh (Jamnia) Canonization of the Hebrew Bible
132-135	Bar Kochba Revolt
200	Mishna edited by Rabbi Judah, the Prince

INDEX OF SUBJECTS

Aharoni, Y. 171, 172 ff.
'Ain Feshka 3
Akiba 166
Albright, William F. 4, 24, 98
Allegro, J. M. 43 ff., 94
Angelology 103 ff.
Antiochus, Epiphanes 94 ff., 110
Apocrypha 7, 53
Assassins 123, 110 ff.
Avigad, N. 53, 172 ff.
Bar-Adon, P., 172 ff.
Bar-Giora 123
Bar Kochba 28, 36, 164 ff. (*See also* Simeon ben Kosiba).
Barnett, Barney 195
Barthelemy, D. 50, 77
Belial 103
Benjamin al-Nihawandi (Karaite) 148
Bentwich, N. 135
Bethar 167
Biberkraut, James 178 ff.
Birnbaum, S. 25
Boethusians 199
Botniya Bar Miasa 192
Burrows, M. 72; Isaiah 85 ff.
Cairo geniza 148
Carbon 14 test 25
Castellion monastery 38 ff.
Cave One 2, 3, 4, 97, 100
Cave Eleven 194
Cave Four 7, 100, 212
Cave Six 7
Celibacy, Essenes 149
Cemetery 17
Chester Beatty Papyri 71
Chronological summary, later discoveries Judean 40 ff.

Clermont-Ganneau, C. 12, 122, 220
Cloths 12 ff.
Codex Ben Asher 80: Codex Petropolitanus 87; Codex Vaticanus 71
Coins 15 ff., 183 ff.
Commentaries 88 ff., 97 ff.
Commodus, Emperor 32
Contracts, Arabic 39; Aramaic 33, 164 ff.
Copper Scroll 43 ff.
Creation 108
Cross, F. M., Jr. 24, 50
Crowfoot, G. M. 25
Cullman, O. 147
Damascus Document 105, 145, 148, 152
Daniel 5, 7, 86
De Langhe, R. 39
Del-Medico, H. 65 ff.
Demetrius 94 ff.
De Saulcy, F., 12
Deuteronomy Scroll of 1883 215 ff.
De Vaux, R. 16, 17, 145, 167
Discoveries in 1951 40: 1952 40; 1955 41; 1956 41
Doctrines, Qumran sect 105 ff.
Dupont-Sommer, A. 67 ff., 145
Earthquake 14
Ebionites 132, 145
Ecclesiastes 86
Ecclesiasticus 212
Ein Gedi 20, 164 ff.
Eleazar ben Simeon (Zealot) 122
Eleazar ben Ya'ir 123, 205, 213
Epiphanius, Bishop of Salamis 3
Essenes 48, 125 ff., 131 ff., 143 ff., 149

INDEX OF SUBJECTS

Essenism, varieties 130
Eusebius of Caesarea 170
Excavations 41 ff., 205-206
Festival of New Oil 197, 199
Festival of New Wine 199
Festival of Unleavened Bread 200
Finkelstein, L. 112
Fragments, biblical 31; Latin 33; New Testament 39
Free will 115 ff.
Gamaliel I, 7
Gaster, T. H. 94
Genesis Apocryphon 2, 52 ff.
Ginsburg, C. D. 219, 220, 223
Goren, Shlomo 188
Greek documents 32
Guthe, H. 218
Habakkuk Commentary 2, 65, 66, 77, 88 ff., 144
Hadrian, Emperor 32, 166, 191
Halakhot (Halakhah) 197, 198
Harding, G. L. 17, 167
Hasidim 110 ff.
Hebrew, Mishnaic 44
Hebrew, rabbinic 197, 222-223
Hebrew University 3
Hebrew University (Isaiah manuscript) 79 ff., 83 f.
Herod Agrippa II, 16, 65
Herod, Archelaus 15, 21
Herod the Great 15, 32, 65, 121, 204, 205, 206, 207, 208, 210
Hezekiah (Zealot martyr) 121
Hillel 117
Hodayot (see Thanksgiving Hymns).
Hyrcanus, John 15, 20, 25
Immortality 108, 116
Isaiah Scroll 2, 69 ff.
Jannaeus 48
Jars (see Pottery).
Jericho 3, 14
Jerusalem, description of heavenly 10
Jesus 160; and Qumran sect 156 ff; ff.; and Teacher of Righteousness 156

Job, in Aramaic 7
John the Baptist 120, 160, 162; and Qumran 154 ff., 202
John of Gischala 123
Jonathan ben Tortha 166
Josephus 14, 112 ff., 143, 144 ; and account of Masada, 204, 205, 206, 207, 208, 209, 213
Jubilees, Book of 55, 212
Judas of Gamala 122
Kahle, Paul 72, 248
Karaites 24, 145, 147
Khirbet Mird 34, 39
Khirbet Qumran, excavations 11 ff.
King, statutes of 201, 202
Kittim (of Egypt) 60 ff., 91 ff.
Knowledge 107
Kohler, K. 127
Lamech Scroll 2, 54 ff. (See also Genesis Apocryphon)
Language, of scrolls 26 ff.
La Sor, W. S. 24
Lauterbach, J. Z. 119 ff.
Lepsius, Richard 218
Lex Talionis 119
Libby, W. F. 25
Linen 25
Magharians 145, 148
Maimonides, Moses, works of 217
Manual of Discipline 107, 137 ff., 151, 152
Manuscripts, nonbiblical 32 ff.
Mar Saba (Saint Sabas) 39
Marda monastery 39 (see Khirbet Mird).
Marianne 32
Masabala Bar Simeon 179 ff.
Masada 123, 167, 204 ff.
Massoretic Text 5; and Qumran Scrolls 69 ff.
Menahem 123
Menahem ben Ya'ir 123
Messiah 157 ff., 160
Messianism 103 ff.
Midrash 52 ff.
Milik, J. T. 18, 50

INDEX OF SUBJECTS

Mishmarot 10
Mishna 198, 201
Mishnaic Hebrew 44
Muhammad el-Dib 1
Nabatean 187 ff.
Nabonidus 86
Nahal Hever 173 ff.
Nahum Commentary 26 ff., 66, 94 ff.
Nazarites 155
Nero 16
Neubauer, Adolf 222
New Testament and Qumran writings 157
Noth, Martin 12
Oral Law 111 ff.
Origen 3
Paleography 25
Palestine Museum 4
Pannuches 134
Parallels, Christianity and Qumran 158 ff.
Paul 117, 160
Pentateuch Scrolls 7
Pentecost 199
Pharisees 111 ff., 199
Philo 126 ff., 132, 143, 144
Phylactery 31
Pliny 131, 143, 144
Polotsky, H. 187
Pottery 12 ff., 25
Prayer of Nabonidus 86
Psalms Commentary 96 ff.
Pseudo-Clementine writings 147
Predestination 106, 156
Quanna-eem (*see* Zealots)
Qumran, library 5; occupation phases 11; scrolls 3; writings 3; writings Christianity 153 ff.
Rabinowitz, Isaac 169
Rechabites 155
Resurrection 116 ff.
Revised Standard Version 76 ff.
Sadducees 117 ff., 199
St. Justin 170
St. Mark's Manuscript 70 ff.

St. Mark's Monastery 2
Salome 32
Salvation 106
Samaritan Pentateuch 5, 75
Samaritans 145, 166; identification with Qumran sect 145 ff., 199
Samuel (Archbishop) 2
Sanhedrin 113, 118
Saul of Tarsus 117
Schlottmann, Constantine 218
Scriptorium 18
Second Temple period 197, 199, 210, 212, 214
Sects, Jewish 109 ff.
Septuagint 5, 71 ff.
Sergius 3
Severus, Julius 166, 191; Alexander 183
Shapira, Moses Wilhelm 215, 217, 218, 223
Shenhar, J. 196
Sicarii 123 ff.
Silva 204, 205
Simeon ben Kosiba 32 ff., 168 ff. (*See also* Bar Kochba).
Simon the Pharisee 162
Six Day War 194, 195, 201
Skehan, P. W. 75
Spirits 107
Sons of Darkness 107, 139
Sons of Light 107, 139
Sukenik, E. L. 2, 58, 101, 194
Synod of Jamnia 34
Synoptic Gospels 153
Talmud 52 ff., 210
Teacher of Righteousness 48, 65, 91 ff., 106, 132, 150, 156
Teicher, J. L., 146
Temple (of Temple Scroll) 200, 202
Temple Scroll 194 ff.
Tetragrammaton 198, 216
Thanksgiving Hymns 3, 24, 99 ff., 137
Theological doctrines 105 ff.
Therapeutae 130 ff.
Thirsus Bar Tinius 180

Timothy 3
Trajan 16
Vallois, H. V. 17
Vermes, Geza 127
Vespasian 14
"Virginian" 194, 195
Wadi Murabbaat 28 ff., 164 ff.
War Scroll 57 ff., 59 ff., 201
Weiss-Rosmarin, Trude 213
Wernberg-Moeller, P. 137
Wicked Priest 91 ff.
Wright, G. Ernest 4
Written Law 114 ff.
Yadin, Yigael 2; description scrolls 43; Genesis Apocryphon 53; Masada excavations 204, 205, 206, 207, 208, 209, 213, 214; Temple Scroll 195, 196, 197, 200, 201, 202; War Scroll 57 ff.; War Scroll Kittim 66 ff.
Yehonatan Bar Baaya 179 ff.
Yehuda Bar Menasha 180
Yeshua ben Galgola 32 ff., 168 ff.
Yeshua ben Gilgula (*see* Yeshua ben Galgola).
Zadok 118, 144 ff.
Zaitschek, David V. 189
Zealots 49, 65, 121 ff.; Masada 205, 207, 208, 209, 210, 211, 212, 214
Zeitlin, Solomon 23, 148
Zodiac 10